Palgrave Studies in Classical Liberalism

This series offers a forum to writers concerned that the central presuppositions of the liberal tradition have been severely corroded, neglected, or misappropriated by overly rationalistic and constructivist approaches.

The hardest-won achievement of the liberal tradition has been the wrestling of epistemic independence from overwhelming concentrations of power, monopolies and capricious zealotries. The very precondition of knowledge is the exploitation of the epistemic virtues accorded by society's situated and distributed manifold of spontaneous orders, the DNA of the modern civil condition.

With the confluence of interest in situated and distributed liberalism emanating from the Scottish tradition, Austrian and behavioral economics, non-Cartesian philosophy and moral psychology, the editors are soliciting proposals that speak to this multidisciplinary constituency. Sole or joint authorship submissions are welcome as are edited collections, broadly theoretical or topical in nature.

Chor-yung Cheung

Hayek and Post-War Chinese Liberalism

Beyond the Enlightenment and National Salvation

palgrave
macmillan

Chor-yung Cheung
City University of Hong Kong
Kowloon, Hong Kong

ISSN 2662-6470 ISSN 2662-6489 (electronic)
Palgrave Studies in Classical Liberalism
ISBN 978-3-031-64887-8 ISBN 978-3-031-64888-5 (eBook)
https://doi.org/10.1007/978-3-031-64888-5

This Palgrave Macmillan imprint is published by the registered company Springer Nature Switzerland AG
The registered company address is: Gewerbestrasse 11, 6330 Cham, Switzerland

Acknowledgements

I first came to learn about Fredrich Hayek's social and political thought in the mid-1970s through the works of Chinese liberals who had gone to Taiwan or to other countries after the Chinese Communist Party established the People's Republic of China in 1949. As a high school student living in a relatively liberal British colony called Hong Kong, I, like many of my peers in local high schools and universities, was curious about the social and political development north of the border in mainland China. Many of us were very much attracted by the critical and passionate writings of the liberals who resided outside the Chinese mainland and strived to keep the tradition of modern Chinese liberal thought alive even though both the Chinese mainland and Taiwan were then ruled by their respective party-states. It was through them that I was introduced to the 1919 May-Fourth Movement in modern China, and I was enlightened by the Movement's aspiration for "democracy" and "science", an aspiration which has led me to a life-long interest in the study of modern social and political theory, both in the East and in the West. As a young intellectual at that time, I was most indebted to the writings of these Chinese liberals, with Hu Shih and Yin Hai-kuang amongst the most influential of them. The publication of this book is a tribute to these pioneering Chinese liberals.

I was fortunate enough to have the opportunity to discuss my initial ideas on Hayek and Chinese liberalism with Lin Yu-sheng (who studied under Yin Hai-kuang in Taiwan and Hayek at Chicago) when he was visiting the City University of Hong Kong in 2013–2014 where I was a member of the then Department of Public Policy. I am very grateful to the late Professor Lin for his comments and encouragement. I must also thank Professors Way Kuo and Paul Lam, formerly President and Vice President (Student Affairs) of the City University of Hong Kong respectively, who allowed me to take a year long sabbatical to work on this project after I stepped down from the position of Dean of Students of the university.

Throughout the years when I worked on this book, the Research Center for Humanities and Social Sciences of Academia Sinica in Taipei has been most generous and supportive. They not only allowed me to use their library to conduct my research and provided me with an office to work in during my visits there, but their Center for Political Thought also invited me to deliver talks on different parts of this book where I could learn from many of the considered comments raised by colleagues. In this respect, I am particularly grateful to Carl K. Y. Shaw, Roy Tseng, I-Chung Chen and Sechin Yeong-Shyang Chien for their insights and support.

An earlier version of Chapter 5 of this book was presented at the 2015 Michael Oakeshott Association Conference held at Hull University in Britain. The draft version of the Appendix of this book was presented at the 2023 Michael Oakeshott Conference in Hungary. Colleagues of the Association have been sources of inspiration for me, and the quality of their respective scholarship is something that I have tried hard to emulate. I have learned so much from the conferences organized by the Association from Noel O'Sullivan, Timothy Fuller, Wendell John Coats, Jr., Paul Franco, Elizabeth Corey, David Corey, Eric Kos, Edmund Neill, Kenneth B. McIntyre, Robert Grant, Kevin William, Gene Callahan, Roy Tseng, Terry Nardin, the late Roger Scruton and Corey Abel, and many others. I also must give my sincerest thanks to Leslie Marsh, who not only introduced me to the Association, but also gave me tremendous support in this book project. An earlier version of Chapter 3 of this book appeared in a book co-edited by Leslie (*Reclaiming Liberalism* 2020), which is also published by Palgrave Macmillan.

I thank Francesco Di Lorio for inviting me to Nankai University in China to give a talk on Hayek and Chinese Liberalism in September 2017. In the winter of 2023, through the kind effort of Francesco and upon the invitation of Professor Matteo Vincenzo d'Alfonso, I gave a talk on Western Thought in China at the University of Ferrara in Italy where I had some very fruitful exchanges with colleagues on this important subject.

In October 2017, I was invited to present a paper on Xia Daoping's liberalism at Hubei University of Economics in China, and I am grateful to Xia Daoping's grandson Xia Ming for his kind invitation so that I could test out some of my ideas developed in this book at the conference.

Last but not the least, I must thank my dearest wife Anne, who has given me full support in all my intellectual endeavours since we met each other almost half a century ago. While writing this book, Anne and I have faced the double challenge of caring for close family members with cancer, and coping with highly unsettling changes in Hong Kong, where a relatively nomocratic territory has been changed into an increasingly teleocratic community. Without Anne's support and companionship, I do not think I could have managed all these alone.

July 2024
Greater London

Contents

1
Introduction: Hayek and Chinese Liberalism

Introduction

This book tries to put forward the following two-pronged thesis. Firstly, it takes Fredrich Hayek's social theory of classical liberalism seriously, arguing that, like what Vikash Yadav did in his *Liberalism's Last Man: Hayek in the Age of Political Capitalism* (Yadav 2023), many of Hayek's social and political ideas are still very much alive, and they continue to be relevant to the twenty-first century, both in the West and in the East. Secondly, the way this book tries to take Hayek's ideas seriously is to focus on some of his leading ideas and to examine how they have been directly or indirectly influencing the development of Chinese liberal thought, particularly since the Chinese Communist Party won the Civil War of China in 1949.

In "Individualism: True and False" (Hayek [1948] 1980, pp. 1–32), Hayek makes it clear that his classical liberalism "is primarily a *theory* of society, an attempt to understand the forces which determine the social life of man, and only in the second instance a set of political maxims derived from this view of society" (ibid., p. 6, emphasis in the original). This does not mean that Hayek's liberal theory is devoid of moral content. Instead, Hayek believes that "there still seems to exist

C. Cheung, *Hayek and Post-War Chinese Liberalism*, Palgrave Studies in Classical Liberalism, https://doi.org/10.1007/978-3-031-64888-5_1

such a philosophy—a set of principles which, indeed, is implicit in most Western or Christian political tradition but which can no longer be unambiguously described by any readily understood term" (ibid., p. 2). In *The Road to Serfdom* (Hayek [1944] 2007), Hayek characterizes one main principle of this philosophy as "the respect for the individual man *qua* man" (ibid., p. 68, emphasis in the original). He points out that this principle acquires its essential features from Christianity and the philosophy of antiquity, and was first fully developed during the Renaissance, with "the recognition of [man's] own views and tastes as supreme in his own sphere…and the belief that it is desirable that men should develop his own individual gifts and bents" (ibid.). The main theoretical endeavor of Hayek, however, is not to spell out fully the moral content of this "respect for the individual man *qua* man." Rather, he believes that the differences between the *true* individualists and the *false* individualists (including the socialists) "ultimately rest on purely intellectual issues capable of a scientific resolution and not on different judgments of value," and he argues that the doctrines advocated by the socialists "can be shown to be based on factually false assumptions," and the whole family of socialist thought can be "proved erroneous" (Hayek 1973, p. 6. See also Hayek 1988).

Hayek's social theory, in other words, is a systematic and profound attempt to explain why social coordination and development in a complex, modern society with maximum respect for each and every individual member's taste, talent, gift, and so on is possible and preferable. Hayek's theory also attempts to spell out what kind of institutional safeguards is required for the protection of individual freedoms, within which self-chosen action and voluntary and spontaneous interaction among the free individuals are respected and can be put into practice as far as possible.

Subsequent chapters of this book will spell out in detail many of the salient ideas of Hayek's social theory of classical liberalism. The chapters will also demonstrate why Hayek's classical liberal ideas are important to the development of post-war Chinese liberalism. In this introductory chapter, however, it is imperative for me to give an overall answer to the central question of this book: Why is Hayek's classical liberalism relevant to modern China? However, before I can give an answer to this question, I must first provide an intellectual and historical context that will make my answer intelligible, and that context requires me to give a brief discussion of the development of Chinese liberalism since the late Qing Dynasty up to the beginning of the post-war period in China.

Chinese Liberalism: From the Late Qing Dynasty to 1949

Liberalism, as a modern Western political ideology, was first introduced to China by Yan Fu (嚴復 1853–1921)[1] at the turn of the twentieth century through his translation of the classical works of some leading eighteenth and nineteenth centuries Western liberal thinkers, such as Herbert Spencer, Thomas Huxley, John Stuart Mill, Adam Smith, Baron de Montesquieu (Schwartz 1964; Huang 2008; Liu, Lin and Wang 1999; Zhou 2017). Benjamin Schwartz, in his pioneering study of Yan *In Search of Wealth & Power: Yen Fu and the West*[2] (Schwartz 1964), describes Yan as the first Chinese literatus who related himself seriously and in a sustained manner to modern Western thought. Liberty as a political concept, and liberal institutions as social practices at that time, were, however, alien to the Chinese culture. There is little dispute to say that political freedom as a value was absent in traditional Chinese political culture, and that is why when translating Mill's *On Liberty* into Chinese, Yan "complains bitterly of the difficulty of conveying the original text in Chinese and of his inability to translate Mill's sentences literally" (Schwartz 1964, p. 134).

However, it will not be right to conclude from the above that liberty and liberal practices are necessarily incompatible with the Chinese culture. Xu Foguan (徐復觀 1904–1982), a leading 20th-century neo-Confucian scholar, argues that the emergence of culture is premised on mankind's ability to develop self-consciousness, and man's reflective consciousness in this regard not only enables man to start to have self-knowledge, but also to begin to make choices in relation to man's life and existence, through which forms of living, practices, customs, and traditions begin to take place. A sustainable culture or civilization presupposes the continual exercise of man's reflective consciousness which, in effect, represents the working, at least to a significant degree, of the human spirit of freedom or free agency, without which civilization will wither (Xu [1988] 2013, pp. 51–52). As Gilbert Murray aptly observes, "Civilized thinking means liberal thinking. Liberality is the inner content of civilization" (Murray 1938, p. 57). Wm. Theodore de Bary has convincingly argued in his *The Liberal Tradition in China* (de Bary 1983) that in the Song and Ming dynasties (960–1279 and 1368–1644, respectively), moral thinking with some liberal orientation (such as the appeal to individual conscience as the final arbiter of moral judgment) and educational practices that were favorable to social pluralism (such as the creation of independent colleges in the society) were quite prevalent among some leading neo-Confucian scholars such as Zhu Xi (朱熹 1130–1200), Wang Yangming (王陽明 1472–1529) and Huang Zongxi (黃宗羲 1610–1695), even though de Bary concedes that collectivism and the lack of socio-economic conditions for political pluralism are evidently dominant in China (ibid., p. 124).

However, one must not forget that Yan's serious attempts to learn from Western liberalism in the Qing Dynasty (1644–1912) had a strong utilitarian purpose. He wanted the Chinese to learn from Western liberalism in order to discover the secret of the West's success in achieving wealth and power at a time when China was repeatedly defeated by Western imperial powers who were keen to scramble for concessions against the Middle Kingdom. The defeats suffered by China since the First Opium War (1839–1842) were far from just military matters. Many progressive Chinese intellectuals, officials, and reform-minded notables at the Qing court believed that China must undergo fundamental social, technological, and political changes in order to cope with the challenge of the West, particularly after a modernized Japan, China's far smaller and previously weaker neighbor who faced the same challenge from Western imperial powers before its 1868 Meiji Restoration, defeated China in the 1894 First Sino-Japanese War and joined the West's scramble for concessions in China.

Schwartz goes so far as to suggest that Yan was so preoccupied with the need for national salvation in the face of these imperialist threats that he altered Mill's original conception of liberty in his translation of *On Liberty* by fitting it into a framework of Spencer's categories of energy and "survival of the fittest," which had effectively turned liberalism into an ideological instrument for national salvation rather than protecting individual rights and setting constitutional constraints against abuses of power. Although Schwartz's thesis of Yan deliberately mistranslating Mill out of the concern for national salvation has been powerfully challenged by some subsequent scholarship on Yan, what appears not to be disputed is the fact that because of the persistent influence of China's traditional collective culture and the concern for national survival, Yan's advocacy of liberalism in the Chinese context was at best vacillating between individualism and collectivism (Huang 2008; Liu et al. 1999; Zhou 2017).

Likewise, there is general agreement by students of modern Chinese political thought that Liang Qichao (梁啓超 1873–1929), the famous constitutionalist reformer and leading pioneer in introducing Western political ideas to China in the late Qing Dynasty and the early republican era, had by and large premised his idea of new and active citizens in China on the need to adopt a collective approach in modern nation building in order to strengthen state capacity (Chang 1971; Lubot 1982; Chow 1995; Yang 2009; Qiu 2019). The following paragraph from Liang on new citizenship is one good example to illustrate this point:

> It is not merely to have rulers, officials, students, farmers, laborers, merchants, and soldiers, but to have ten thousand eyes with one sight, ten thousand hands and feet with only one mind, ten thousand ears with one hearing, ten thousand powers with only one purpose of life; then the state is established ten-thousand fold strong…When mind touches mind, when power is linked to power, cog to cog, strand around strand, and ten thousands roads meet in one center, this will be a state. (quoted from Chang 1971, p. 100)

The collapse of the Qing Dynasty and the establishment of a republic in China in 1912 ended the political institution of universal kingship, which can be traced back to the Shang Dynasty (17th BCE–11th BCE), in China (Ching 1997; Liu 2006). It did not, however, bring legitimate, sustainable, and constitutional rule to the new republic (Price 1990;

Gao 2022), which was plagued by military strongman politics (1912–1916), brief reversals back to monarchial, albeit ineffective, rule (1916 and 1917), warlordism (1916–1928), and an authoritarian party-state engaging in a civil war with a revolutionary party (1928–1949). On the other hand, the outbreak of the First World War in 1914 eventually brought China to side with the Allies and declared war against Germany in 1917. But at the 1919 Paris Peace Conference after the Great War, the Allies, who won the War, made the decision to allow Japan to retain territories in China's Shandong province that had been surrendered by Germany to Japan in 1914 during the War instead of returning the territories to China. Such a decision triggered the outbreak of the famous May Fourth students protests (Chow 1960) in China, where thousands of university students in Beijing protested on the streets on the fourth day of May 1919 to demand the Chinese government not to accept the decision. They also made petitions to the Allies, urging them to respect the territorial sovereign right of China and not to yield to the principle of "might is right."

The impact of the above great historical events on the development of Chinese liberal thought is two-folded. Firstly, while many of the May Fourth generation of Chinese liberal intellectuals were as eager as their mentors like Yan and Liang to try to learn from the West about the secret of achieving wealth and power, the political incompetence and corruption of the successive Chinese warlord governments, and the failure of the new republic to establish a stable constitutional framework in China, led many of them to shun practical politics. Instead, they now believed that before they could reform Chinese politics, they need to reform the traditional, submissive, and passive mindset of the Chinese people. The following paragraph, written in 1919 by one of the most prominent student leaders of the May Fourth protests Luo Jialun (羅家倫 1897–1969), perhaps captured the mood of many of the Chinese liberals of the period best:

> We agree fully with [the] French positivist philosopher [Auguste] Comte, who said: If you want to reform politics, you must first change habits of mind. His words are particularly apt for the sorry situation of contemporary Chinese politics and society, which is caused by an obstinate

> mentality…Chinese mentality today had three characteristics: it is slavish, autocratic, and chaotic. Our thought revolution aims to change slavish mentality into independent thinking, to change autocratic mentality into egalitarian thinking, to change chaotic mentality into logical thinking. (quoted from Schwarcz 1986, p. 94)

In fact, two years before the May Fourth students protests, Luo's teacher at Peking University, the leading Chinese liberal from the May Fourth period up to his death in 1962 Hu Shih (Hu Shi/胡適 1891–1962) and the Dean of School of Arts and Letters of the same university Chen Duxiu (陳獨秀 1879–1942), initiated the New Culture Movement, in which, among other things, they argued for the adoption of the Chinese vernacular language to replace the classical Chinese for literary writings. They believed that the former was a living language, liberating both in style and in content, and was down to earth, even ordinary people could understand it. Whereas the classical language was both timid and dead, works written in the classical language were not only elitist, but also full of cliches and were devoid of real-life emotions and experiences. In their view, such a language and its literature were directly or indirectly in support of the submissive and passive mentality of the Chinese. As we shall see below, this turning away from practical politics had also radicalized the Chinese liberals' cultural critique, and they believed that such a critique was necessary since what China at that time required was nothing short of a "thought revolution."

The May Fourth protests and the New Culture Movement together are now commonly regarded as the May Fourth Movement in modern Chinese history (Chow 1960; Schwarcz 1986). When commemorating the May Fourth in 1933, Hu characterized this Movement as China's Renaissance, which, to him, was a conscious movement not only to use the vernacular language to replace the classical language, but also to consciously apply rationality as a standard to critically examine the problems of the Chinese tradition, so that the individuals, men and women of China, could be liberated from many of the irrational, obsolete, and oppressive chains embedded in the autocratic Chinese culture. Hu described this as a conflict between freedom and authority, reason against tradition. Earlier, Hu also called for the use of reason to initiate a transvaluation of all traditional values in China, and to promote modern human values and life against oppression. To Hu, the Chinese Renaissance was a movement of humanism (Yu 1999, p. 3). In other words, for the Chinese liberals, the May Fourth era heralded the advent of a "dare to think independently" and a "dare to engage in thought revolution" movement so that new and rational thinking and practices could be introduced to the Chinese society, making the Chinese free from their traditional, submissive habits, and mindset. To the May Fourth intellectuals, this was a cultural revolution, and the way to do it was to subject the whole Chinese tradition, particularly Confucianism with its paternalistic socio-political relationships, to the most critical scrutiny, and to demand the adoption of two modern practices in China that had been absent in its traditional culture: democracy and science.

Yu Ying-shih (Yu Yingshi/余英時 1930–2021) argues that although Hu was right to point out the parallels between Europe's Renaissance and China's May Fourth Movement in introducing the use of their respective vernacular languages to replace the classical ones, the heavy reliance on rationality, and the passionate use of scientific/positivist reasoning and modern Western values in mounting a comprehensive critique of the traditional Chinese culture by the May Fourth intellectuals in effect made the Movement look more akin to the Enlightenment than the Renaissance (ibid., pp. 4–5. See also Li 1987, pp. 7–49, and Schwarcz 1986). Consequently, the turn away from the corrupt politics of the practical world in China and the eagerness to fundamentally change the traditional mindset of the Chinese had radicalized many of the liberals in the May Fourth era in their thought revolution. This revolution had led to a comprehensive critique of the Chinese tradition, which was unprecedented in Chinese history, and this was, after its vacillation between individualism and collectivism, the second prominent characteristic of Chinese liberalism in pre-war China.

According to Lin Yu-sheng (林毓生 1934–2022), the May Fourth era's radical anti-traditionalism was then a widely shared phenomenon among the Chinese intellectuals. In his *The Crisis of Chinese Consciousness: Radical Antitraditionalism in the May Fourth Era* (Lin 1979), Lin demonstrates that apart from the leading liberal Hu Shih, his colleague Chen Duxiu (who was another leading liberal in the early period of the

May Fourth, though he turned to Marxism-Leninism a few years later), and Lu Xun (魯迅 1881–1936) (the most prominent left-wing literary figure in China during the May Fourth period) all adopted an explicitly totalistic rejection stance against the Chinese cultural heritage. Lin calls this "totalistic iconoclasm" (ibid. pp. 5–7). He argues that despite its radicalism, this frame of mind of the May Fourth intellectuals, in the final analysis, was profoundly though unconsciously influenced by the deep-rooted traditional Chinese mode of holistic thinking, which assigned primary responsibility to cultural and intellectual ideas in social and moral changes, though this time round the "ideas" concerned were not the traditional Confucian virtues, but a wholesale adoption of science and democracy from the West aiming to totally replacing the Chinese culture.

However, given the military and territorial threats from Japan and the Western imperial powers, and given the incompetence of successive governments in Beijing and the internal chaos created by warlordism, the turn to cultural radicalism of Chinese liberalism in the May Fourth era did not eclipse the need to continue to seek wealth and power for national salvation in China. The success of the Bolshevik Revolution and the ideological teaching of Marxism in Russia in 1917 provided a ready-made, practical, and ideological model, at least it seemed so to many Chinese intellectuals at that time, for fundamental, comprehensive, and revolutionary changes in a society pregnant with political crises. In the light of this, some radical leaders in China became keenly aware of the relevance of the Soviet's success and started to learn from Marxism-Leninism. People like Chen Duxiu had become even more radicalized as a result, and believed that rather than stopping at thought revolution, political revolution of the Marxist-Leninist type was what was required by China. Chen eventually founded the Chinese Communist Party in 1921 and started fully engaged in revolutionary politics. In other words, to many in China, liberal Enlightenment of the May Fourth, while culturally radical, did not go far enough. Direct and revolutionary political action was what was required (Qiu 2019, Chapter 5). Even the Father of the 1911 Republican Revolution Sun Yat-sen (Sun Zhongshan/孫中山1866–1925), who continued his revolutionary endeavors to try to end the warlords' rule in China after the establishment of the Republic of China, saw the need to reorganize his Chinese Nationalist Party along the Leninist party-state approach. In the early 1920s, under Sun's leadership, the Chinese Nationalist Party started cooperating with the Soviet Russian experts in China and the newly formed Chinese Communist Party to consolidate the revolutionary forces in China to further Sun's fight to unify China under the leadership of the Chinese Nationalist Party. The need for national salvation and direct political action, as the philosopher Li Zehou (李澤厚 1930–2021) argues, once again took center stage, it eclipsed the liberal's Enlightenment and thought/ cultural revolution (Li 1987, pp. 32–33). However, this time round, the endeavors for national salvation were armed with a far more radical, action-oriented, and comprehensive ideology Marxism-Leninism, which went far beyond the liberals' cultural radicalism.

The reformed Chinese Nationalist Party, under the leadership of Chiang Kai-shek (Jiang Jieshi/蔣介石 1887–1975), who became the party leader after Sun Yat-sen died in 1925, managed to formally unified China by defeating the warlords in the Party's Northern Expedition by 1928. A relatively stable central government was then established in Nanjing under the one-party rule of the Chinese Nationalist Party. Chiang also launched a bloody purge against the Chinese Nationalist Party's minor partner, the Chinese Communist Party during the Northern Expedition in an attempt to eliminate any possible competition from another Leninist type of revolutionary party in Chinese politics. The purge forced members of the Chinese Communist Party to flee to the more remote areas of China to regroup, where they continued to conduct their guerilla warfare against the Nationalist government in what they called the Long March so that they could continue their socialist campaign in China in a civil war that would eventually end in their victory in 1949 against the militarily stronger Nationalist government.

After the establishment of the Chinese Nationalist Party's one-party rule in China and the outbreak of the Chinese Civil War in the more remote areas of China between the Nationalist government and the Chinese Communist Party, the Chinese liberals could no longer avoid real-world politics. Also, there was a looming military threat from Japan whose ambition was to establish a Japanese Empire in the Pan-East Asia region, and the first step taken by the Japanese was to invade the North-Eastern part of China Manchuria in 1931 and established a puppet Manchurian government there. This was followed by a fully fledged invasion of China by the Japanese from 1937 onwards, and many parts of the Chinese mainland were then under Japanese occupation while the Nationalist government put up its resistance against the Japanese in its provisional capital Chongqing in the South-Western part of China.

In the light of all these developments, the Chinese liberals, first and foremost, needed to respond to the authoritarian one-party rule of the Nationalist government. In this connection, under the leadership of Hu Shih, the Chinese liberals started a debate on human rights in China in 1929 by criticizing the Nationalist government's one-party rule. Hu took the Chinese National Party to task for their failure to have a timely introduction of constitutional rule in China to protect human rights as promised earlier by the proposed 3-step approach to constitutionalism (i.e. military rule, guided constitutional rule, and fully fledged constitutional rule) under the late Sun Yat-sen's official ideology entitled Three People's Principles (i.e. the Principle of the People as a Nation, the Principle of the Rights of the People, and the Principle of People's Livelihood. See Sun 1985). Hu was ably joined by another leading liberal Luo Longji (羅隆基 1898–1965), who in the second half of the 1920s studied politics under Harold Laski, a London School of Economics' politics professor and a leading member of the British Labour Party. Luo, having returned to China after 1928, claimed himself as the Chinese student of Laski, and had contributed a lot of arguments in support of Hu's clamor for the implementation of constitutional rule and the protection of human rights in China under the Nationalist regime. At the same time, Luo started to develop a conception of human rights and constitutionalism which was premised on the liberal idea of the autonomous self by "treating man as man" in Chinese liberalism (Luo 2022, particularly Volume 2. See also Cheung 2022.12.04 and the Appendix of this book). Both these ideas, constitutionalism and "treating man as man," in my view, have become leading theses in the development of Chinese liberal thought up to the present time.

The Civil War between the Nationalist government and the Chinese Communist Party—with the former justifying their rule by Sun Yat-sen's Three People's Principles and by reviving the traditional respect for Confucianism, and the latter striving for the ultimate adoption of Marxism-Leninism in China, arguing that socialism represented genuine democracy and true freedom for the people with the aim to abolishing all capitalist exploitations—also made it imperative for the Chinese liberals to differentiate themselves, both ideologically and politically, from these two dominant forces in Chinese politics.

In responses to the above challenges, the Chinese liberals continued their radical cultural critique of Confucianism, to the extent that Hu Shih, in the 1930s, even adopted another cultural radical Chen Xujing (陳序經 1903–1967)'s proposed idea of "wholesale Westernization" of China in order to catch up with the West (Chen 1976). In fact, earlier in 1923 in the famous Science and Metaphysics Debate (Chang et al. 2008) between the Chinese liberals and the cultural conservatives who identified themselves with many traditional Chinese values, the liberals already accused the conservatives who still insisted on upholding Confucian ethics as unscientific and regressive, criticizing them of dragging the feet of China in her march toward modernization. As an alternative, the liberals proposed the adoption of a scientific life view, and they believed that the use of the scientific method would enable China to modernize and to solve many of the problems facing the Chinese society. In other words, a totalistic anti-traditionalism joined hands with the belief in the almost omnipotent power of science in the context of the pursuit of knowledge for social progress, and this became another prominent aspect of Chinese liberalism at that time.

Apart from the demand of constitutionalism in China and the critique of one-party rule under the Nationalist government, the Chinese liberals also disagreed with the Chinese communists on the need to use violent revolutionary means to achieve a democratic and modern China. Hu Shih's famous research-based, piecemeal socio-political reform approach was proposed as the preferred alternative to the ideas suggested by the then leading communist thinker Li Dazhao (李大釗 1889–1927) who introduced Bolshevism to China in 1919. Li believed that revolutionary ideology such as Bolshevism was what was needed as a blueprint for comprehensive changes to help China to be transformed into a genuine democracy and a modern state (Lin 2019, pp. 183–191). As a pre-war Chinese liberal, Luo Longji was far more politically active than Hu Shih, and he was on the left wing of the then Chinese liberalism. Luo, however, also rallied for a gradual, peaceful approach for democracy in China. Lou was a founding member of the then important liberal-oriented political party called China Democratic League, which was established in 1941 during the War against the Japanese. The League played an important, though eventually unsuccessful, political role between the end of the Second Sino-Japanese War (1937–1945) and the breakdown of the peace talk by the end of 1946 between the Nationalist government and the Chinese Communist Party when Luo and other politically active liberals tried hard to bridge over the differences between the nationalists and the communists.

After the Second Sino-Japanese War, the League was opposed to the continuation of the Civil War by the two parties, and they tried hard to work out a compromised approach, in which all the three major parties (with participation from some minor parties too) should form a constitutional national assembly to enact a constitution for China that was acceptable to all, after which a multi-party coalition government could be formed to join hand to rebuild China. In other words, Chinese liberals like Luo were both against the Nationalist government's one-party rule and the Chinese Communist Party's violent means to capture political power in China at that time. The fact that Luo called himself the Chinese student of Laski whose British Labour Party managed to win the British parliamentary election in 1945 immediately after the Second World War (1939–1945) and to form a moderate socialist government in the UK to initiate comprehensive social welfare reform spoke volumes about how some of the leading Chinese liberals' social democratic inclination was inspired by the British experience of welfarism at that time (Xu 2021, pp. 49–68). In this sense, it is important to note that pre-war Chinese liberalism was significantly influenced by the more moderate version of socialism or the Western ideology of social democracy, which supported state-led redistribution for greater equity and economic equality. In his excellent *The Intellectual Foundations of Chinese Modernity: Cultural and Political Thought in the Republican Era*, Edmund S. K. Fung rightly observes that "from May Fourth on, liberalism and socialism were intimately intertwined in the minds of many liberal intellectuals [in China]" (Fung 2010, pp. 191–192). In particular, Fung's analysis shows that while the pre-war Chinese liberals were at one with their Western counterparts in upholding individual freedom, constitutionalism, and the like, "they were not opposed to…the exercise of state initiative to develop the economy and to regulate the market simultaneously" (ibid., p. 259). Even Hu Shih recalled that in the 1930s, he believed that "socialism is a logical sequence of the democratic movement" (Lin 2013).

One more challenge to pre-war Chinese liberalism needs to be mentioned here. As regards the looming military threat from Japan in the early 1930s, the Chinese liberals were also torn between the need for national survival and the development of democracy in China. In another famous debate of the time on democracy and dictatorship, we find that many Chinese liberals were of the view that for the sake of national survival, they preferred to support the one-party dictatorship under Chiang Kai-shek, whose Chinese Nationalist Party was regarded as the only centralized, credible political force of the time in the nation to fight against the Japanese. Although they admitted that this was a contingent measure, it was necessary since, given the backwardness of China and her people, it would take too long for democracy to be entrenched in China, and the threat of foreign military invasion was nothing if not imminent. Leading liberals like Hu Shih and Luo Longji, however, did not agree with their liberal colleagues in this regard, and they were most insistent that protecting human rights and building democracy in China were not inconsistent with the need to resist a possible Japanese invasion (Zhi 2010).

While I am acutely conscious of the fact that the brief discussion of the above political context in modern Chinese history that affected the twists and turns of the development of pre-war Chinese liberalism is far too skeletal for expert students of modern Chinese history, I hope I have sufficiently outlined some central ideas that were prevalent in modern Chinese liberal thought in the pre-war period. Perhaps, it is not impertinent to say that pre-war Chinese liberalism was shaped largely by what could be called "the politics of the felt need," if I can borrow from the British philosopher Michael Oakeshott a term that he made famous in his discussion of rationalism in politics (Oakeshott 1991, p. 9). National salvation was an urgent concern that few Chinese liberals could afford to ignore when they were trying to learn from Western liberalism. Yan Fu's and Liang Qichao's vacillation between collectivism and individualism in the late Qing Dynasty was echoed by the vacillation between dictatorship and democracy by the Chinese liberals before the outbreak of the Second Sino-Japanese War. When the pre-war liberals perceived the traditional culture as the main obstacle deterring the development of democracy and science in China, this politics of the felt need of the Chinese liberals prompted them to take a radical, cultural turn in their liberal ideas and developed what Lin Yu-sheng calls the extraordinarily totalistic anti-traditionalism in their thought revolution during the May Fourth era. This wholesale critique of the traditional culture was partnered with an incredible faith in the power of the method of science, even though this liberal rationalism and radicalism were outflanked by the even more radical and political ideology of Marxism-Leninism.

The introduction of the idea of individual freedom, the emphasis on the individual's self-autonomy, and the stress on the ability to think independently nevertheless did help the Chinese liberals to focus on a conception of the self that required institutional protection of individual human rights by constitutional rules. The theme "treating man as man" has since become a central tenet of Chinese liberalism, and the question of how to establish constitutional government in China has been an on-going concern for the Chinese liberals ever since. Although pre-war Chinese liberals since the May Fourth era continued to launch scathing attacks against the Chinese tradition, their approach in politics was in the main gradual, favoring moderate and peaceful reforms over violent revolution and synoptic changes. Like their moderate socialists or the social democratic counterparts in the West, many pre-war Chinese liberals were in favor of economic equality, they believed that political freedom could co-exist with economic equality in a future democratic China. Some may suggest that such a belief is more consistent with the more egalitarian ethics of the Chinese tradition on economic matters. While this suggestion is not unreasonable, I suspect that it is also the case that the pre-war Chinese liberals' faith in state intervention reflected the influence of the politics of the felt need at that time, in which active political intervention to address urgent socio-economic challenges related to national survival was often regarded as necessary to rescue China from national demise.

Not long after Japan surrendered in 1945, the Nationalist government and the Chinese Communist Party resumed the Civil War after a brief but failed attempt to achieve national peaceful reconciliation to enact a new constitution for a coalition government in China. Benefitted from the Japanese invasion and with the help of the Soviet Union, the Chinese Communist Party had grown in strength after the Second Sino-Japanese War. It eventually defeated the Nationalist government in the Civil War and established the People's Republic of China on the Chinese mainland in 1949, and the defeated Chinese Nationalist Party was forced to withdraw to Taiwan. The victory of the Chinese Communist Party meant that a series of revolutionary socialist campaigns and programs to build a new China were about to commence on the Chinese mainland.

There were good reasons to believe that Chinese liberalism in the post-war era would have had a dim prospect. While the end of the Second World War did bring the world the demise of fascism, Nazism, and Japanese militarism, it also heralded the beginning of the Cold War, in which two power blocs representing two competing ideologies, capitalism and socialism, started to engage in a comprehensive and fierce confrontation for global supremacy. The defeat of the Nationalist government in the Civil War on the Chinese mainland by the Chinese Communist Party and the establishment of the People's Republic of China in 1949 to replace the Nationalist government's Republic of China meant that henceforth, China in the main belonged solidly to the socialist camp, and revolutionary socialism, or Marxism-Leninism-Maoism rather than liberalism appeared to be the answer to China's pursuit of national salvation and modernization. Many pre-war Chinese liberals, in view of the oppression against political dissents by the Chinese Nationalist Party and corruption in the National government, did choose to side with the Chinese Communist Party in the 1940s (Luo 2022, Volume 4 pp. 168–200; Han 2015). After 1949, more than a few of them even started to sincerely embrace socialism rather than liberalism in the People's Republic (Qian 2017). In Taiwan, where the Nationalist government found refuge after their defeat in the Civil War, what was foremost in the mind of Chiang Kai-shek was not constitutional development as promised under Sun Yat-sen's Three People's Principles before the Civil War (Nie 2017), but the implementation of martial law on the island[3] and how he could gather enough military power to launch a counter-offensive on the mainland to reverse the result of the Civil War. However, this was an objective that Chiang nevertheless did not manage to achieve in the end.

In the light of the above, many were right to ask if liberalism was still relevant after 1949 in China. The answer, however, turned out to be a yes. What is even more interesting was the fact that although Hayek was then an internationally renowned economist in the West and was famous for his debates on economic theory with John Maynard Keynes in the 1930s (Caldwell 2004), very few Chinese intellectuals, some notable exceptions notwithstanding (Chow 2011), heard about Hayek in pre-war China, not to say to anticipate that they were about to be influenced by his classical liberal thought shortly. So, what first made Hayek's classical liberalism relevant in post-war China?

Hayek and the Critique of Totalitarianism

In the late 1920s and 1930s, while Hayek, as a trained professional economist, was justly famous for his study of monetary theory and the Great Depression of 1929, the industrial cycle, the subjective theory of value, the critique of socialist calculation, and some methodological as well as epistemological issues in the study of economics (Caldwell 2004), what made him first becoming internationally important as a polymath thinker was the publication of what he called his "political" book *The Road to Serfdom* (Hayek [1994] 2007) in 1944, in which he powerfully argued that both Hitler's national socialism and Stalin's communism were variants of totalitarian politics, the practice of which, when pressed to the logical end, not only would lead to the total control of the society by the state, but also would deprive all citizens their individual freedom.

The post-war liberals in Taiwan, some of whom belonged to the liberal wing of the Chinese Nationalist Party under Chiang Kai-shek, found *The Road to Serfdom* doubly attractive, because its arguments were, on the one hand, most pertinent in their critique against what was being practiced in communist China after 1949, and, on the other, equally powerful in criticizing many of the state-centered and authoritarian policies practiced by the then Nationalist government in Taiwan.

In this regard, post-war Taiwan's leading liberal journal *Free China* (《自由中國》), which was founded in 1949 by leading Chinese liberals like Hu Shih and Lei Chen (Lei Zhen/雷震 1897–1979), who was a former senior official in the Nationalist government but wanted to establish an opposition party in Taiwan to develop democracy there, published many of its critical Chinese editorials and articles written by prominent liberal writers like Yin Hai-kuang (Yin Haiguang/殷海光 1919–1969) and Xia Daoping (夏道平 1907–1995), criticizing what was happening under the authoritarian rule of the then Nationalist government in Taiwan and the then increasingly totalitarian politics imposed by the party-state on the Chinese mainland. These Chinese liberals were inspired by the ideas and arguments they learned from Hayek, and *The Road to Serfdom* was first translated by Yin into Chinese and published, in serial format, in *Free China* in 1953–1954, indicating that the influence of Hayek's ideas on these post-war liberals in Taiwan was on the rise. Lei's idea of forming an opposition party in Taiwan and the journal's critical articles against the Taiwanese regime eventually proved to be too much for Chiang to stomach, and *Free China* was banned by the Nationalist government in 1960, and Lei and one other editorial member staff were arrested on the charges of subversion, and they eventually were sentenced to prison for 10 years. Although the journal was banned and Lei was imprisoned, the influence of Hayek's ideas in Taiwan continued as we will see in Chapter 2 of this book.

Hayek's critique of totalitarianism did not manage to reach the mainland intellectuals publicly since 1949, not to mention during the Great Proletarian Cultural Revolution (1966–1976) because of strict political censorship on the mainland. It was only after the death of Mao Tse-tung (Mao Zedong/毛澤東 1893–1976) and the implementation of the "reform and opening" policy adopted by Deng Xiaoping (鄧小平 1904–1997) in the late 1970s that China heralded a period of social and cultural relaxation on the Chinese mainland, making it possible for the mainland intellectuals to enjoy a relatively liberal environment, in which they could again eagerly read many of the foreign and non-communist literature to continue their calling in seeking modern solutions to overcome the challenges facing China in her road to modernization. The horrors of totalitarian politics experienced in person by many of the mainland intellectuals during the big famine of the Great Leap Forward of 1958–1962 and the political purges of the Great Proletarian Cultural Revolution made Hayek's critique prophetically, albeit retrospectively, both overwhelming and persuasive to them. The fact that Hayek's critique was published well before the totalitarian horrors experienced by the mainland intellectuals under communist China speaks volumes about the theoretical vigor of Hayek's intellectual analysis in this regard. The same can be said of Hayek's life-long criticism of socialism, which started well before the Berlin Wall fell in 1989. That is why many Chinese intellectuals on the Chinese mainland have since taken Hayek's liberalism very seriously, whose social and political theory appeared to spread fast on the Chinese mainland soon after Deng's "reform and opening" policy to fill out the theoretical as well as ideological vacuum left by the loss of faith in Marxism-Leninism-Maoism in China (Gao 2017, pp. 218–220; Deng 2004; Liu 2000).

Hayek's critique of totalitarianism and his defense of liberalism, as I said earlier in this chapter, are supported by a systematic and powerful theory of society, from which Hayek derives his arguments justifying the value of freedom, the respect for the individual, and many liberal and spontaneous social and political institutions. As a social theory, Hayek's critique of totalitarianism is not primarily based on moral or ideological grounds. Instead, he offers a social-scientific explanation on the impossibility of synoptic, centralized social planning to achieve the intended political and economic ends of socialism (Hayek [1948] 1980, pp. 119–208). To Hayek, in any developed, complex, and diverse society, such an impossibility is not just practical, but epistemological. It is not only that there is no centralized authority capable of gathering all the fragmented and circumstantial information and knowledge possessed by each and every individual in the society in order to come up with one centralized plan to serve the different and diverse needs of all. What is more fundamental is the fact that these individual preferences, tastes, information, and knowledge are anything but static, and they are never given objectively out there as such; often they will be emerged and used only when they are being put into practice by individual actors in their spontaneous social interaction. They are, therefore, circumstantial, interactive, teleological/conventional, contextual, and dynamic, making it impossible for any central authority to know abstractly or in advance for certain what the individual social actors each would like to choose or act (Hayek ibid., Chapters 1–5, Horwitz 2001). While society often requires collective action, Hayek's individually based social theory denies the theoretical validity of a "collective" mind, and any centralized authority performing the role of a single mind for all to design and develop a comprehensive plan for a most rational and perfectionist society is nothing but hubris (Hayek [1952] 1979), and any attempt to implement such a comprehensive plan will require measures that will deny the autonomy of the individual, and this effectively is treating the individuals as means, serving some arbitrary, pre-determined ends favored by those who hold political, coercive power (Hayek 1960, p. 21). The understanding of this systematic and profound liberal social theory has helped the post-war Chinese liberals to develop, firstly in Taiwan, and subsequently on the Chinese mainland, a more critical and relatively more sophisticated liberalism in the Chinese context, which was unrivaled by pre-war Chinese liberalism (Ren 2004, pp. 1–21; Gao 2017, pp. 217–251). Consequently, post-war Chinese liberalism has, as a result, stood far more firmly on the ground of individualism rather than vacillating between collectivism and individualism like their pre-war mentors. Chapter 4 of this book below will elaborate on this important development in more detail. Post-war Chinese liberalism is also far more sensitive to the incompatibility between rationalistic state intervention and the spontaneous adaptation required for a liberal social order to cope with the always changing and dynamic external environment. Post-war Chinese liberals have, as a result, abandoned the pre-war consensus among themselves on the importance of the so-called economic equality and have since paid more attention to the unintended consequences created by social interaction among the individuals. Chapter 2 below will have more on this. Overall, Chapters 2–4 of this book together are my attempt to develop a more adequate account of the relevance of Hayek's theoretical critique of totalitarianism to the development of Chinese liberal thought in post-war Taiwan and in the era of China under Mao Tse-tung and beyond.

Spontaneous Social Coordination: Result of Human Action, Not Human Design

Hayek's epistemological critique of totalitarianism is justified by a critique of Rationalism with a capital R, or what he calls Cartesian Rationalism or Constructivism (Hayek 1967, Chapter 5; Hayek 1973, Chapter 1; 1978, Chapters 1–2). In the context of post-war Chinese liberalism, Hayek's negative critique of the impossibility of centralized socialist calculation and the chaos and suffering created by the coercive implementation of the command economy prompts the Chinese liberals to seriously consider the danger of radical utopian politics that aims to solve all socio-economic problems in one go. This, in my view, has inspired some leading Chinese liberals to start to explore the origins and the nature of radical and utopian thinking in modern China (Lin 2019, pp. 95–153; Lin 2020, pp. 3–74), and to examine whether this kind of radical utopianism is linked with the metaphysically perfectionist assumption of the Sage King idea, which is central to the political thinking of China since the classical period (Chang 1989, pp. 3–78; Chang 1990). I believe that the development of this liberal critique in Chinese political thought is important at least for two reasons. Firstly, it alerts the Chinese liberals of the danger of radical politics, and their preference for a gradualist and evolutionary approach in political reform is now grounded both in theory and in the painful experience many have suffered under political radicalism and Maoist utopianism in modern China. Secondly, China's radical utopianism appears to be linked with a mode of thinking which is not only holistic and moralistic, but it also assumes a belief in the primacy of adherence to a supreme moral and even utopian ideal before taking radical actions for social and political changes. It is a mode of thinking that is described by Lin Yu-sheng as privileging cultural and intellectual ideas and values in social and moral changes for the better, which has been inherent in the Chinese mode of thinking for a long time (Lin 1979, pp. 10–55). However, Hayek's epistemological critique of totalitarianism is premised on a social theory that is in great contrast with such a holistic and moralistic mode of thinking, and it argues that social coordination and development are achieved mainly not because of human design, whether intellectual or moral, but because of human interaction via rule-following conventions, practices, and institutions in a trial-and-error process, and the task of social theory is to explain how the unintended consequences of social interaction are both important and intelligible, and why they are related to spontaneous social coordination. Chapters 3 and 4 of this book will talk more about how Hayek uses the price mechanism in a free market as an illustration to show how his social and economic theory helps to explain the achievement of spontaneous social coordination, under which individual social actors/market participants can try to freely achieve their respective individual pursuits as far and as much as possible.

In other words, Hayek's theoretical critique of totalitarian politics, together with his explanation of why many of the social institutions and practices that help to sustain a civil order in society are the result of human interaction rather than rationalistic synoptic design (Hayek 1967, Chapter 6), not only helps the Chinese liberals to better understand the mode and the potentially catastrophic nature of radical utopian thinking in modern China, it also inspires the Chinese liberals to better understand the spontaneous, immanent, and evolutionary nature of sustainable social interaction and coordination. Hayekian liberalism also focuses their minds on one important point about real-life politics and policy consideration, and that is "The pursuit of unattainable goals may prevent the achievement of the possible" (Hayek 1976). This is a theoretical insight that Lin Yu-sheng has clearly taken up (Lin 2020, pp. 64–65) when he criticizes the unattainability of some Chinese utopian thinking and stresses the need to, when contemplating feasible and realistic social and political changes, learn from the Scottish Enlightenment (which is different from the rationalistic French Enlightenment), from which Hayek has derived many of his insights when developing his social theory in explaining spontaneous social coordination (Hayek 1967, Chapters 6–7; 1978, Chapters 15–16).

Given the impossibility of rationalistic, synoptic social planning, how is sustainable social coordination possible in Hayek's social theory? One important explanation advanced by Hayek in his social theory is that what renders individually oriented social coordination possible is man's ability to follow abstract rules, even though many individuals often time may not be aware of them when they interact with each other. In the essay "Rules, Perception and Intelligibility," Hayek makes the following observation:

> The most striking instance of the phenomenon from which we shall start is the ability of small children to use language in accordance with the rules of grammar and idiom of which they are wholly unaware. (Hayek 1967, p. 43)

Hayek then continues to say:

> Rules which we cannot state…do not govern only our actions. They also govern our perceptions. The child who speaks grammatically without knowing the rules of grammar not only understands all the shades of meaning expressed by others through following the rules of grammar, but may also be able to correct a grammatical mistake in the speech of others. (ibid., pp. 43–45)

The ability to use language for communication is vital for social interaction and coordination. Human action and perception, Hayek suggests, are in fact always rule guided. In the realm of practical skills, for example, there are a lot of social practices or human actions that are not the products of rational design. But they are nevertheless successful in the sense of fulfilling human expectations via interaction in many instances. Like the grammatical rules example, one does not need to know in a billiard-ball game how to construct the mathematical formulas that will give the directions of travel of the balls that will score most points under the circumstances before one is a good billiard-ball player (ibid.). These incidents show that the ability to act successfully is not necessarily derived from the ability to explicitly demonstrate by "reason" why it is successful. Rather, to use Gilbert Ryle's oft-celebrated statement, there is an important realm of human phenomena that is most appropriately regarded as "knowing how" without "knowing that" (Ryle 1963, Chapter 2. See also Polanyi 1962, Chapters 4–5).

In these examples, the rules of our language and of mathematical calculation can be followed by us all when we put them into practice, even though we may not be able to articulate them while acting. They are essential in coordinating interpersonal interaction and communication, even if we are not explicitly aware of them or in a position to understand the logic or principle behind them. For the functioning of a complex society, it is evident that rules of many different kinds are required to make spontaneous social interaction and coordination possible. These may include many of the rules of human conduct, such as prudential rules like "save for the rainy days"; moral rules like "keeping promises"; and rules of just conduct (i.e. laws) that prohibit murder. If the individual's autonomy is respected in a society, given the dynamic and contextual nature of individual preferences and the dispersed and circumstantial nature of the knowledge and information possessed by different persons, the rules that are capable of creating or maintaining a spontaneous social order must have the ability to coordinate the diverse actions of the separate individuals and to reconcile, according to certain mutually subscribed procedures, most if not all of the different and even conflicting ends pursued by separate and distinct individuals and social organizations.

While man is to observe these rules in his actions even if he is not conscious of them, the selection, adoption, and the sustainability of these rules will, according to Hayek, depend on their ability to adapt to "the solution of recurring problems situations faced by the society concerned and thereby help to make the members of the society in which they prevail more effective in the pursuit of their aims" (Hayek 1976, p. 21). In other words, while the characteristics of these rules help to coordinate diverse human actions, it is their long-term effectiveness in improving and sustaining the complex social order that ensures their prevalence. That is why Hayek calls many of these general rules in society "multi-purpose instruments" (ibid., p. 4). They are instrumental, not in the sense of necessarily helping an individual social actor to directly achieve his personal preference or chosen end. They are instrumental in the sense that they help to *coordinate* the pursuit by different individuals of their separate, chosen ends in their interaction. Although these rules alone do not guarantee the satisfaction of any individual's specific chosen preference, the sustainability of these "multi-purpose instruments" depends very much on whether they manage to develop an ever better problem-solving or coordinating capacity in the evolution of the social order, particularly when there is a need for such an order to make improvement in the light of competition and so on.

What are the distinctive attributes of these rules that help to make the spontaneous formation of a social order possible? In the first place, an order in which the ever-changing individual ends of its members can be coordinated must be an order that can attain any degree of complexity (Hayek 1973, p. 38). As it is impossible either for any individual or organization in a complex society to know the expectations of all the actors in entirety, or for a single actor to know all the particular relevant circumstances of time and place in social interaction, these rules of the spontaneous order must be able to coordinate most if not all the separate individuals' and organizations' pursuits of their respective, diverse, dispersed, and even conflicting ends without the need to resort to any rationalistic planning or coercion. The correspondence of individual ends in the social order must be achieved by mutually accepted abstract rules that can satisfy different individual expectations as far as possible, and they also must act as a guide for further interaction. In other words, unlike commands or specific instructions that aim at specifiable results, the first distinctive attribute of these rules must be that they are end-independent (i.e. not aiming at any specific end of any individual or any pre-determined end-result); instead, they must be capable of maintaining the abstract relations among individual members of the society in their interaction. These relations are abstract because the rules, unlike commands, are not formulated in such a way that they are applicable primarily to a here and now concrete situation, but to an unknown number of future instances, and the applicability of these rules is not restricted to any pre-defined specific individual, they are equally applicable to all members so long as their interaction happens to fall within the conditions and jurisdiction that are spelt out by the rules (Hayek 1976, p. 35).

Those common rules, institutions, and social practices that constitute a spontaneous social order should all possess these end-independent and abstract attributes. Such a social order, which presupposes pluralism and diversity, also requires a relatively clear demarcation of a private realm where the individual can make his free and autonomous decision, in contrast to a public realm where the interpersonal relations are to be regulated by some common, abstract, and end-independent rules and practices. In this regard, Hayek likes to refer to David Hume's three fundamental laws of nature to characterize the kind of practices required for the spontaneous social order: "that of the stability of possession, of transference by consent, and of the performance of promises" (quoted in Hayek 1960, p. 158). Some prominent examples of these rules and practices discussed in Hayek's social and political theory are the price mechanism in a free market, the moral value of the dignity of the individual, and the rule of law and constitutionalism. How these rules and practices make spontaneous social coordination possible will be further discussed in Chapters 3 and 4. Furthermore, how such a social theory helps Hayek to derive his defense of individual freedom and constitutionalism, and how they have impacted on the development of post-war Chinese liberalism's critique of revolutionary radicalism will be discussed in Chapter 6 below.

Tradition, Constitutionalism, and Human Agency

Hayek's critique of Rationalism and his theory of convention-based, rule-following, spontaneous, and evolving social coordination point to a liberal order that is the result of human action but not human design, though they do not exclude the possibility that when people begin to recognize the benefits or competitive advantage of such an order and its social practices for better social coordination, articulated efforts to make improvements in a gradual, incremental, and trial-and-error manner can always be attempted. To the Chinese liberals, the appreciation of these Hayekian theoretical insights has triggered a conservative turn of Chinese liberalism in the post-war era. As I have said earlier, since the May Fourth Movement, there was a dominant tendency among many Chinese intellectuals (liberals or otherwise) to adopt what Lin Yu-sheng calls an approach of "totalistic anti-traditionalism" in their efforts in nation building and in their pursuit of science and democracy in order to cope with the challenge of modernity in China. Whatever their respective different ideologies, the common consensus among these intellectuals (except the cultural conservatives) then was that the traditional Chinese culture was the main obstacle to achieve these important goals in modern China and hence, nothing short of the total abandonment of the Chinese tradition was what was required. Although from the perspective of Hayekian liberalism, it is impossible to cast away one's tradition in *toto* and to start afresh in one's social reform, even the leading Chinese liberal of the May Fourth period Hu Shih then demanded nothing less than the wholesale or maximal westernization in order to turn China into a modern state. Post-war Chinese liberals, after having learnt from the critical thought of Hayek and witnessed the horrors of totalitarian politics as practiced on the mainland in the 1950s–1970s, have given up their totalistic anti-traditionalism and started to re-examine the relationship between tradition and the pursuit of liberal values in China.

The conservative turn of post-war Chinese liberalism, together with the critique of radical utopianism by the Chinese liberals, in my view, has given rise to the following three major theoretical developments in post-war Chinese liberalism, all of which will be further explored later in this book with a view to outlining a research agenda for the development of Chinese liberal thought for the future.

Firstly, if a liberal social order cannot be developed without the partnership of many of the established, traditional practices of a society, the fact that there is a lack of individualistic, liberal values and practices in the Chinese tradition poses a particularly acute challenge to the Chinese liberals who want to introduce liberalism to modern China (Qiu 2014). One possible response to this challenge is to argue that there can be a constructive synergy between liberalism and Confucianism (traditionally the dominant ideology of China) so that a certain version of liberal Confucianism can be developed to satisfy the dual requirement of liberty and cultural identity for modern China. A related but different response is to attempt a "creative transformation of the Chinese tradition" by identifying those remanent elements in the Chinese culture that are still having the potential to be re-vitalized and modernized and to transform them and make them consistent with (or at least not contradictory to) the value of freedom. In this regard, Lin Yu-sheng's contribution is perhaps the most important, though he has mainly touched upon the social or cultural, instead of the political, aspect of his proposed creative transformation in this regard.

The second theoretical development differs from the first by arguing that, in fact there is a tradition of constitutionalism emerged in modern China, though this tradition is secondary to the dominant trend of radical revolutionism, it has nevertheless been there since the late Qing Dynasty and it is still going on, even though very intermittently. In other words, in the past 170 years or so, apart from the radical politics of revolutions, modern China has also developed quite a tradition of constitutionalism, which aspires to establish social and political institutions for the protection of individual rights and the development of democracy. In this regard, Taiwan since the 1990s is the most obvious achievement of this after the successful democratization of the island. A thorough understanding of this important democratic and constitutional development in the Chinese context is the way forward for the further development of Chinese liberalism. One focus for this approach is how the principles of the political constitutionalism of the liberal kind can be made gradually accepted and practiced in the Chinese context and what are the challenges ahead. In this regard, I believe that the works of Gao Quanxi (高全喜) (2003, 2016, 2017, 2022) are most interesting. If, as Hayek contends, human beings are rule-following actors in social interaction and coordination, how to improve the rules for constitutional politics in China perhaps is a very Hayekian approach in trying to transform China into a constitutional democracy if the social and political conditions are favorable. I shall discuss more on this in Chapter 6 below.

Last but not the least, underlining Hayek's critique of totalitarianism and his theory of the spontaneous social order is his moral and political individualism: "the respect for the individual man *qua* man" (Hayek [1944] 2007, p. 68, emphasis in the original). Whatever its shortcomings or inconsistence, Chinese liberalism also shares this fundamental concern of treating man as man, or respect for the autonomous individual. How some post-war Chinese liberals have enriched this conception under the influence of Hayek's "true individualism," and how individualism may be made gradually embedded in the Chinese culture will be further explored in Chapters 4 and 5.

Perhaps, it should be added at this point that while Hayek's theoretical insights have been instrumental in helping many post-war Chinese liberals to develop their liberal thought, it is incorrect to think that his is the only significant influence. Readers of this book can find in the Appendix that there are other leading Chinese liberals who have contributed substantially to the development of a more coherent conception of human rights and constitutionalism in the Chinese context. One prominent post-war example is Chang Fo-chuan (Zhang Foquan/張佛泉 1908–1994), whose liberalism is benefitted more from British idealism and Ernest Barker's political thought (Chang [1993] 2005) than from Hayek's classical liberalism. In the Appendix, Chang's liberal ideas, together with some others', are discussed in the context of Oakeshott's idea of civil association and free agency, and I believe that the discussion there addresses issues that are related to many of the concerns that the main chapters of this book also address.

Yadav is right to point out that while Hayek's critique of totalitarian politics and Constructivism was most pertinent in the twentieth century, Hayekian liberals in the West will need to catch up with the new intellectual challenge posed by what Yadav calls "political capitalism," in which authoritarian states in the world now have adopted a kind of capitalism that endorses the market mechanism and economic globalization, yet at the same time they have managed to continue to exert a tight and top-down authoritarian control in the political realm to preserve their power in their respective party-states (Yadav 2023, also see *The Economist*, 2023.12.02–08, pp. 65–66). In my view, Yadav has done a good job in further developing Hayekian liberalism in his book to meet the new challenge of the twenty-first century. I hope that what I am going to say below will also help to contribute to the enrichment of Hayekian liberalism. If successful, this is a contribution made in the Chinese context, and this may help to demonstrate that Hayek's ideas continue to be alive and relevant, not only in the West, but also in the East.

Notes

1. For the benefit of those who are not familiar with Chinese history, Chinese historical figures, thinkers, and authors analyzed and discussed in the main body of this book, when they are first mentioned, will be provided with their year of birth and year of passing away (if applicable) as far as possible.
2. I follow the Pinyin romanization system to transliterate the Chinese names of the Chinese people mentioned in this book, unless the person cited already has his/her own proper or widely accepted name in English or in another Chinese transliteration system. In the latter case, the Pinyin name of the person cited will also be mentioned in brackets when he/she is referred to for the first time in the book. In the case of Schwartz's book title cited here, since he did not follow the Pinyin system to transliterate Yan Fu's name, Yan's name in Schwartz's book is transliterated as Yen instead of Yan. In addition, when Chinese characters appear in this book, they will be in the version of Chinese traditional characters, not in the simplified version of Chinese characters.
3. The Nationalist government under Chiang promulgated the government's first constitution for the Republic of China in 1947, but after having implemented the constitution for about five months, the Nationalist government in May 1948 added certain emergency provisions to the constitution, which effectively was a declaration of martial law to cope with the imminent threat from the Chinese Communist Party whose People's Liberation Army was about to take over control of most parts of the Chinese mainland. The martial law provisions were not lifted until 1991 in Taiwan (see Gao 2022 Volume 2, pp. 189–191).

2

The Road to Serfdom and Cold War Liberalism in Taiwan and Mainland China

The Road to Serfdom and Post-War Chinese Liberals

The Road to Serfdom (Hayek [1944] 2007) is Hayek's first major work that has exerted a lasting intellectual impact on post-war Chinese liberalism. Hayek's ideas firstly influenced some leading liberals in the then Nationalist governed Taiwan in the early 1950s, and subsequently, his thought also became very popular among many reform-minded intellectuals in communist China when Deng Xiaoping adopted the "reform and opening" policy on the mainland in the late 1970s after the end of Mao's Great Proletarian Cultural Revolution.

The Road to Serfdom, which came out in 1944, was first introduced to the Chinese liberals in post-war Taiwan by David Chow (Zhou Dewei/周德偉 1902–1986), who studied at the London School of Economics under Hayek and Lionel Robbins from the autumn of 1933 to early 1936 (Chow 2011, pp. 347–351). According to Chow (2004, p. 287), he organized a bi-weekly discussion group in the winter of 1951 at home with some leading Chinese liberals in Taiwan after the then Nationalist government, having defeated by the communists in the Civil War, fled

C. Cheung, *Hayek and Post-War Chinese Liberalism*, Palgrave Studies in Classical Liberalism, https://doi.org/10.1007/978-3-031-64888-5_2

to the island province. It was then that Chow invited Yin Hai-kuang, a leading Chinese liberal in Taiwan in the 1950s and 1960s, to translate *The Road to Serfdom* into Chinese. Yin's selected translation came out, in serial form, in 1953–1954 in the then leading liberal journal *Free China*, and it managed to immediately persuade many Chinese liberals associated with Taiwan, including the leading liberal since the May Fourth period Hu Shih, to accept many of Hayek's theoretical arguments. I will go back to this point for a fuller discussion later in this chapter.

On the Chinese mainland, partly because of Hayek's thesis of the impossibility of socialist calculation and partly because of his attack on totalitarianism, the Chinese Communist Party started to pay attention to Hayek's ideas very early on after the establishment of the People's Republic of China in 1949. Hayek's *Prices and Production* was translated into Chinese on the mainland in 1958, and the mainland translation of *The Road to Serfdom* came out in 1962. Both, however, were only for restricted circulation among senior party cadres for internal ideological critique purposes in Mao's China. This notwithstanding, mainland scholars believe that these internal circulations helped to "spread Hayek's thoughts in Mainland China" in the pre-reform era (Li et al. 2017, p. 214).

While the Chinese liberals in Taiwan were persuaded by Hayek's theoretical arguments through reading *The Road to Serfdom* in the 1950s, many mainland intellectuals, when they were able to read Hayek for the first time in the 1980–1990s, found *The Road to Serfdom* nothing short of prophetic, though paradoxically in a somewhat retrospective manner. This was the case because what Hayek analyzed in the book in 1944 was corroborated more than once in their tragic personal experience during the Great Chinese Famine (also known as the Great Leap Forward) in 1958–1962 and the political upheavals of the Great Proletarian Cultural Revolution from 1966–1976. "This book had a huge impact on me," (Stephens 2013) said Yang Jisheng (楊繼繩 1940–), a leading mainland liberal journalist, now retired, whose prize-winning book *Tombstone: The Great Chinese Famine 1958–1962* (2012) chronicles the first major man-made catastrophe in communist China that led to an estimated 30 million people died of starvation under the totalitarian rule of the Communist Party. Yang's father was one of the victims died in this catastrophe. Yang remembers vividly Trotsky's statement quoted by Hayek in the book: "In a country where the sole employer is the State, opposition means death by slow starvation"[1] (Hayek [1944] 2007, p. 147). In Chapter 3 below, more will be said on how the 1958–1962 Famine and the Great Proletarian Cultural Revolution had turned Gu Zhun (顧準 1915–1974) from a believer in communism to embrace liberalism.

Laski vs. Hayek

One immediate impact of *The Road to Serfdom* on the Chinese liberals in Taiwan in the 1950s was that Hayek's arguments managed to convince many of them on the importance of economic freedom in a liberal democracy. In the preface to Yin Hai-kuang's selected translation of *The Road to Serfdom*, there is one oft-quoted passage telling the readers how Yin finally came to realize that without economic freedom, political freedom (i.e. democracy) alone would not be able to stop the slippery slope to serfdom in a state-controlled economy. In the first half of that passage, Yin gives us a vivid account of why to many Chinese liberals at that time, they believed that political freedom was compatible with economic equality[2]:

> I am a liberal. Like many post-May Fourth liberal leaning young people, my adoption of the liberal persuasion at that time started from the political dimension with little conscious thinking. There is an economic dimension to liberalism too. The economic aspect of liberalism has been under serious attack and criticism from the socialists. The mainstream liberals, including those whose ideas are derived from British liberalism of the Benthamite kind, have failed to defend the orthodox economic thinking of liberalism. They by and large have abandoned economic freedom in order to seek a compromise with socialism. At the same time, the communists have used the demand for "economic equality" to ferociously attack liberalism. Under the threats of such a critical, shocking, and urgent situation, also partly out of the mental drive to alleviate the above-mentioned threats, many Chinese intellectuals with a

> liberal leaning have gradually arrived at the position of advocating "political democracy and economic equality" together [as a compromise]. (Yin trans. [1944] 2009, pp. 1–2)

Yin was frank enough to admit that he was one of these liberals in China before. Even when he was adamantly opposing the Chinese Communist Party during the Chinese Civil War as the chief editor of the then Nationalist controlled the *Central News* (《中央日報》) in 1948, he was supporting nothing less than democratic socialism:

> In the search for a bright road for China's future…the consensus is that China must go down the "democratic socialist" road. For democratic socialism is the child born in wedlock between democracy and socialism, having the blood of democracy and the blood of socialism. It combines the best of both worlds to create an ideal society. (quoted from Fung 2010, p. 253)

After having read Hayek's *The Road to Serfdom*, however, Yin was convinced by Hayek that he was then mistaken:

> I have not properly studied political science, not to say economic science for that matter. Therefore, while I felt rather uncomfortable with the thought about [the compatibility of political democracy and economic equality], it was for me at most only a kind of "feeling" at the time, and I could elaborate nothing further. When my thinking fell into a state of bewilderment because of this, suddenly I came across Professor Hayek's *The Road to Serfdom*. My doubts and worries then disappeared. Hayek's theory has rehabilitated the liberal economic theory from socialism; it has hence saved liberalism, and he has further extended his theory on a moral foundation. When one's rice bowl is being forcefully controlled by those in power, where can one speak of freedom? Hayek's rehabilitation of liberalism is really no small achievement. (ibid., p. 2)

Before we go to further explore why most pre-war Chinese liberals favored economic equality or security over economic freedom, let's not forget that *The Road to Serfdom* originated from a memo written by Hayek in the early 1930s to the then Director of the London School of Economics Sir William Beveridge, whose 1942 report for a comprehensive welfare reform provided the blueprint for the post-war British Labour government to establish its ambitious welfare state in the UK through central economic planning. In the memo, which subsequently was expanded into a journal article, Hayek disputed the then popular claim among progressive intellectuals of the West that fascism represented the dying gasp of a failed capitalist system against the rise of democratic socialism. To Hayek, the error of the democratic socialists was that they mistakenly believed that only by thorough, rational planning of the state could we save mankind from the cyclical economic boom and bust disasters inherent in capitalism (Hayek [1944] 2007, p. 1. See also Hayek 1994, Part III). In the Introduction of *The Road to Serfdom*, Hayek turned the democratic socialists' argument to its head, contending that "the rise of fascism and Nazism was not a reaction against the socialist trends of the preceding period but a necessary outcome of those tendencies" (Hayek [1944] 2007, p. 59). This was the case because, according to Hayek, the almost absolute faith in rationality in the pursuit of some high ideals through central economic planning, a faith which was shared both by the socialists and by the fascists, sooner or later would require the state to unambiguously engage in the nationalization of the means of production, which was exactly what socialism meant in the 1940s; and the need to attempt to ensure the central plan to achieve the ultimate ideals and be freed from "irrational" or "unplanned" disruptions would eventually force the state to take over total control of the society by increasingly coercive means. That was why both fascism and socialism would, if unstopped, lead us to totalitarianism, producing just the opposite of what many of the democratic socialists had been striving for (ibid., p. 60).

Although the prime targets of Hayek's criticism in *The Road to Serfdom* were Nazi Germany and Soviet Russia (less directly for the latter at that time since it was a wartime ally to the West while Hayek was writing the book [see ibid., p. 40]), he was equally critical of the then British Labour Party whose political program through the parliamentary route to socialist planning and nationalization of enterprises, in his view, would not only undermine the liberal ethos of the British people, but would possibly be forced to go down the slippery slope of totalitarian control if the government prepared to achieve and protect all its intended socialist goals and objectives at all costs. In *The Road to Serfdom*, Hayek had launched some scathing attacks against Harold Laski, his London School of Economics colleague in politics and a leading intellectual member of the then British Labour Party, criticizing many of his proposals as "proclaiming the doom of the freedom of the individual" (ibid., 208).

Specifically, Hayek had in mind the British Labour Party's 1942 pamphlet *The Old World and the New Society* for post-war Britain, in which the party advocated that "there must be no return to the unplanned competitive world of the inter-War years, in which a privileged few were maintained at the expense of the common good" (ibid., 12). Laski described market competition as "mad," the result of which brought poverty to all peoples and was responsible for the outbreak of war (ibid., 208 n. 52). In spearheading these ideas, Laski urged the British Labour Party to continue to adopt the governmental program of "[n]ationalization of the essential instruments of production before the war ends [and] the maintenance of control over production and distribution after the war" (ibid., 13) in order to eliminate capitalist exploitation for the enhancement of the economic security of the people. Failing that, Laski argued, "liberty is not worth having" (ibid., 156 n. 9). Hayek pointed out in *The Road to Serfdom* that Laski was so determined to protect economic security over liberty that for him "the continuance of parliamentary government would depend on [the Labour government's] possession of guarantees from the Conservative Party that its work of transformation would not be disrupted by repeal in the event of its defeat at the polls" (ibid., 105n. 4).

It must be pointed out at this juncture that most pre-war Chinese liberals, particularly throughout the period of the 1940s, were more convinced of Laski's ideas than that of the free market liberals of the West. Lin Jianhua (林建華), in his book-length study of Chinese liberalism in the 1940s, observes that "Chinese liberals in the 1940s all aspired to [US President] Franklin D. Roosevelt's "Four Freedoms."[3] On the other hand, the British Labour Party's integration of Fabian socialism and the labor movement and its success in getting hold of governmental power through peaceful means also appeared to have served as a model for many Chinese liberals (Lin 2012, p. 3. See also Chapter 4 of Lin 2012).

I think it is probably no exaggeration to say that in the pre-1949 era, apart from a few intellectuals trained in economics or were directly influenced by Hayek, such as David Chow, Tsiang Sho-Chieh (Jiang Shuojie/蔣碩傑 1918–1993 who was Hayek's second Chinese student after Chow at London School of Economics in the 1940s) and Xing Muhuan (邢慕寰 1915–1999) (who attended Hayek's Chicago seminar in 1946) (see Zhang 2012, p. 19; Wu 2015, pp. 206–207), Hayek's *The Road to Serfdom* and his idea of economic freedom failed to impress most mainstream liberals in China.

Quentin Pan (Pan Guangdan/潘光旦 1899–1967), a leading educationalist, sociologist, and a Central Committee member of the China Democratic League which represented many pre-1949 mainstream Chinese liberals, disagreed with Hayek's thesis that economic freedom and economic planning were incompatible after he had read *The Road to Serfdom* soon after its publication. Pan criticized Hayek's idea as radical and biased (Zhang 2012, p. 31). Laski's another Chinese student Wu Enyu (吳恩裕 1909–1979) argued in 1946 that Hayek's idea was outdated, and he doubted if liberalism with an individualistic foundation was ever possible again with the growing trend of socialism (ibid.). Perhaps the most typical view adopted by the pre-1949 Chinese liberal was best articulated by Fu Sinian (傅斯年 1896–1950). Fu was a prominent member of the liberal wing of the Chinese Nationalist Party, a leading historian and the one who led the student protest movement on May Fourth of 1919 in Beijing against the unfair treatment of China by the Western powers and Japan at the Paris Peace Conference. In his 1945 article remembering President Roosevelt after the sudden death of the latter, he not only praised the contributions made by Roosevelt's "Four Freedoms" to the cause of new liberalism, but Fu also argued that without economic equality, freedom was not real, not to say other equalities. Fu further separated liberalism from capitalism, saying that while the former had helped to create equality before the law to the people, the latter promoted huge economic inequality, which also led to the evil of imperialistic expansion to the developing countries (Fu 1945, p. 110).

Fu's anti-capitalist and anti-imperialist sentiments were widely shared by pre-1949 Chinese liberals. Edmund S. K. Fung observes that "[Chinese pre-1949 liberals] were…in the main 'revisionist,' statist liberals with democratic socialist leanings" (Fung 2008/2009, p. 572). Most of them were statist because they embraced the western ideology of liberalism primarily for the sake of national salvation and nation building to strengthen the state capacity and power of China in order to fend off imperialist invasion of all kinds, though many of them did not wish to resort to violent revolutionary means to bring political change to China. To them, while democracy was important, equally important, if not more, was for the state to be strong to modernize itself, and to help to alleviate poverty and backwardness of the nation by organized political power. That was why a statist approach rather than an individualist approach to liberalism was always to be preferred.

One clear illustration of the statist orientation of the Chinese liberals was the 1933–1935 debate on the question of enlightened dictatorship versus democracy among the liberals themselves. After the Japanese annexation of the North-Eastern part of China (Manchuria) in 1931, many Chinese liberals, including very close friends of Hu Shih like historian Tsiang Tingfu (Jiang Tingfu/蔣廷黻 1895–1965) and scientist Ting Wen-chiang (Ding Wenjiang/丁文江 1887–1936), believed that only by granting dictatorial power to the state would China be able to cope with the challenge of national salvation (Zhi 2010; Han 2015, p. 145). Although in the debate Hu Shih resisted to concede to his friends' arguments in favor of dictatorship in China, it is interesting to point out that for him, even the communist experiment of the then Soviet Union was classified as "democratic development" rather than "dictatorship" (Zhi 2010, p. 232). It is important to note that Hu Shih in the pre-war period regarded the democracy movement of the 18th–nineteenth centuries in Europe as inseparable from the mid-nineteenth century's socialist movement there, believing that the latter was just the continuation of the former in another, more advanced stage (Hu 1928, pp. 38–39) Since Hu always believed that Western civilization, when compared with the East, represented a higher water mark of the development of modernity (ibid., pp. 31–32. See also Hu 1926), and his evolutionary ethics was such that "socialism is a logical sequence of the democratic movement" (see Lin 2013, p. 63), his difference with the other liberal friends in this democracy versus dictatorship debate was far less fundamental than the difference between statist liberalism and classical liberalism. This, however, was going to change soon, to the extent that in the early 1950s, after Hu had studied Hayek's *The Road to Serfdom*, Hu openly made a confession that he now accepted that socialism was just one aspect of totalitarian communism, and that without economic freedom, individual freedom would be hugely compromised.

The Confession of a Chinese Liberal: Hu Shih

On March 5, 1954, Hu Shih delivered a famous speech entitled "Talking about *The Road to Serfdom*" (〈從《到奴役之路》說起〉) (Yin trans. [1944] 2009, pp. 183–189) in Taipei at a welcoming reception organized by *Free China*, in which he not only acknowledged that Hayek's book was an important contribution to liberalism and individualism, he also confessed that he was persuaded by Hayek that socialism of all stripes was against freedom (ibid., p. 184).

In his speech, Hu made the following important points in re-evaluating liberal democracy.

First of all, Hu referred to his previous July 1941 speech "Conflict of Ideologies" made at the University of Michigan of the United States, in which he argued that revolution as a means to bring about comprehensive and fundamental social changes required the most dictatorial kind of political power to achieve its goals, and he regarded this as qualitatively different from democracy. Hu further alluded to the respective experiences of the extreme rightist Nazism and the extreme leftist Stalinism to demonstrate their anti-democratic, totalitarian nature, in which these regimes could not maintain their power without resorting to radical and dictatorial measures such as concentration camps, rounding up of political prisoners, forced labor, and so on. It is clear that in the 1940s, with totalitarian politics on the rise, Hu started to retract from his sympathetic view of the 1930s over the Soviet's "democratic" experiment and his position on this was apparently reinforced by having read Hayek in the late 1940s or early 1950s. Hu was now clear that liberal democracy was incompatible with Nazism and communism (ibid., p. 187). We may add that the success of the Chinese communist revolution on the mainland and the establishment of the communist regime in China in 1949 had further strengthened Hu's position on this.

Secondly, in his confession speech, Hu also made known the fact that he was influenced by a friend[4] through the discussion they had in the past two years, and he now came to appreciate Hayek's argument that so long as they shared the conviction in economic central planning, socialism, fascism, and communism would all lead to totalitarian control of the means of production and destroy individual freedom if they insisted on achieving their political objectives. The difference in this among these ideologies was only a matter of degree. Hu now also appeared to endorse his friend's observation that it was wrong to assume that socialism was the more advanced stage and the inevitable future of democracy. On the contrary, Hu now believed that it was likely that left-wing political ideologies would lead to the road of serfdom as Hayek argued (ibid., pp. 185–186). In his November 24, 1953, diary entry, Hu said that Hayek's thesis of the incompatibility of freedom and socialism was "commendable." He also referred to Hayek's citation in *The Road to Serfdom* of Johann Christian Friedrich Holderlin's statement: "What has always made the state a hell on earth has been precisely that man has tried to make it his heaven." In the diary, Hu insisted that he was a liberal who believed in a sound conception of individualism. Therefore, he would not be able to accept any kind of socialist principle and belief. (Lin 2013, p. 63).

Let us not forget that in a 1935 article in commemorating the May Fourth Movement, Hu equated his sound conception of individualism to liberalism, which advocated critical thinking, nurtured an independent personality, and attempted to develop the individual's potential to the full (Hu 1935, pp. 244–245). But at that time, however, he continued to have reservations about the economic aspect of individualism, which failed to avoid the result of economic inequality (ibid., p. 243). While he started to criticize Soviet Russia's suppression of freedom of thought at that time, he still praised the communist revolutionaries as fighters who fought for individual freedom (ibid., p. 246). Indeed, soon after the Cold War started and the Nationalist government and the Chinese

Communist Party were engaged in a fierce civil war in China, Hu, in an important article written in 1947, had already made it very clear that he would side with the democratic world against the communist bloc for the sake of freedom. But even at that time, Hu was still of the view that democratic socialism was consistent with freedom and socialized economic policy like those pursued by the British Labour Party was something to be commended (Hu, 1948, p. 168).

By 1953–1954, however, Hu, while still upholding his conception of sound individualism, no longer regarded socialism of any kind being compatible with individual freedom. In his confession speech, he went all the way to endorse the view expressed by another Taiwanese intellectual in a discussion of Hayek and Ludwig von Mises that capitalism not only would not collapse, but it instead would also have a bright future (Yin trans. [1944] 2009, p. 184). At the end of the speech, Hu asked rhetorically whether the hardworking Chinese people would prefer to rely on themselves each as an individual to develop a free economy, or whether, with a clear intention to allude to the first five-year plan (1953–1957) implemented by the Chinese Communist Party on the mainland at that time, the five hundred million Chinese people's economic future and livelihood should be planned and determined by a few leaders instead (ibid., pp. 188–189)?

With this change of attitude, Hu was also critical of the Nationalist government's policy of nationalization in Taiwan (ibid., p. 185), and he urged that the liberals in Taiwan should launch a fundamental critique of the Nationalist government's economy policy, since the liberal economy of the free market was the correct approach (ibid., p. 189), and open criticism against the government would demonstrate that Taiwan, unlike the mainland, did enjoy freedom of speech (ibid., pp. 183–184).

Cold War Liberalism and Post-War Taiwan

Judging from his 1954 confession speech, it is not unreasonable to say that Hu's conversion had a lot to do with the political success of the Chinese Communist Party and Hu's understanding of the horrors of totalitarian politics as witnessed in Nazi Germany and Soviet Russia.

Given the more or less pre-war consensus of the importance of economic equality over political freedom among mainstream Chinese liberals, Hayek's criticisms of the progressive intellectuals in the West over their failure to appreciate the dangerous logic of central economic planning as explained in *The Road to Serfdom* should certainly have played an important role in persuading Hu to accept Hayek's warning of the end-result of totalitarian rule from the path of socialist politics. What is less clear was on what theoretical grounds did Hu come to terms with Hayek's critique of socialist planning and why he now was willing to embrace liberal capitalism?

According to David Chow, he had the opportunity to meet with Hu not long after Hu had delivered his speech. At the meeting, Hu told Chow that one of his friends wrote to him urging him not to change his view on capitalism even though he now agreed with Hayek's critique of communism. At a subsequent meeting, Hu further asked Chow to provide him with a reading list on some leading contemporary anti-communism literature, and Chow introduced the works by Mises, Wilhelm Röpke, Karl Popper's *Open Society and Its Enemies,* and some other works of Hayek to Hu, though Hu admitted that he was too out of touch to the latest development in this field then (Chow 2004, pp. 288–290).

Perhaps Hu and many Chinese intellectuals were all struck by the success of the communist revolution in China, and they all feared that the establishment of the People's Republic of China meant that the prospects for freedom and democracy would be completely lost in this dictatorial regime. Critical and historical events like these, together with the Cold War, were enough to create a general anti-totalitarian sentiment among these intellectuals, and for the post-war Chinese liberals in particular, such a sentiment would draw most of them to become sympathetic with the arguments developed by different public intellectuals in the West who shared the same kind of liberal temperament, even though these intellectuals, such as Karl Popper, Isaiah Berlin, Raymond Aron, Hayek, and so on, might come from different intellectual traditions with different theoretical outlook, and not all of them were involved in the study of political theory even though they were mostly shaped by the liberal culture of Europe (Nardin 2015, pp. 2–3).

I believe that it is probably true to say that Hu had never articulated an adequate theoretical explanation on his conversion.[5] Wang Yuan-yi (王遠義 1959–) powerfully argues that while Hu had unambiguously stood on the side of freedom and democracy in post-war China against communism, this leading Chinese liberal failed to enrich his liberalism even after having convinced by Hayek. To Wang, this speaks volumes about the superficiality and limitation of Hu's liberalism when compared with the profundity of Hayek's social theory (Wang 2012).[6]

In fact, even Yin Hai-kuang, the one who first translated *The Road to Serfdom* into Chinese in the early 1950s and had more or less become a Hayekian Chinese liberal since, failed to properly grasp the theoretical significance of Hayek's critique of central economic planning, as I would try to show in the latter part of this chapter.

In the next section, I shall spell out, as precisely and adequately as I can, the core arguments of Hayek's critique of central economic planning found in *The Road of Serfdom*, arguing that a proper understanding of these arguments will help us to fill out the theoretical void left by Hu's conversion, and help to correct some initial misunderstandings made by some post-war liberals in Taiwan over Hayek's theory, the clearance of which can pave the way for a better appreciation of these Chinese liberals' adoption of Hayek's epistemological thesis against socialism and the moral thesis of respecting "the individual *qua* man instead of merely as the member of an organized group" (Hayek [1944] 2007, p. 218) as they first learned from *The Road to Serfdom*.

Hayek's Critique of Central Economic Planning

The Road to Serfdom was the first book published by Hayek which went beyond technical economics. Hayek described it as a "political book" (Hayek [1944] 2007, p. 37), which, with hindsight, heralded the beginning of Hayek's subsequent intellectual development as a polymath. In fact, Hayek's criticism against central economic planning happened prior to *The Road to Serfdom*. He and Mises began to argue for the impossibility of socialist calculation from an economic point of view in the

1920s and 1930s, a topic I will return to in the next chapter of this book when we examine Gu Zhun (who is now regarded by some as China's Hayek) and his defense of the market economy under communist China in the 1950s. The main focus of Hayek's criticism of central economic planning in *The Road to Serfdom* is to try to demonstrate that planning in a directed economy is such that if pursued consistently and vigorously to its logical end, it will require the state to exert total control over the population in order to achieve a pre-determined goal or end-state, the nature of which is bound to be arbitrary and controversial, with the government exercising coercive power to force any possible dissenting voices who are either against the goal or against the adoption of the chosen means to achieve the goal to fall in line and to oblige.

Hayek's analysis starts with the differentiation of two qualitatively different kinds of planning: namely, (1) planning in the sense of a systematic application of reason to social problem, and (2) planning in the sense that the concrete action of the different individuals—what he is to do and how he is to do it—is to be decided by a supreme central planning agency (ibid., Chapters 4–6, and Hayek 1994, p. 194). To Hayek, the first kind of planning, with the conception of "reason" properly understood, is both reasonable, unavoidable, and consistent with individual freedom. It is partly because of this that the idea of planning has so much appeal to our common sense. The second kind of planning, however, requires central direction according to some preconceived social blueprint, which in the end requires some individual mind to decide for the rest of us what we have to do at each moment in order to achieve what is promised in the blueprint, even though it is almost impossible to achieve consensus about the concrete ends pursued in the blueprint, the realization of which is also far from certain.

Originally, *The Road to Serfdom* was meant to be the last part of Hayek's grand intellectual project on the abuse of reason conceived in the 1940s. The first three parts of the project, according to the original plan, were, firstly, an overview of the individualistic theories of the eighteenth century (i.e. the Scottish Enlightenment, etc.), with the second part on the intellectual hostility toward these individualistic theories, which was to be followed by an historical account of the spread of anti-individualist ideas from their origins in France, Germany, England, and beyond, and finally, with the last part focusing on the examination of the decay of reason in the twentieth century under fascism and communism (Caldwell 2004, pp. 240–241). This perhaps over ambitious project was never completed though, but many of Hayek's publications at that time can be regarded as closely related to his critique of Rationalism and the abuse of reason project. For example, several of the essays published in his *Individualism and Economic Order* (Hayek [1948] 1980) fall into the first part, with *The Counter-Revolution of Science: Studies on the Abuse of Reason* (Hayek [1952] 1979) belongs to the second and third parts, and, as said before, *The Road to Serfdom* being the concluding part of the intended project.

We have already dealt with some of the fundamental criticisms launched by Hayek against totalitarianism in Chapter 1 of this book, and it is important to remember that when Hayek talks about the first kind of planning in *The Road to Serfdom*, the application of reason is no synoptic or scientistic "reason." Instead, it is the use of reason, whether tacit, practical, or explicit, for the provision of an institutional framework or for a system of general, non-instrumental rules equally applicable to all and intended to be permanent (though not immune from revision in the light of necessary change), within which decisions as to what to do and how to earn a living are left to the individuals, with more or less effective coordination being carried out by no central authority, but by established social practices and interactive mechanisms (such as established moral rules or the price mechanism), which are mostly the results of human actions but not human design. Subsequent chapters of this book will examine these important Hayekian theses and how they have impacted on the development of post-war Chinese liberalism. Meanwhile, the rest of the current chapter will mainly concentrate on why Hayek believes that planning of the second kind ultimately is totalitarian in nature and as such is anti-democratic to say the least.

To Hayek, economic central planning aims to replace free exchange with "the deliberate organizations of labors of society for a definite social goal" so that the allegedly "whims and fancies of irresponsible individuals" (Hayek [1944] 2007, p. 100) will not be allowed to create chaos, waste or even "mad competition" (ibid., p. 208 n. 52) for the benefits of the privileged few at the expense of the many. These various kinds of collectivism, communism, fascism, or socialism, Hayek argues, "differ among themselves in the nature of the goal toward which they want to direct the efforts of society," but they are united in organizing "the whole society and all its resources for [an] unitary end and in refusing to recognize autonomous spheres in which the ends of the individuals are supreme" (ibid., p. 100). Needless to say, there must be a central planning authority within a collective of this kind to establish the "deliberate organizations of labors," to determine what the "unitary end" or "social goal" should be, and to be in charge of the resources available to the collective for the implementation, according to a centralized plan, of concrete actions and strategies for the attainment of the common end/goal. The information and knowledge which guide the organization of labor, the determination of the common goal, the implementation and production activities leading to the attainment of the goal, and so on are ultimately dependent on the centralized authority, not on the combined knowledge of the separate individuals' spontaneous interaction and coordination in the end (see also Hayek 1994, p. 196).

The first and foremost question that needs to be resolved in the economic central planning approach is how in a single and centralized plan to determine the so-called common or social goal for all. Hayek notes that it is far from adequate if the central planners come up only with vaguely defined terms like the "common good," the "general welfare," or the "general interest" to stand for some definite social goal under the central plan, since they are too imprecise to help to determine a particular course of action in the planning and implementation process.

If one admits that the welfare and the happiness of millions of the people cannot be measured on a single scale of more or less, and the happiness of a man or the welfare of a people depends on a great many of the things that can be provided in an infinite variety of combinations, we can direct all our activities according to a single plan only if we presume that there is in existence a complete ethical code in which all the different human values are allotted their due place and that every one of our separate needs is given its rank in an order of values which must be complete enough to make it possible to decide among all the different courses which the planner has to choose. However, to Hayek, "The essential point...is that there is no such complete ethical code exists" ([1944] 2007, p. 101).

Why is it that there does not have such a complete ethical code to exist? Hayek's arguments in providing answers to this question are crucial for a better understanding of some important aspects of his social theory and classical liberalism.

To start with, Hayek thinks that "strictly speaking, scales of value can exist only in individual minds," and he regards this as one fundamental fact on which the whole philosophy of individualism is based (ibid., p. 102). This obviously puts Hayek's discussion of scales of value on a Kantian footing where respect for the individuals means respecting them as autonomous beings who set moral ends for themselves even though one may have different views and evaluation as regards those ends (Baron et al. 1997, pp. 10–15).

Hayek goes on to say that such scales of value of the individuals must be "partial" (Hayek [1944] 2007, p. 102). This is the case because "it would be impossible for any mind to comprehend the infinite variety of different needs of different people which compete for the available resources and to attach a definite weight to each," and "it is impossible for any man to survey more than a limited field, to be aware of the urgency of more than a limited number of needs" (ibid.). The partiality of individuals' scales of value not only makes a complete ethical code for the central planners impossible, but also means that different individuals may hold quite different scales of value, be they more self-centered or largely altruistic. Some of these scales may also be inconsistent with each other and honest people could sincerely disagree with each other in this regard.[7]

In the light of the above analysis, if central planners press on economic central planning regardless, that means that they are going to impose their own preferred, partial, and arbitrary scales of value, in a hierarchical order, if necessary, onto the whole community and force the rest of the people to accept their ends as the social ends for all. As such, the arbitrary scales of some override the individual's scale of value should the individual differ from the planner's preferred scales, which, given the diverse interests and needs of the people in general, clearly means that there is no respect for the individual. Instead, the central planners prioritize their chosen scales of value in the name of "common good" and implement them in a single plan obliging all the people to follow.

In order to make their single plan effective, dissenting or different voices/scales of value, together with any departure from the single plan happened or expected to be happened anywhere in the community, cannot be allowed. They need to be suppressed, if possible, by coercion when needed, until the planners' pre-determined end (regarded as a "common" purpose for all under the single plan) is achieved. This, if pressed to its logical extreme, will be the certain road to serfdom according to Hayek, and is against the kind of individualism that is defended in Hayek's classical liberalism.

Although in *The Road to Serfdom*, Hayek did not spell out in detail his defense of individualism, he did highlight the importance of "the respect for the individual man *qua* man" (ibid., p. 68). He pointed out that this individualism acquired its essential features from Christianity and the philosophy of antiquity, and was fully developed during the Renaissance, with "the recognition of [man's] own views and tastes as supreme in his own sphere…and the belief that it is desirable that men should develop his own individual gifts and bents" (ibid.). It is to the credit of people like Yin Hai-kuang that this important idea was consciously picked up by post-war Chinese liberals in Taiwan. In my quotation of Yin's preface to his translation of *The Road to Serfdom* above, we can find that Yin specifically referred to Hayek's contribution to articulate his liberalism on a moral foundation, and he, together with his colleague Xia Daoping in *Free China*, subsequently further developed this thesis of "respect for the individual man *qua* man" as one essential moral pillar for Chinese liberalism, a topic that I will further examine in Chapter 4 of this book. Perhaps, Hu Shih was also impressed by Hayek's defense of individualism in *The Road to Serfdom* when he reiterated his commitment to a sound conception of individualism and would not accept any version of socialism after having studied Hayek's book in his diary entry of November 24, 1953.

Hayek's argument of the non-existence of a complete ethical code also has important implications for democracy in his analysis on the problems of economic central planning. While agreement among individual scales of value is difficult if not impossible to achieve, Hayek believes that "people are most likely to agree on common action where the common end is not an ultimate end to them but a means capable of serving a great variety of purposes" (ibid., p. 102). Here, perhaps it is more accurate to say that the means capable of serving different individual purposes are better to be described as a set of *general, common rules* or procedure rather than "common action," it is clear from the context of Hayek's statement that he believes that while an imposed "common" purpose under a single plan to be carried out by the state is a problematic road likely to lead to serfdom, planning in the first sense of the word as explained above for the provision of an institutional framework or for a system of general, non-instrumental rules equally applicable to all to facilitate free interaction and personal pursuit of individual objectives is the pre-condition for a liberal state to prosper. Hayek calls this "Planning and the Rule of Law" in *The Road to Serfdom* (Chapter Six), and he further develops this theme subsequently in *The Constitution of Liberty* (Hayek 1960) and in the first volume of *Law, Legislation and Liberty* (Hayek 1973). I will examine this important topic when we discuss how Hayek's idea in this area has influenced the development of liberal constitutionalism in China.

Hayek's criticism of economic central planning and his preference for planning for the rule of law brings him to stress that if we really treasure democracy, we should restrict governmental power within areas where agreement is possible. He believes that democratic government is discredited mainly because "democracy having been burdened with tasks for which it is not suited." "Government by agreement is possible" says Hayek, "only if government action is confined to subjects on which people have common views" (Hayek 1994, p. 205). The non-existence of a complete ethical code for all means that if central planners insist on carrying through the single plan for the fulfillment of their self-imposed "common" purpose to the state, the government "shall either have to coerce people to agree, or to abandon government by agreement, or both" (ibid.). Therefore, the price to be paid for democratic government is to limit the functions of the government to the establishment of a common institutional framework or set of general and non-instrumental rules for the pursuit and fulfillment of individual purposes. This is what Hayek calls nomocracy (or, constitutional/rule-based government), as in contrast with teleocracy, or government by a "common" purpose (Cheung 2014a). Hayek believes that contrary to the common claim that democracy will not tolerate economic freedom/capitalism, it is the merit of economic free competition that "it reduces the necessity of agreement to a minimum compatible with the diversity of individual opinions which will exist in a free society" (Hayek 1994, p. 205). To that extent, Hayek argues that "only capitalism makes democracy possible. And if a democratic people come under the sway of an anti-capitalistic creed, this means that democracy will inevitably destroy itself" (ibid., pp. 205–206).

It seems clear that Hayek's theoretical arguments about central economic planning and democracy in *The Road to Serfdom* were just the opposite of what the pre-war Chinese liberals believed. It is not far off the mark to say that the fact that post-war Chinese liberals in Taiwan managed to fundamentally revise their position on economic equality and individual freedom was largely in debt to Hayek's influence, even though Hu Shih did not spell out the theoretical reasons behind his conversion in 1954, and some Chinese intellectuals in Taiwan, including Yin Hai-kuang, initially were still a bit confused. For example, in the explanatory notes in his translation of *The Road to Serfdom*, Yin still claimed that while he now accepted that political freedom was prior to economic equality, the latter could still be regarded as a subclass of human rights, which, theoretically speaking, could require the government to discharge the duty to achieve a certain pre-determined, end-state kind of wealth redistribution. Yin's understanding here, I think, is still teleocratic rather than nomocratic in nature. To do this redistribution, the government must be given enough power to interfere with and override the results of the free exchanges of the individuals, as well as to allow those who are in public offices to impose their preferred level of economic equality over the whole population in an arbitrary and controversial manner (see Yin trans. [1944] 2009, pp. 111–116; Cheung 2018, pp. 192–198; Jiang 1968, pp. 157–170). This initial confusion notwithstanding, it is true to say that Hayek has replaced Laski and became one leading influence in the development of post-war Chinese liberalism in Taiwan after the publication of *The Road to Serfdom*.

As regards Hayek's influence on the mainland, although Chinese liberalism largely disappeared since the Chinese Communist Party, led by

Mao Tse-tung, took over the mainland in 1949, the fact that Hayek's *Price and Production* and *The Road to Serfdom* were translated for internal reference on the mainland into Chinese in 1958 and 1962 respectively indicated that even the Chinese Communist Party was aware of Hayek's theoretical influence in economics and in political study well before Deng Xiaoping opened up China for economic reform in late 1970s.

In the preface to the 1962 mainland translation of *The Road to Serfdom,* the translators openly acknowledged that Hayek was a very influential thinker of capitalism in the West (Teng & Zhu trans. [1944] 1962, p. 1). Although, to the best of my knowledge, there has little evidence to show that Hayek's social and political theory had any direct impact on the intellectual development of Mao's China (1949–1976), one extraordinary fact was that Hayek's critique of socialist calculation and his idea of nomocracy had some important parallel developments in the People's Republic even at the heydays of totalitarian rule there, and this was to be found in a dedicated communist revolutionary turned liberal thinker called Gu Zhun in the period when socialist central planning was vigorously introduced and enthusiastically implemented in China. Gu Zhun now is credited with the honor of being the first mainland Chinese economist who argued for the indispensability of the price mechanism for economic coordination even under socialism and advocated market reform in China as early as the mid-1950s, some even refer him as China's Hayek in this regard (Wu 2005, in Luo ed. 2017, p. 184; Bottelier 2018, p. 132). It is to the liberal lessons of Gu Zhun's thought that we must now turn.

Notes

1. Yang's book (2012) won the Manhattan Institute's Hayek Prize in 2013, and his views on Hayek and China can be seen in the interview he gave to *The Wall Street Journal* in "Reading Hayek in Beijing," May 24, 2013, by Bret Stephens at http://www.wsj.com/articles/SB10001424127887324659404578501492191072734, accessed on February 25, 2020.

2. The English translation of the Chinese text here is mine. Throughout this book, except otherwise specified, the translation of the English text into Chinese is mine.
3. Roosevelt's "Four Freedoms" are: freedom of speech, freedom of worship, freedom from want, and freedom from fear. Hayek, however, very much worries about Roosevelt's "Freedom from Want" (Hayek 1960, p. 421 n. 1). To Hayek, the full realization of this "freedom" probably requires the state to centralize the control of the process of production and distribution of goods in accordance with a pre-determined, acceptable level of want satisfaction, leading to the kind of nationalization of the means of production that makes the road to serfdom unavoidable.
4. Hu did not mention the name of his friend in the speech because the friend was a government official in Taiwan then. I think it is reasonable to say that judging from the historical context and the evidence related to the exchanges between Hu and David Chow at that time, this friend was David Chow, Hayek's first Chinese student at London School of Economics (see Chow 2004, pp. 286–290; Wang 2012, p. 229 n. 148).
5. Hu Shih passed away in 1962, at the age of 70.
6. Space here does not allow me to fully elaborate this important point. But I basically agree with the sophisticated arguments developed by Wang Yuan-yi in (Wang 2012).
7. In early 2020, the world was under the attack of the pandemic COVID-19 and some governments in the developing world faced the moral dilemma of locking down cities to prevent the spread of the infectious virus with insufficient provisions of food or allowing normal productive activities to be continued at the risk of a large number of people being infected with the deadly disease. As the then Prime Minister of Pakistan Imran Khan said, "If we shut down the cities…we will save [people] from corona at one end, but they will die from hunger." One wonders if there is a complete ethical code to help to determine which course of action to take without disagreement under such circumstances and uncertainties.

3

"China's Hayek" and the Liberal Lessons in Gu Zhun's Thought under Totalitarian Rule

From "Venture Communist" to "China's Hayek"

Gu Zhun is relatively unknown to the outside world. Even in the Chinese-speaking world, those who are not familiar with the development of liberal thought in China in the post-war period seldom hear about Gu Zhun and his thought.

Gu was born in Shanghai, China's most economically developed city before the communist takeover. He started to apprentice as an accountant at the age of 12 under the mentorship of the then Harvard-trained Pan Xulun (潘序倫 1893–1985), who is regarded as the father of modern accounting in China. Gu was a successful young professional at that time and authored several widely circulated textbooks on accounting. Upon Pan's recommendation, Gu became a professor of economics at the Shanghai College of Commerce. However, he chose to join the Chinese Communist Party when he was 20 because the Nationalist regime failed to resist Japan's invasions to China. Before Gu

An earlier version of this chapter appears in Cheung (2020).

C. Cheung, *Hayek and Post-War Chinese Liberalism*, Palgrave Studies in Classical Liberalism, https://doi.org/10.1007/978-3-031-64888-5_3

became a communist, he was radicalized through his contact with the young printers of the Shanghai Commercial Press during his liaison with them for his books' publication. These printers, according to an historian of Shanghai at Berkeley, "were among the most radical of Shanghai's organized workers" (Yeh 2007, p. 199). Gu was also influenced by one former senior schoolmate at Chinese Society for Vocational Education who joined the then communist and unionist-infiltrated Labor University where Gu picked up Western radical political thought like anarchism and the idea of capitalist exploitation of the laborers. It was from about that time that Gu gradually started to embrace the idea of violent revolution in China and regarded his professional accounting work of serving the capitalists in Shanghai as a kind of disgrace (Gu 2002a, pp. 15–20; Yeh 2007, p. 199).

Late in 1934, because of his radical ideas and political activities, Gu was forced to flee his home from possible persecution to Shanghai's foreign concessions where the Chinese government did not have jurisdiction. At around the same time, Gu formed the Society for Progress with his former classmates of Chinese Society for Vocational Education and his young associates in the accounting profession, and the Society eventually became a spontaneous Marxism-Leninism cell under the Chinese Communist Party. After joining the Chinese Communist Party, Gu became a leading cadre in the Shanghai and East China region. He, however, needed to flee again in 1940, this time out of Shanghai and went finally to Yanan, the revolutionary base of the Chinese Communist Party, in 1943. In April 1949, Gu returned to Shanghai triumphantly with the People's Liberation Army. He was tasked with the responsibility of taking over the financial and taxation departments of the municipal government of post-civil war Shanghai (Gu 2002a, pp. 65–149; Yeh 2007, pp. 200–204).

Although Gu Zhun's time wielding at the helm of taxation and public finance of liberated Shanghai was far from long (1949–1952), his excellent professional knowledge, his good old-boy network with Shanghai's accounting and finance elites who had been working with him and his mentor, together with his pragmatic strategies helped him not only to come up with creative policies and measures to implement a smooth takeover, but also to restore Shanghai's war-torn economy and fill up the coffers of the nation by increased tax revenues soon after the Civil War. By March 1951, tax receipts in Shanghai, through Gu's insistence on the implementation of his specialist system of taxing on the profit on capital, had already swelled to almost eleven times their level of 1950. When compared with the ideologically more orthodox bottom-up democratic assessment method as advocated by some other cadres, Gu's system appeared to be less politically correct by indirectly allowing the capitalists' profit motive to thrive in a newly created socialist state. But the success of Gu's professionally oriented system managed to provide the new state with increased and durable sources of revenue for the urgent tasks of national reconstruction and funding the war in Korea, to which the People's Republic of China was firmly committed at that time. To Gu, the democratic assessment method was arbitrary, allowing members of different trade associations to ascertain rather subjectively how to apportion their respective shares of tax payment to fulfill the state imposed overall quota of tax revenue. Gu's taxation system eventually got the blessing of Mao and was practiced nation-wide.[1]

Christopher R. Leighton has given us an excellent account of Gu Zhun in Shanghai in 1949–1952 (Leighton 2014). It is interesting to note that Leighton calls Gu a "venture communist." He argues that Gu confounds some general assumptions about communist cadres, since "while he may have been a cadre, Gu Zhun was also something of an entrepreneur (of economic related ventures more than actual commercial firms, to be sure), conversant with the language and processes of business, and accomplished at introducing novel ways to novice audiences...Not all cadres were bent on wiping away Shanghai's [capitalist] past; taxes could be an exciting, modernizing innovation, and within the party some evangelists for economic change imagined a different sort of socialism" (ibid., p. 120).

For Leighton, Gu was never a doctrinaire communist. To Gu, the Western-style accounting methods were a tool. While the capitalists might use it to protect profit, the communists could wield it to raise state revenues or wrest back imperialist owned property (ibid., p. 130). Leighton further shows us that Gu was never a fan of the Soviet-style centralized command economy from day one. Instead, he and other like-minded cadres in this period pursued "a decentralized, locally based system of socialist enterprise, overseen by regional governments with budgetary independence from the central government" (ibid., p. 136), in which the locally controlled state enterprises each should implement "enterprise-type accounting" to tighten fiscal control for effective and economically efficient management as much as possible (ibid., p. 137).

Gu's did not stay long enough in his leadership position in Shanghai to allow his scheme mentioned above to succeed, though Leighton regards it as having set a very early "precedent for decentralization and market socialism" for Deng's reform era (ibid., p. 136). Somewhat unexpectedly and without any pre-warning, Gu was abruptly removed from office in early 1952 during the Five Anti Campaign launched by Mao. The Campaign was to fight against the "capitalists" in the Party and on the mainland on charges of bribery, tax evasion, theft of state property, and economic information. However, Gu was never accused of any substantial "capitalist" crimes in the Campaign, and no specific charges were raised. The Shanghai party committee only accused him of "grave individual heroism" and "disregarded organizational discipline" (Gu 2002a, pp. 209–213). While here we see many signs of an idiosyncratic communist cadre in Gu Zhun with unorthodox views on how to pursue socialism on Chinese soil, his substantial and well-articulated departure from doctrinaire socialism came a few years later in 1957 when he first challenged the then orthodox view of the dispensability and temporality of the law of value and the price mechanism under socialism in his theoretical article "A Tentative Discussion of Commodity Production and the Law of Value under the Socialist System" (2002b, pp. 77–133).[2] In the article (hereinafter called "Tentative Discussion" in this chapter), he argues that socialism could not do without the law of value, the price mechanism or using money as a circulating medium for exchange. This is because without following the law of value in economic production, there is no rational basis for socialist planning, not to say a more effective and efficient utilization and allocation of resources. This was a challenge that in many ways similar to Ludwig von Mises' and Friedrich von Hayek's critique of socialism in the famous socialist calculation debate in the 1920s and 1930s in the West (Hayek [1948] 1980, pp. 119–208).

Economic Calculation and Socialist Planning

Mises is the first theorist who argues that since it is not possible to have economic calculation under socialism as understood by Marx and Engels, the system of socialist central planning is "just a system of groping about in the dark" (1963, p. 699). To Mises, socialism is a system of social cooperation without a market, in which private property is replaced by collective ownership, with the state owning all the means of production. Production is purely for use in accordance with a centralized command plan and not for exchange. Commodities under such a system will eventually be abolished since all consumption goods are only for socialized use. Money is no longer required as there is no need for any medium of exchange to be circulated, and the price mechanism is superfluous because values of the products only reflect the useful labor time for their production. Exchange value has allegedly become irrelevant.

Mises believes that under socialism, economic calculation is logically impossible since without the price mechanism and money as the medium of exchange, there is no common standard to compare the relative economic efficacy of different products, services, and factors of production in a society. It is therefore unclear how socialism can make improvement to its economic performance to better serve the needs of the people.

To Mises, the Marxian labor theory of value is problematic not only because it is never clear if there exists any universally valid scale to define what is skilled and what is simple labor and to conduct conversion between the two, it is also because if value is defined as the amount of socially useful labor time for production, it is far from adequate since it fails to take all other non-labor factors of production into account in determining the true value of a product. "What is ultimately decisive for the solution of the problem of the feasibility of using labor as a basis of economic calculation," says Mises, "is the question whether one can assimilate different kinds of work to a common denominator without a valuation of the products by the consumer" (1981, p. 115). Mises points out that with the abolition of private property and the market, it is doubtful if the central planners can come up with a rational plan for production and distribution for all that can serve the respective preferences of the producers and consumers.

Hayek's contribution to this debate is to develop Mises' logical critique into an epistemological critique, spelling out the indispensable part plays by circumstantial knowledge (such as market participants' here and now but always dynamic preferences) in economic decision and social coordination, and why the contextual and interactive nature of this kind of knowledge (e.g. market players' decisions are dependent on their anticipation of what other players may decide) makes central planning impossible ([1948] 1980, pp. 77–91). To Hayek, "[t]he economic problem arises…as soon as different purposes compete for the available resources" (ibid., p.123), and it is unclear on what rational basis a central planner can rely on to determine which purpose should be chosen in his plan over other competing purposes to better suit the needs and demands of the citizens.

A close examination of Gu's "Tentative Discussion" shows that he came up with similar views on this question of economic calculation, even though there is no evidence to suggest that when he wrote the article in 1956–1957, he had the privilege of having learned from Mises and Hayek in the famous socialist calculation debate of 1920s and 1930s.[3]

Gu argued that on matters like this, it was more important to empirically examine the issues involved (i.e. looking at the actual practice of state socialism we found in the USSR and China) rather than dogmatically assuming that Marxism had already solved all the economic problems under socialism once and for all. In "Tentative Discussion," Gu was not only courageous enough to point out the contradictions committed by Stalin (2002b, p. 96) and the inadequacy of classical Marxist theory on this matter, he in effect advanced the thesis that without the price mechanism in the market, there was no rational basis to come up with a common yardstick to measure and compare the relative economic efficacy of different products, services, and factors of production in a society. Like what Mises and Hayek had argued, Gu believed that central planning alone would not provide us with the necessary information for economic allocation, production, and coordination.

Gu admitted in "Tentative Discussion" that classical Marxism argued that in theory, market exchanges among individuals would be abolished and money as a medium of exchange was therefore superfluous under socialism. Money would then be replaced by coupons which represented the useful labor time contributed by the workers concerned in productive work. Workers could use the coupons to redeem the allocated consumption products they deserved to get under a socialist economy (ibid., p. 79). However, Gu reminded us that the historical experience in Soviet Russia demonstrated that the efforts in introducing the labor coupons to replace money in the country after the October Revolution failed, and Lenin was forced to reverse this policy by 1921. Money as a medium of exchange had since been reintroduced and it remained in place in the USSR and in socialist China (ibid., p. 83). On matters like this, Gu thought that instead of being dogmatic, one should be open-minded and learn from our actual experience, since Marx and Engels were not in a position to know about all the subsequent developments occurred in the socialist states with ready-made answers to the new problems we might have encountered subsequently (ibid., p. 88).

Gu argued that money as a medium of exchange had many functions that could not be replaced by labor coupons. For example, as a general medium of exchange, money allows consumers to use it to buy different kinds of products and services since it provides a common numerical standard for exchange. Also, through savings, interests, credits, loans, and other related financial tools, money can be developed into a credit system that facilitates delayed or advanced spending and investment if the people or enterprises find it desirable to do so. However, the crucial point is that money, together with the price mechanism and the law of value, provides a common standard in economic calculation to help to determine what rational economic decisions shall be made to enhance productivity and better distribution of resources.

Gu noted that classical Marxism did not anticipate the need of doing economic calculation under socialism. Quite the contrary, it postulated that products produced under socialism would only have use value since all the products produced under socialism were only for socialized use, not for exchange (ibid., pp. 104, 108–109). However, Gu argued that if socialism aimed to increase a society's overall productivity and to improve the well-being of the people, we could not simply rely on a pre-determined central plan to come up with information about the relative economic efficacy of a certain product when compared with its substitutes before making the most economically rational decision for production and resource distribution. Instead, we would have to rely on economic calculation to ascertain the relative economic efficacy of the concerned product before a production and distribution decision was made. This, in effect, is the same as admitting the inevitability of the economic problem under the circumstances, a theoretical point recognized by people like Hayek, who believes that "decisions of this sort will have to be made in any conceivable kind of economic system, wherever one has to choose between alternative employments of given resources" so that the advantages deriving from the most economically use of given resources can be taken ([1948] 1980, p. 123).

Why the most economical use of given resources cannot be planned in advance? Gu's answer was that it was because the level of labor productivity changes all the time, depending on many contingent and changing factors, such as the more efficient use of given resources due to technological breakthrough, the change in the length of necessary labor time, the improved skillful use of production facilities, the reduction in management cost, variation of time in the cycle of production, the extent of using recyclable materials, so on and so forth (2002b, p. 85). Gu believed that only through economic calculation could we capture this kind of dynamic information to help planners to come up with a rational approach in economic planning. Gu argued that historically, it had been proven that treating the whole society or country as one accounting unit in economic calculation was not viable (ibid., p. 97). Instead, each enterprise should be treated as one separate and independent accounting unit, each possessing its own fund and balance sheet to do the calculation. Where necessary, a big enterprise should also be subdivided into different independent sub-units for the same accounting purposes. This, in effect, amounts to suggesting that there should be decentralization in the management of enterprises, with each enterprise enjoying its autonomous status in economic calculation. This eventually was a reform measure adopted under the Deng era for the development of "market socialism" after the late 1970s.

Gu's idea is that the price of a product is a numerical index expressed in the form of a circulating currency that represents the value of a product. If the currency is relatively stable, the price of a product, when compared with the value of that product, is relatively more stable, though the sum total of all the prices in a society in the end must equal the sum total of the values of all the products produced in that society. If the price of a particular product in that society is higher than the value of the product concerned, it will be balanced out by the lower than value price of another product in the same society in the end. In a society's division of labor, the necessary labor spent on a particular product is not a constant, and hence the value of the product may vary from time to time as explained above. The value of that particular product is also not the same as the average useful labor time spent on all the products of the society too, and it is through this relativity in values, which ultimately are translated into the relative prices of different products in the market, that helps to determine the relative economic efficacy of different products (ibid., pp. 106–111).

Gu said that the pure income in an accounting unit through the sale or transfer of products was not a pre-known data. Instead, it is through economic calculation, reflecting the changes in the unit's productivity level and the demand and supply situation in the economic process, that the enterprise concerned can come up with the actual data, which is the total income minus the cost of production (including workers' salary, expenses for resources and facilities for production, maintenance and management fees, depreciation, taxation, and so on) (ibid., pp. 155–173). The same kind of product or its substitute may be produced by different accounting units, but the pure income of each of them may vary, depending on their ability to control costs and to meet new demands. If the enterprises or producers are in a position to adjust the price of the product in accordance with their productivity level and with the demand and supply situation found in the market, those with higher productivity and earn more pure income will be in a position to adjust the price of the product to facilitate more production and sales, aligning the price more with the adjusted value of the product. This in effect is bringing market competition back into the economic process.

The dynamic nature of economic calculation and the static nature of central planning were clearly recognized by Gu in "Tentative Discussion":

> Economic calculation's ability to make adjustment helps economic planning to obtain data that cannot be obtained by statistical surveys, and it is on the basis of these data that future economic planning is to be made. For example, when a society's level of consumption is raised, production of consumption materials should in parallel be expanded accordingly. However, amongst the different and diverse kinds of consumption goods, which ones should be expanded, the extent of expansion, and the proportion of expansion amongst different consumption goods are all important data that cannot be reliably found just by consumption surveys, no matter how meticulous these surveys are. Yet by observing the movements in the retail market of consumption goods, by identifying which products are very much sought after and which are not, and by looking at the price adjustments made in the sales of these products, one can detect all the changes happened in demand and supply and, in accordance with which, one could adjust one's production decisions. Similarly, in each production enterprise, the sales situations and the related price and profit adjustments happened to its products are important indicators telling us the degree of equilibrium achieved between product production and consumption and the changes in productivity level. Information of these kinds is all very useful for future economic planning. Society's re-production process is a continuous process and the annual production plan for the society does not come out of the blue. The information and data generated from economic calculation form one fundamental basis for economic planning. Without these, no economic planning can be made. (ibid., p. 99)

While Gu mostly adopted socialist ideas and terminology in advancing his arguments for economic calculation under socialist planning in "Tentative Discussion," the logic underlying his analysis was in many respects consistent with the critique of socialist calculation as separately developed by Mises and Hayek, though Gu did not go all the way to analyze in what ways were the decentralized, independent accounting units (i.e. enterprises) different from the privately owned enterprises and how these state-owned but independent units could be autonomous and state-directed at the same time when doing economic calculation. Likewise, Gu's insistence on economic calculation did not go all the way to deny socialist planning, even though it was clear from his arguments that the two were by nature logically rather incompatible.

The publication of "Tentative Discussion" in 1957 eventually earned Gu the honor of being regarded by many as the father of socialist China's market reform (Bottelier 2018, p. 132), though its more immediate impact was that partly because of this, he was purged by the party as a rightist (i.e. a reactionary who opposed the revolution). He was expelled from the party in the autumn of 1957 (Gu 2002a, pp. 225–250). Although Gu was not the only first-generation economist (Bottelier 2018, pp. 125–138) since the establishment of the People's Republic to advocate the importance of the market in building socialism after 1949, his "Tentative Discussion" was the most critical and comprehensive theoretical treatise before the Great Proletariat Cultural Revolution to openly examine the limits of central planning and the necessity of introducing economic calculation in communist China.[4]

Hayek is of the view that "the differences between socialists and non-socialists ultimately rest on purely intellectual issues capable of a scientific resolution and not on different judgments of value," and he believes that the doctrines advocated by the socialists "can be shown to be based on factually false assumptions," and the whole family of socialists thought can be "proven erroneous" (1973, p. 6). When it comes to Gu's understanding of the relationship between economic calculation and socialist planning, I think it can be said that he was far closer to Hayek than to Mao and the then Chinese Communist Party. This is one reason why he is labeled by some today as "China's Hayek" (Ma 2010, in Luo ed. 2017, pp. 328–348). But the subsequent political purges against him and his experience during the Great Leap Forward and the Great Proletarian Cultural Revolution helped to convince Gu that communist idealism was not the answer to China's modernization. Instead, liberal empiricism was what was needed if one wanted to avoid the horrors of totalitarianism.

Famine, Politics in Command, and the Horrors of Totalitarian Rule

Not long after Gu was expelled from the party in November 1957, he was sent to labor camps for re-education. He was first sent to a camp in Hebei province (May–December 1958), and later to the remote rural area of Shangcheng (March 1959–February 1960) in Henan where he experienced one of the worst famines in human history. That was the Great Chinese Famine of 1958–1962, in which close to 30 million people were estimated to have died in the food crisis (Sen 1999, p. 181; Lin and Yang 2000, p. 145).

In November 1961, Gu managed to remove his rightist label and resumed his work in the Economic Research Institute of the Chinese Academy of Science. But he was purged as a rightist again in September 1965 before the start of the Great Proletarian Cultural Revolution. This time, his wife divorced him and later committed suicide. His children disowned him as father and refused to see him again throughout his life.

Gu, however, did not stop reflecting on the communist experience of China during these difficult times. Most of his critical reflections in these two "re-education" periods can be found in his diaries from October 1959–January 1960 and October 1969–September 1971 (Gu 1997, 2002d), respectively, with the former chronicling how the Famine killed many of the rural peasants in Shangcheng, and the latter recording his personal suffering after having learned of his wife's suicide. These diaries also contained his analysis that the politics in command kind of revolutionary approach adopted by Mao would eventually need to give way to economic reform and a policy of open door if China wanted to avoid further economic catastrophes and to build a strong nation.[5]

Although Gu's diaries were no systematic studies of the communist experience of China in those periods, his analysis was sharp as his critique profound. For example, a careful reading and reconstruction of his observations there could help to vindicate Amartya Sen's subsequent entitlements approach in explaining the cause of famines in modern society where both property and democratic rights are absent (Sen 1981; Zhang 1998, in Luo ed. 2017, pp. 191–212). One famous quote of Hayek is from Leon Trotsky: "in a country where the sole employer is the State, opposition means death by slow starvation" (Hayek [1944] 1972, p. 119). Gu's analysis in his diaries echoed this observation. It showed that in a country where the sole employer and power holder was the party, and the party upheld politics in command with a wartime economy imposed on the peasants with a view to achieving rapid industrialization in the urban cities at the expense of the rural areas, death by slow starvation for many peasants in the countryside was probably inevitable, even though the overall food supply may still be sufficient to feed the whole population. Absolute control in this period was supplemented by ruthless political campaigns and oppression against the "class enemies," in which Gu was labeled as one of them.

In Gu's Shangcheng diary (Gu 1997, pp. 1–131), three things came out very prominently. They were, firstly, hunger, food, and death by starvation. Secondly, hard labor by the rural people and those who were undergoing "re-education" in the labor camps even at the time of food crisis. Thirdly, Gu's reflection on the cause of the Famine and how communist oppression inevitably led to general moral depravity, which was reminiscent of what Hannah Arendt has to say about totalitarian domination: the killing of the juridical person in man, the murder of the moral person in man, leading finally to the killing of man's individuality (Arendt 1973, pp. 437–459).

We learn from Gu's December 1959 diary entries that there were 79 members in his hard labor team, most of them were under "re-education" in Shangcheng (Gu 1997, pp. 71–72). He reported that in the summer of 1959, a few team members started to look bloated because of malnutrition. This was to increase to over 40 in September and October, which later jumped to over 70 in November/December 1959 when the famine in Shangcheng sunk in and hit the population hard (ibid., pp. 47–48). Gu subsequently recorded that out of the 79 members in the hard labor team, three of them died of starvation (ibid., p. 119). This, on its own, already indicated the seriousness of the famine, and we should be mindful that even under such a situation, most of them in the team (except the leading cadres who were there to enforce party rules) were required to do whole day hard labor work most of the time. Gu himself was required to engage in all day hard labor work in 190 days out of the 199 days while he was with the team in Shangcheng (ibid., p. 82).

However, when compared with the local peasantry, the situation in the hard labor team looked like "heaven" and a "safe haven." This was the case because while food was scarce, its supply had not been stopped for the team (ibid., p. 13). On the contrary, out of the 13 members in Gu's vegetable farming sub-unit in his hard labor team, there were six local members, out of which five had family members died of starvation at that time (ibid., p. 87). In his December 17, 1959, diary entry, Gu recorded that a member in another sub-unit named Huang had his wife, father, elder brother, and two kids died of starvation within a matter of one and a half months. At least four local members in the hard labor team had more than one family member died of starvation (ibid., pp. 51–52 & p. 94). In fact, there were horrendous news of cannibalism in Shangcheng as recorded in Gu's December 22, 1959, entry, in which a husband ate his wife after he had killed her, and an aunt ate her niece after the latter had passed away (ibid., p. 58).

Gu estimated that in that winter, if the then 420,000 population of Shangcheng could be reduced by 70,000 to 350,000 before local food supply was expected to improve next spring, it would be a very good thing already (ibid., p. 53). Gu observed that hunger would drive people to do whatever necessary for survival, such as cannibalism, prostituting, lying, flattering in order to get favor, falsely accusing others in return for food, and so on (ibid., p. 118). In his January 14, 1960, diary entry, Gu was tormented by the fact that he stole food in order to combat hunger many times while he was in the hard labor team (ibid., p. 113). Gu described Shangcheng as a land full of wailing and despair (ibid., p. 74) where it was not uncommon that half of the members of an agricultural production team in the rural area died. Gu also noted that while the situation in Henan was bad, the province further south in Hubei was even worse (ibid., p. 119 and p. 130). That spoke volumes of the serious situation in this Famine during the Great Leap Forward.

But the situation in the urban areas was very different. Gu was allowed to leave the labor camp in Shangcheng on December 28, 1959, after having served in the hard labor team for 199 days. He, together with other released members of the team, stayed in the county town area of Shangcheng until January 17, 1960, before returning to Beijing. Throughout these weeks, Gu no longer faced starvation. Food supply for him and his colleagues was not a problem then. They even had the opportunity of visiting a designated model village Changchunyuan south of Shangcheng. Gu found that Changchunyuan had a population of 20,000 with 20,000 acres of good quality farmland. Although it was a remote village, the food supply was abundant. Unlike peasants in other rural areas who were required to help with massive infrastructural projects, such as highway and big dam construction, people in Changchunyuan were not required to do the same. A nearby village called Daquandian also enjoyed a similar privilege and was relatively well off (ibid., p. 90).

Even in the badly affected areas, as we have seen above, the hard labor team was in a better situation than the ordinary peasantry in Shangcheng. Although members in the team were mostly rightists and were undergoing socialist "re-education," most of them were from the big cities. The team and the labor camp were managed by the party with relatively secure though reduced food supply. The ordinary peasants, on the contrary, did not enjoy this treatment. In addition to facing reduced supply, the peasants had to fulfill the official procurement quotas before they could have food to eat. Also, within the team, the leaders and those who were close to or favored by the leaders never had the problem of having adequate food supply.

For example, Shen Wanshan was the party secretary responsible for re-educating the members of Gu's hard labor team. Not only that he could eat whatever he wanted, he also occupied the best acre of land in the camp, which could produce high-quality vegetables, with members of the team helping him to do many of the necessary chores in the field (ibid., p. 3). Gu described Shen as a "dictator" and "emperor," saying that while members who planted the melons in the field were thieves if they picked the melons without formal permission, Shen could pick them anytime he liked for private use. His family members could take whatever food they wished in the collective kitchen anytime, which was a forbidden area for other team members. Similarly, those who had the fortune of working in the collective kitchen or were being favored by Shen were a privileged few with no problem of having adequate food supply (ibid., p. 8 & p. 37).

In his diary, Gu did not subscribe to the view that the main cause of the Famine was the sudden drop of total food supply, even though China did suffer from drought and bad harvest then (ibid., p. 58). Instead, he believed that it was the result of a centralized, tightly controlled political system imposed by the Chinese Communist Party, with the aim of speeding up China's industrialization by creating a kind of semi-military type of wartime economy to exploit a backward, massive, and overpopulated rural sector in order to squeeze enough surplus for urban modernization.

Gu argued that China had long been a vast agricultural country with the peasantry living on a subsistence kind of economy. Any rapid population growth in the countryside would easily lead to overpopulation without a corresponding growth of food supply, unless there was a great improvement in agricultural productivity, which could only be achieved by agricultural mechanization in a large scale. This situation fitted well into the Malthusian trap and the related theory of population (ibid., p. 48). In order to cope with this problem, Gu believed that the Chinese Communist Party under Mao wanted to solve the problem of rural overpopulation and the need for rapid industrialization in one go by following Stalin's collectivization program of the 1930s. In the Chinese context, what was introduced was a rigid household registration system, in which there was a strict control for people's movement between the urban and rural areas and from one's registered household location to other locations. Secondly, in the rural areas, people's communes, a kind of semi-military production and labor formations, grouped all the peasants into different units, the organization of which were modeled after the military for mass mobilization to help to build great infrastructural projects for the state during their off-peak agricultural seasons. According to Gu's diary, 70 million people nation-wide were organized for this purpose in 1959 to exploit the cheap and massive labor force in the rural areas for rapid modernization.

In the communes, collective kitchens were established with food rationing and consumption under tight control. When overall food supply was a problem, the collective kitchens would be hit seriously since the party adopted a policy of favoring the urban areas in order to facilitate urban development and rapid growth in heavy industry (ibid., pp. 58–59 & p. 86). Another serious problem for the rural areas in the Great Leap Forward was that under the euphoria of rapid transition to socialism promoted at the time, many local authorities had largely exaggerated many of their alleged production quotas in order to demonstrate their revolutionary zeal and achievement, the result of which was that local rural food supply was further diminished because of the need to fulfill the inflated quota requirements. Lin and Yang's 2000 research showed that while 1959s overall food supply dropped by 15%, China's net grain export (presumably to earn foreign currency) continued to reach historical height. In addition, the total procurement of grain output by the central authorities also reached a peak since the quota-output ratio of 25.9% in 1958 was raised by inflated quotas to 37.7% in 1959. "As a result," Lin and Yang said, "the excessive procurement severely reduced the food supply to which rural people were entitled" (Lin and Yang 2000, pp. 143–144) during this serious food crisis.

Gu at that time did not have the benefit of having access to the relevant macro data that Lin and Yang later have in analyzing this Famine. But what he observed in his diary was essentially confirmed by Lin and Yang's more systematic work almost 40 years later, in which they argued:

> In 1953, the central government introduced a system of Unified Procurement and Unified Sale for grain and oil-bearing crops, which brought all grain procurement and distribution under its direct control, as a way to suppress food prices...Accompanying the Unified Procurement and Unified Sale was a rigid household registration system, which deprived the rural population of the right to move to urban areas and thereby put the country-to-city migration under the government's tight control. The aim of these schemes was to extract as much agricultural surplus as possible to facilitate the heavy-industry-oriented development strategy that had resulted in an increased demand for grain and other agricultural products for urban food consumption and exports. (ibid., p. 139)

Under such a central command policy, when there was a sudden drop of overall food supply, the rural areas had to bear the crux of the food crisis since they were only entitled to the residual grain. The result for this was 30 million deaths by slow starvation. Gu speculated that this perhaps was Mao's conscious policy to control the problem of overpopulation in rural China (Gu 1997, pp. 108–109). He further suggested that the accompanying political persecution campaign of the Anti-Rightist Movement served the political purposes of mass mobilization against "class enemies" in a crisis situation. The official line was always that the food problem was essentially an ideological, not a practical, problem (ibid.,

p. 97) because, as always, politics was in command to serve revolutionary cause to build socialism.

Gu's "re-education" experience in Shangcheng convinced him that the kind of socialism practiced by the Chinese Communist Party at that time was to centralize the whole nation's strengths for wartime-like construction so that the privileged minority could live a normal or luxurious life (ibid., p. 37). He pointed out that while the labor cost in the communes was squeezed to a bare minimum, big and small industrial enterprises in the urban areas could be built by the party whatever the costs, with the remaining surplus going to finance the construction of the Great Hall of the People next to the Tiananmen Square of Beijing and other grand buildings for national celebrations (ibid., pp. 70–71). To Gu, such kind of political control and economic centralization was bound to produce abuse of power, grave disparity, and corruption. He believed that the kind of "re-education" offered in the hard labor team would bring nothing but moral depravity (ibid., p. 107). In his December 29, 1959, diary entry, Gu mentioned the last speech made by party secretary Shen to his team members before they were released. In Gu's view, the essential point made in Shen's speech was to warn them that when compared with the overall achievements of the Chinese Communist Party, what the members went through and suffered in the hard labor team—i.e. lying, hunger, death—was nothing, and they, after their release, would have to mind their words in the future if they wanted to avoid further political incorrectness, which would be consequential (ibid., p. 76).

Gu's 1959–1960 and 1969–1971 diaries contain many entries describing how he and his fellow members in the labor camps suffered political oppression and moral depravity. But two things stand out most clearly that are close to what Arendt describes as attempts for total domination (1973, pp. 437–459) by totalitarian rule.

The first was the so-called thought exposure exercises, in which the accused were constantly required to expose their innermost "evil" thoughts to the Party and to the people in public if they wanted to have a chance for rectification. The accused were also required to participate in thought exposure exercises against other rightists and to join criticizing and accusing the latter openly. The more active they participated in these mutual criticisms and exposures, the more politically correct they would be as perceived by the party (Gu 1997, pp. 15, 20, 24–25). The second was that refusal to admit guilt and even committing suicide by the accused were no escape, for these would only be regarded as proofs that they were die-hard counterrevolutionaries in life and in death. This would likely bring adverse consequences to family members or close colleagues of the accused.

In Gu's November 12, 1969, diary entry, there is a very tragic and moving description of how he received the news about his wife's death in Beijing while he was about to be sent to a labor camp in Henan for "re-education." Gu's wife, as we now know, took her own life in April 1968. Gu did not learn about this piece of sad news for over one and half years. Though he had suspected that something terribly wrong must have happened to her, the party refused to inform him about this for a long time since he was a second-time rightist. This is what was written down by Gu in his diary when the news was broken to him:

> When I learned about this fatal news, I was both surprised and not surprised. I was surprised because since she loved the children so much, how could she leave this "mother committing suicide" label to the family? I was not surprised because she had written a will in the autumn of 1965. And in May 1967, it was then clear that she was no longer strong enough to cope with all the pressure she had to face. When Yang told me about the news, I said, "Why committing suicide? She did not allow me to do that, saying that people like me committing suicide would harm people [who were related to me]. Now, why she wanted to harm people?" All I want to know now is how she died. Zhao said that they would try to find out this for me. I then went to get my portion of meal to eat [in the canteen]. After having eaten a few mouthfuls of rice, I was overwhelmed by my feeling of great sorrow. I buried my face down in the rice tray and burst out crying. But I still tried to restrain myself, making every effort to finish my meal. I need to stay alive… (ibid., p. 160)

Gu's entry here reminds me of Arendt's acute analysis of total domination:

> Totalitarian terror achieved its most terrible triumph when it succeeded in cutting the moral person off from the individualist escape and in making

> the decision of conscience absolutely questionable and equivocal…when even suicide would mean the immediate murder of his own family—how is he to decide? The alternative is no longer between good and evil, but between murder and murder. (1973, p. 452)

Although Gu was spared the fate of choosing between murder and murder in his case, his children no longer recognized him as father. Until his death in 1974, Gu was never to meet them again.

Gu observed that the so-called thought exposure exercise was both a divide-and-rule tactic and a kind of political blackmail, with the former attempting to destroy one's moral self, and the latter to exert control over the accused since if the accused wanted to beg for rectification, they would need to fully cooperate in these exercises (1997, pp. 20 & 40). By the same logic, Gu realized that thought exposure must start with admission of "guilt" by the accused in order to stand any chance of being accepted. The more serious the "guilt" and the "eviler" the counter-revolutionary thought and action the accused confessed, the more politically correct one might be (ibid., 24). If we remember that Gu had written over 200,000 words for self-confession (2002a), we cannot say that Gu refused to participate in this morally corrupt undertaking. But what was remarkable was that deep inside his soul, Gu had not been crushed by these attempts at total domination. He remained critical through and through to examine what had gone wrong with an idealistic revolution which he had so enthusiastically embraced when he was a young professional.

From Revolutionary Idealism to Liberal Empiricism

Gu's post-1949 experience in communist China had changed his outlook and political belief fundamentally, transforming him from advocating revolutionary idealism to embracing liberal empiricism. "Today," Gu wrote in 1973, "when people in the names of the martyrs have changed revolutionary idealism into conservative, reactionary authoritarianism, I am determined to embrace the most thorough kind of empiricism and pluralism and to fight against this type of authoritarianism to the end" (2013, p. 187).

Given the vicissitudes of Gu's life, he did not have the opportunity to produce systematic work on the horrors of totalitarian domination and his conversion to liberal empiricism. Some of his family members (his younger brother in particular) and colleagues nevertheless managed to keep his diaries, private correspondence, reading notes, and some unpublished papers safe for publication in the 1990s, which contained many of his important, albeit fragmented, reflections on post-revolution China. When commenting on the 1990s posthumous publication of Gu's works, historian Yinghong Cheng says, "in his loneliness and having no access to the resources of Western liberal literature, Gu worked to seek answers for the questions related to Marxism and revolution...[t]he result was an unintended crossover between his thoughts and some fundamental liberal ideas...[This] showed the world the fact that even in the darkest years of intellectual suffocation, some seeds of liberal ideas still survived [in communist China]" (2008, pp. 385–386).

In this concluding section, I am going to summarize some of the more important thoughts of Gu that can be regarded as crossovers to liberalism.

My analysis in the socialist planning section of this chapter should have made it quite clear that when Gu was still a member of the Chinese Communist Party, his idea on economic calculation and on the price mechanism, the law of value, and market exchange had already put him more on the side of Mises and Hayek in the theoretical debate of socialist central planning and market reform, though Gu's discussion was very much formulated in socialist jargons. Equally important was the fact that very early on, Gu supported financial and managerial autonomy of local enterprises under a socialist state. Intellectually speaking, the remarkable thing about Gu was that he probably was the first mainland Chinese economist who dared to openly challenge some central tenets of Marxism and Stalinism in economic theory and demanded solid empirical corroboration in order to ascertain the validity of classical socialist thought. Gu was always a fighter against dogmatism.

Gu's reflection on the horrors of the labor camps and the Great Chinese Famine in his diaries not only paralleled Sen's entitlements approach in explaining famines in modern societies, but it was also a damaging indictment against the deprivation of the basic rights of the people and the blindness and dangers of a top-down, pre-determined command plan for forced modernization and industrialization. Gu's reflection demonstrated the moral bankruptcy of the attempt to exert total domination over dissension, since total domination required total power, which would easily lead to total abuse of power, encourage hypocrisy, double standards and, in the end, promote corruption of the moral self.

In the last two years (1973–1974) of his life, Gu and his younger brother Chen Minzhi (陳敏之 1920–?)[6] exchanged a lot of letters discussing many issues, both academic and political, of common concern. Chen subsequently edited Gu's letters to him into a book and published it under the title *From Idealism to Empiricism* (Gu 2013). In this book, Gu examined the important question of what happened after the revolution. Here Gu alluded to the main character Nora of Henrik Ibsen's famous play *A Doll House*, who decided to take control of her own fate by leaving her husband and family in pursuit of the meaning of life in the then male-dominated Norwegian society. The important question for Gu was: "what happens after Nora has left?".

Gu noted that since the seventeenth century, there had been two revolutionary traditions. One was England's Glorious Revolution and the American War of Independence, the other the 1789 and 1870 French Revolutions. Gu pointed out that the first tradition triggered the development of capitalism, while the latter, bringing two empires and five republics to France, attempted to replace capitalism with socialism without success (2013, p. 136). It was until 1917 that the revolutionary force in Russia was strong enough to smash all opposing resistance to the vanguard party by revolutionary dictatorship. One thing common to the two French Revolutions and the 1917 Revolution was that they both had an ultimate goal, which was to establish an ideal society of socialism on earth. Gu linked the origin of this "ultimate goal" tradition to Christianity, which not only postulated a divine standard of perfection and the ultimate good, but also believed that Christ was destined to return to the world and bring with Him perfection on earth. Following this tradition, the earthly revolutionaries were there to bring the ultimate good of communism to earth too. Gu argued that while to start with, most revolutionaries were democrats, in the end, for the sake of the realization of the "ultimate goal" of the revolution and the ultimate good, they invariably resorted to all necessary coercive means, including sacrificing democracy, imposing dictatorship and Stalinist tyranny to achieve heaven on earth (ibid., pp. 137–138).

While this formulation of the argument here may be crude, it can be regarded as spelling out the folly of an embryonic idea of establishing a kind of modern collective state called "enterprise association" or "teleocracy" as postulated by Oakeshott and Hayek (Oakeshott [1975] 1991; Hayek [1978] 1990).[7] Gu's reservation of this "ultimate goal" approach of the revolution is threefold. Firstly, historically speaking, not only the "ultimate goal" has never been realized, but what has been realized is usually the opposite. The following, as one example, was what Gu wrote in 1973:

> With the victory of the 1917 revolution, Lenin assured the Russian youths of that generation that communism would be realized within their lifetime. However, many of those youths by now would have been dead. For those who are still alive, what they now see is that while the Soviet navy is cruising around the world, their living standard is worse than Czechoslovakia. They also witnessed the protests initiated by the wife of [the dissident] Andrei Sakharov and her persecution [by the USSR Communist Party]. As for today's definition of communism, it is increasingly inconsistent with and divergent from Marx's definition in *The Communist Manifesto*—"we shall have an association, in which the free development of each is the condition for the free development of all"—to the extent that it is increasingly difficult to understand what it really means. (2013, p. 138)

Gu reminded us that while Lenin promised direct democracy after the revolution and set up the Soviets in the factories then, sooner rather than later, direct democracy was replaced by centralization of power. The history of the USSR and the People's Republic of China so far had both corroborated the same trend of post-revolutionary dictatorship (ibid., p. 134).

Gu's second reservation is this. At best, the idea of the "ultimate good" cannot be a fixed and static one. Since a static concept implies no further development, it is the end of human progress and is far from satisfactory. In other words, the "ultimate good" in the end is by nature a moving and slippery target that can never be achieved. The more we pursue it, the farther it will move away (ibid., p. 138). Thirdly, Gu found it doubtful if we could demonstrate a priori that the "ultimate good" postulated must be the truth and could not be challenged. Such an assumption could easily be slid into dogmatism (ibid., p. 169). The only way to prove if our judgment of the so-called ultimate good was valid, Gu argued, was to subject it to further empirical test, which must be open-ended, with different possible results and interpretations (ibid., p. 170).

For the above reasons, Gu preferred the empirical and pluralistic approach and argued that the English and American Revolutions, whatever their shortcomings, had embodied the open-ended empirical tradition of freedom and democracy, even allowing dissenting voices and political opposition to exist so long as they subscribed to a common set of procedural rules for peaceful co-existence. For this tradition of revolutions, there is no "ultimate goal" pre-determined. It only postulates a process of continuous interaction trying to make improvements (ibid., p. 138). While Gu's discussion here again is sketchy when compared with what Oakeshott and Hayek postulate as "civil association" or "nomocracy" in their discussion of the liberal state in their political philosophy (Oakeshott [1975] 1991; Hayek [1978] 1990), it is perhaps not unreasonable to say that what Gu preferred was clearly closer to nomocracy than teleocracy.

Not long before Gu died in December 1974, he said that even Mao accepted the fact that it was inevitable that there were rival factions in revolutionary parties. The liberals would certainly argue that if there are no institutionally accepted arrangements to resolve factional conflicts after the revolution, revolutionary dictatorship by those in power will lead to endless internal political struggles which, in the end, are self-destructive and self-defeating. To them, it is better to follow the American Revolution's example of allowing opposition factions to develop into different political parties and allow them to peacefully compete for office. Gu came to admit that there was no perfect institution as such on earth.

The logic of this points to the conclusion that any system that can inherently develop a capacity of self-correction is far better than a system that leads to self-destruction, although how one can bring about this to a particular political community is a different matter.

The publication of Gu's works in the 1990s has revived much interest in liberalism in mainland China (Cheng 2008; Zhu 1999, pp. 151–170; Qian 2017, pp. 667–708 & 943–1021; Luo 2017). Gu's courage, foresight, and the crossovers of his ideas to some fundamental values of liberalism at a time when China was under totalitarian rule attracted a lot of attention among the intellectuals then. They started to reconnect China's political discourse to liberalism, a discourse that had been severed for over four decades since the communists took over the mainland. I think it is legitimate to say that having experienced the horrors of totalitarian politics on the Chinese mainland has made the Chinese liberals fully aware of the fact that without the protection of individual liberty and human rights, the pursuit of national salvation and revolutionary idealism can easily turn into the road to serfdom, particularly under a party-state regime with centralization of the power of economic planning and political control. Coupled with Hayek's influence on post-war liberals in Taiwan as explained in the last chapter, one can see that unlike pre-war Chinese liberal thought, the need to develop constitutional protection of the individuals has increasingly become a more fundamental conviction of the Chinese liberals in the future development of post-war Chinese liberal thought.

Subsequent chapters of this book will continue to explore what has happened after this revival of interest in liberalism, but it is not without ironies to say that China's policy of supporting economic globalization and international free trade under Deng would not have been conceivable if there has been no liberal turn in the ideology in the Chinese Communist Party's pursuit of socialism with Chinese characteristics. Gu's example, nevertheless, shows that liberalism, even under the most adverse circumstances, can still find its strengths and adherents among some of the most outstanding Chinese intellectuals after all.

Notes

1. According to Leighton (2014, pp. 133–135), Gu's specialist system of taxation comprised the compilation of an updated and detailed list of commercial taxpayers in Shanghai, on the basis of which he ranked the tax paying entities and companies into three tiers, from large enterprises to peddlers, with each group having different treatment in terms of taxing their profit or income. Gu instituted several control mechanisms to ensure proper tax payment, with investigation teams set up to double check the companies' vouchers and compared them with the accounts in their books. He also created tax-paying mutual aid groups for taxing small- and medium-sized capitalists. In December 1951, Chen Yun (陳雲 1905–1995), the leading official responsible for economic policy in Beijing, opined in a central Party meeting that Gu Zhun's method was correct with Chairman Mao's endorsement.
2. The Chinese title of this article is〈試論社會主義制度下的商品生產和價值規律〉.
3. To the best of my knowledge, there is no reference in Gu's works to indicate that he had the benefit of having read Mises and Hayek in his lifetime, although in his reading notes and diaries (Gu 1997, 2002c), we find that he had read the following non-Marxist economists from the West: Cannon, Pigou, Smith, Keynes, Sraffa, Fisher, Böhm-Bawerk, Veblen, Clark, List, Marshall, and Rostow. In addition, Gu did translate Schumpeter's *Capitalism, Socialism and Democracy*, volume two of Joan Robinson's *Collected Economic Papers*, and most of Mill's *Principles of Political Economy* into Chinese in the 1960s. But Gu did not manage to finish translating Mill's work due to his persecution in 1968 (Luo 2017, p. 69), and the translated works of Schumpeter and Robinson were published only posthumously after the Great Proletarian Cultural Revolution in 1979 and 1984, respectively. In the January 2, 1970, entry of his diary, Gu did mention that he had read Oskar Lange's textbook of political economy (Gu 1997, p. 179). But he did not refer to the debate on market socialism between Lange-Taylor and Hayek in the late 1930s and early 1940s there.

4. Other market-oriented first-generation economists at that time include Sun Yefang (孫冶方 1908–1983) and Xue Muqiao (薛暮橋 1904–2005), both were key economic advisers to Deng Xiaoping during the reform period after the Great Proletarian Cultural Revolution. Sun is famous for being the first Chinese mainland economist who advocated the indispensability of the law of value in socialist economy in the 1950s (Sun 1979, pp. 1–14), but Sun personally acknowledged to his colleagues and students that he was influenced by Gu while developing this idea (Zhang 1993, in Luo ed. 2017, pp. 24–25). In the 1960s, Xue put a lot of emphasis on the price mechanism for macroeconomic management under socialist planning, but Gu went beyond Xue's idea by emphasizing that the price mechanism will have to follow the law of demand and supply closely in order to function well (Gu 2002b, pp. 155–173).
5. Judging from the different writing styles of these two periods of Gu's diaries, I agree with the observation that his 1959–1960 diary was written without the conscious fear of being discovered, while his 1969–1971 diary was written in a way that was mindful of the danger of being used for further political persecution against him. During the Great Proletarian Cultural Revolution, Gu was forced to write over 200,000 words of confessional statements (2002a), reexamining his life's "capitalist" and "counter-revolutionary" ideas and actions and how he was prepared to "wholeheartedly" and "thoroughly" transform himself through "re-education" to become a new man again.
6. Unlike his brothers and sisters, Gu used his mother's maiden name as his surname in the family while his siblings all followed his father's surname.
7. For my further discussion on the nature of teleocracy vs. nomocracy/enterprise association vs. civil association, see Cheung (2014a) and Chapter 6 of this book.

4

True Individualism, Dispersed Knowledge, and Treating Man as Man in Chinese Liberalism

Individualism, Not "The Doctrine of Self-Centeredness"

In China's traditional, centralized, and hierarchical order, individualism, if literally and straightforwardly translated into Chinese (個人主義), does not have a good reputation. Cultures are complex entities. When two distinctive cultures meet, a lot might be lost in translation in their respective attempts to understand the complexity of each other, particularly in areas where there are few overlaps between the two. Even as late as in the early 1980s, a leading sinologist in the United States John K. Fairbank could still make the following observation:

> To say that liberalism rests on individualism under the supremacy of law is more sensible and gratifying than to say, as one does in Chinese, that the doctrines of spontaneous license (*ziyu zhuyi* [自由主義]) rest on the doctrine of self-centeredness (*geren zhuyi* [個人主義]) under the supremacy of administrative regulation (*falu* [法律]). (quoted in Pye 1985, p. 192)

C. Cheung, *Hayek and Post-War Chinese Liberalism*, Palgrave Studies in Classical Liberalism, https://doi.org/10.1007/978-3-031-64888-5_4

It is not just the traditionalists or reactionaries in China who fault individualism as selfish or self-centered. Radical revolutionaries like Mao Tse-tung also view individualism and liberalism with hostility. For example, in his 1937 essay "Combat Liberalism" (Mao 1961, pp. 31–33), Mao denounced liberalism as opportunistic, arguing that the liberal ideology rooted in petty bourgeoisie's selfishness and always placed personal interest above the interest of the revolution. He called for the elimination of liberalism in the ranks of the revolution.

In his "The Development of Individualism in Modern China" (Chow 1995), William C. L. Chow argues that since China was exposed to the challenges of the West in mid-nineteenth century, "the lack of an individualistic concept of man is doubtless the most obvious point that distinguishes Eastern from Western culture" (ibid., p. 78).

While Confucius was a great educator who did not make any class distinction when it came to learning, and his idea of Confucian personality was, at least conceptually speaking, not inconsistent with the values of moral autonomy of the self, self-cultivation and self-development, the actual, hierarchical, and socio-political circumstances of pre-modern China were such that only the educated and cultivated elites, the gentlemen, were supposed to be leading the way to social harmony and moral and political excellence, and the self is always grounded in the complex web of interpersonal relationships of the familial kind. Furthermore, these gentlemen, even in Confucius's teaching, were to be sharply distinguished from the ordinary folks who were regarded as little men. William Theodore de Bary has made a valid point when he examines the lack of individualism in China:

> For one thing we should distinguish between individualism and "individuality." The existence of the latter does not always imply the presence of the former. Many flourishing cultures have recognized individuality in arts and letters, for instance, without affirming an equal right to individuality of expression in other fields of endeavor or among all classes of society. Aristocratic societies have often encouraged more individuality among the elite than the democracies have tolerated among the masses. (quoted in Chow 1995, p. 79)

As I have explained in Chapter 1 of this book, even the commitment to individualism by liberal-minded Chinese intellectuals who were pioneers in introducing liberalism to modern China is always being questioned. Benjamin Schwartz argues that Yan Fu was so preoccupied with the need for national salvation in the face of scrambling for concessions of China by Western imperial powers that Yan altered John Stuart Mill's original conception of liberty in his translation of *On Liberty* by fitting it into a framework of Herbert Spencer's categories of energy and "survival of the fittest," which had effectively turned individualism into a means of national salvation. Likewise, there is general agreement by students of modern Chinese political thought that the famous constitutionalist reformer of the late Qing and early republican era Liang Qichao had by and large premised his idea of new citizens on the need of nation building for a modern Chinese state.

I have no intention here to go over the grounds again in the well-documented debate about the primacy of individualism versus the primacy of national salvation in early modern Chinese liberalism (Schwartz 1964; Chang 1971; Schwarcz 1986; Li 1987; Yu 1999; Huang 2008; Qui 2014, 2019). This is not because this issue is not a significant one in modern Chinese political thought. Rather, it is my contention that Hayek's idea of individualism is a sophisticated and multi-faceted one, a proper and thorough understanding of which helps one to go beyond the apparent dichotomy of individual freedom and national salvation. Furthermore, the post-war Chinese liberals, at least the more profound ones, have managed to learn from many of the insights deriving from Hayek's idea of individualism and classical liberalism and developed a conception of individualism that places central importance to the dignity of the individual, and this conception is also at the same time sensitive to, though not uncritical of, the Chinese cultural context. In this regard, I think Xiong Zijian (熊自健), in what is probably the first article-length Chinese study of Hayek's thought and post-war Chinese liberalism in Taiwan (Xiong 1992), is right to observe that through a study of Hayek's thesis of true and false individualism and the moral basis of liberalism, post-war Taiwanese liberals like David Chow, Yin Hai-kuang, and Xia Daoping have started to develop an idea of individualism that echoes what Hayek said in *The Road to Serfdom* of respecting the individual man *qua* man, an idea which is not premised on an appeal to the primacy of an abstract individual or on a wholesale rejection of the traditional Chinese culture.

Individualism: True and False

One important point I cannot help but to repeatedly stress is that a key to understanding Hayek's idea of true individualism as against rationalistic pseudo-individualism is to remember that it is a theory of society ([1948] 1980, p. 6). It is a theory that is sophisticated and multi-faceted, comprising epistemological, methodological, political-cum-institutional as well as cultural-evolutionary arguments to substantiate its claims.

Gerald F. Gaus, in analyzing Hayek's complex views on social evolution and reason, reminds us that one must recognize that many of Hayek's ideas are so inter-related that if one just focuses on one or two elements of his theory without appreciating the fact that they are often embedded in a more or less coherent system of ideas, one is almost bound to misunderstand him (2006, p. 254). I agree with Gaus on this important point. In what follows, I shall try to spell out the essential and inter-related aspects of Hayek's social theory of individualism and see how they have inspired the post-war Chinese liberals to develop their idea of individualism and enrich the theoretical contents and plausibility of Chinese liberal thought.

In discussing the two contrasting traditions of individualism in modern Western thought, why does Hayek characterize one as true and the other as false?

One reason given by Hayek is that the individualism that he defends, that is, the individualism of Mandeville, Hume, and other thinkers of the Scottish Enlightenment of the eighteenth century, Burke, de Tocqueville, and Lord Acton, is true because it is the only individualism that is "consistent," and it is the "only theory which can claim to make the formation of spontaneous social products intelligible" ([1948] 1980, p. 4 & p. 10). Throughout Hayek's academic career, he maintained that "the differences between socialists and non-socialists ultimately rest on purely intellectual issues capable of a scientific resolution and not on different judgments of value," and he believed that the doctrines advocated by the socialists (false individualists included) "can be shown to be based on factually false assumptions," and the whole family of socialist thought could be "proved erroneous" (Hayek 1973, p. 6).

The tradition of individualism favored by the Encyclopedists, Rousseau, and the physiocrats is regarded as false by Hayek because, in his view, it has adopted a very expensive, mistaken, Cartesian conception of Reason (with a capital R), and this false individualism believes that one can trace "all discoverable order to deliberate design" to be guided by Reason, which "is always fully and equally available to all humans and that everything which man achieves is the direct result of, and therefore subject to, the control of individual reason" ([1948] 1980, p. 8). To Hayek, while true individualism is acutely aware of "the limitations of the individual mind which induces an attitude of humility toward the impersonal and anonymous social process by which individuals help to create things greater than they know," false individualism "is the product of an exaggerated belief in the powers of individual reason and of a consequent contempt for anything which has not been consciously designed by it or is not fully intelligible to it" (ibid.).

It is clear from the above that Hayek tries to justify his defense of true individualism and his attacks against false individualism first and foremost on epistemological grounds. More specifically, he argues that there are at least two insurmountable limitations of reason that make false individualism erroneous. The first one is the constitutional limitation of human reason, and the second one is the fragmented, circumstantial, and dispersed nature of useful and personal information/skills in social interaction that makes complete command of knowledge in society and rational design of a social order by any central agency impossible. In other words, in social theory, exhaustive and synoptic knowledge on social interaction is out of the question, and human ignorance and unintended consequences in the social process are something that are not avoidable, though this does not mean that because of that social coordination is not to be achieved.

Let us now examine Hayek's epistemological arguments and see how they affect his understanding of a defensible conception of individualism.

The Epistemological Thesis[1]

Hayek's social theory is very much indebted to the Scottish Enlightenment thinkers. In particular, Adam Ferguson's following observation on the unintended consequences of human action is perhaps singularly important to Hayek:

> Like the winds, that come we know not whence, and blow whithersoever they list, the forms of society are derived from an obscure and distant origin; they arise, long before the date of philosophy, from the instincts, not from the speculations, of men. The croud of mankind, are directed in their establishments and measures, by the circumstances in which they are placed; and seldom are turned from their way, to follow the plan of any single projector…Every step and every movement of the multitude, even in what are termed enlightened ages, are made with equal blindness to the future; and nations stumble upon establishments, which are indeed the result of human action, but not the execution of any human design. (1995, p. 119)

While social establishments are seldom the results of the design of any single person, these establishments, nevertheless, originate in the interaction of the individuals in society:

> Mankind, in following the present sense of their minds, in striving to remove inconveniences, or to gain apparent and contiguous advantages, arrive at ends which even their imagination could not anticipate, and pass on, like other animals, in the track of their nature, without perceiving its end. He who first said, "I will appropriate this field: I will leave it to my heirs; did not perceive, that he was laying the foundation of civil laws and political establishments. He who first ranged himself under a leader, did not perceive, that he was setting the example of a permanent subordination, under the pretence of which, the rapacious were to seize his possessions, and the arrogant to lay claim to his service. (ibid.)

To Hayek, Ferguson's insights here pose a number of important questions for the understanding of society. If social establishments are not the results of human rationality, in what sense are they the products of man? What are the nature and range of man's unavoidable ignorance in social interaction? Given such unavoidable or radical ignorance of man, how is it that individual interaction can still lead, albeit unintentionally, to all kinds of social cooperation and well-established social practices?

To tackle these problems, Hayek proposes a theory of mind to help to support Ferguson's insights. To begin with, he argues that far from being independent of civilization, the development of the human mind is, in reality, very much dependent upon it:

> Man did not simply impose upon the world a pattern created by his mind. His mind is itself a system that constantly changes as a result of his endeavour to adapt himself to his surroundings...[T]he growth of the human mind is part of the growth of civilisation; it is the state of civilisation at any given moment that determines the scope and the possibilities of human ends and values. The mind can never foresee its own advance. (Hayek 1960, pp. 23–24)

The fact that the growth of the human mind is part of the growth of civilization implies that the two, in fact, evolve concurrently, with the latter providing the context for the former to acquire meaning and value, while the former, in interacting with the natural and social environments, modifying existing social practices by exploring new ones or adapting to the more successful ones through evolution to cope with the challenges human beings face (Hayek 1973, pp. 17–19).

In other words, Hayek denies the possibility of a Cartesian mind that exists independently of social institutions and arrives at conclusions purely by logical deduction from explicit and demonstrable premises. Civilization as human artifact, in Hayek's view, is artificial not mainly because of deliberate human decision, but because of human convention (ibid., pp. 9–11 & pp. 20–21).

From the concurrent evolution of mind and civilization, Hayek goes on to suggest that there are two inherent limitations of human knowledge, one circumstantial, and one logical. Looking at his argument for the logical limitation of human knowledge brings us to one of the fundamental premises of his theory of mind, for the mind (or the mental order), to Hayek, is a mechanism of classification in which external stimuli we perceived are related to other stimuli or to our past experience in accordance with the classification structure of the mental order, in relations of which we make sense of human interaction and the external environment, and from which we derive our meanings and values to guide human action.[2]

To Hayek, "a question like 'what is x?' has meaning only within a given order, and within this limit it must always refer to the relation of one particular event to other events belonging to the same order" ([1952] 1976, pp. 4–5). In other words, what Hayek is saying is that meaning does not lie in the so-called nature or essence of the thing as such. Rather, what is meaningful is necessarily relational, and our mind can comprehend things out there only within a classification framework already existed, though such a framework is not necessarily deliberately established (Gray 1998, pp. 5–6). In this regard, Hayek maintains that the way to demonstrate whether a person is color-blind is not by ascertaining how "red" looks to him in any absolute sense, but by ascertaining instead whether and how it differs from various other shades of "red" and from "green" ([1952] 1976, p. 31).

From such a perspective, it is not difficult to understand that Hayek does not recognize the existence of any "absolute" qualities of sensations. Instead, he describes such a presupposition as a "phantom-problem" in the philosophy of mind, (ibid., pp. 30–36) for "any question about the nature or character of particular sensory qualities" should necessarily arise as "a question about the differences from (or the relations to) other sensory qualities; and the extent to which the effects of the occurrence of any other qualities determines the whole of its character" (ibid., p. 35). Such a conception of mind as an "order of events" or "a complex of relations" implies that "all the attributes of sensory qualities (and of other mental qualities) are relations to other such qualities, and that the totality of all these relations between mental qualities exhausts all there is to be said about the mental order" (ibid.).

The relations that constitute the mind must be abstract in nature,[3] for to identify the differences between the sensory qualities involved means only to highlight the relevant, not all, attributes of the qualities concerned. As Hayek says, "we never act, and could never act, in full consideration of all the facts of a particular situation, but always by singling out as relevant only some aspects of it" (Hayek 1973, p. 30). Thus, abstraction, which necessarily involves classification, "is not something which the mind produces by processes of logic from its perception of reality, but rather a property of the categories with which it operates—not a product of the mind but rather what constitutes the mind" (ibid.).

As a result, the mind, as a mental order of classification and abstraction,

> [m]ust possess a structure of a higher degree of complexity than is possessed by the objects which it classifies...therefore, the capacity of any explaining agent must be limited to objects with a structure possessing a degree of complexity lower than its own...it means that no explaining agent can ever explain objects of its own kind, or of its own degree of complexity, and, therefore, that the human brain can never fully explain its own operations. (Hayek [1952] 1976, p. 6)

This conception of the logical limitation of the mind for complete self-explanation is supported, Hayek suggests, by Georg Cantor's theorem in the theory of sets, according to which in any system of classification there are always more classes than things to be classified, which presumably implies that no system of classes can contain itself (Hayek 1967, pp. 61–62). Given the fact that mind and civilization develop concurrently, it is only logical for Hayek to contend that it is not possible for the mind to stay outside society and shape the development of the latter in accordance with some separate and preconceived ideas of the former. In other words, there is no Archimedean point in man's self-understanding.

It is society or civilization, Hayek writes, that gives the context of meaning for the mind, whose capacity to make sense of the environment is inherently dependent on many of the practices in our civilization and society. Thus, the idea of a Cartesian mind is absurd, and any social engineering deriving from such a conception of mind is, to say the least, extremely misconceived, since it puts the cart before the horse. In other words, Hayek's conception of individualism in never atomistic, it does not rely on the assumption of an abstract, asocial self to make sense of it.

While the Cartesian conception of mind is untenable, this does not mean that there is no rational or explicit knowledge. Hayek readily accepts that scientific knowledge, particularly for those parts of knowledge dealing with some relatively simple physical phenomena in many instances, is capable of precise and demonstrable explanation and prediction of particular events from explicit and clear premises. However, in the more complex endeavor of social interaction, Hayek maintains that there is an equally important body of knowledge that is not explicit in the normal sense of the word, for this non-rational kind of knowledge, or "tools" as Hayek loosely calls it, consists in a large measure of forms of conduct which man habitually follows without knowing why:

> They consist of what we call 'traditions' and 'institutions,' which [man] uses because they are available to him as a product of cumulative growth without ever having been designed by any one mind. Man is generally ignorant not only of why he uses implements of one shape rather than of another but also of how much is dependent on his actions taking one form rather than another. He does not usually know to what extent the success of his efforts is determined by his conforming to habits of which he is not even aware…Concurrent with the growth of conscious knowledge there always takes place an equally important accumulation of tools in this wider sense, of tested and generally adopted ways of doing things. (1960, p. 27)

In the light of the above, true individualism is not hostile to tradition or to the kind of non-rational knowledge. In this respect, Hayek's true individualism is sensitive to the beneficial effects of established practices, and any wholesale repudiation of one's cultural tradition is not consistent with this conception of individualism. In the Chinese context, it is clear that post-war Chinese liberals, after having accepted Hayek's idea of true individualism, can no longer endorse the pre-war liberals' wholesale attack on the Chinese tradition (see Lin 1979) in their liberalism. We will further examine this in the next chapter when we are talking about the conservative turn of post-war Chinese liberalism.

Furthermore, there also exists, apart from these "tools," a wide spread of particular and local knowledge that is necessarily dispersed. This is so partly because much of this is knowledge of particular circumstances of time and place, and partly because whether a piece of information is useful or not very often depends on individual's subjective judgment or interpersonal choices:

> It is with respect to this [knowledge of particular circumstances of time and place] that practically every individual has some advantage over all others because he possesses unique information of which beneficial use might be made, but of which use can be made only if decisions depending on it are left to him or are made with his active cooperation...The shipper who earns his living from using otherwise empty or half-filled journeys of tramp-steamers, or the estate agent whose whole knowledge is almost exclusively one of temporary opportunities, or the *arbitrageur* who gains from local difference of commodity prices—are all performing eminently useful functions based on special knowledge of circumstances of the fleeting moment not known to others. (Hayek [1948] 1980, p. 80, italics in the original)

Hayek's thesis is that if omniscient man is nowhere to be found, individuals must be allowed to have free play in their trial-and-error type of separate endeavors before one can find out whose attempts are more promising in the process. The key to social development is not how comprehensive a society's plan is, but whether a society has managed to develop effective social coordination that can maximize the beneficial effects of separate individual's actions. This lends strong support to an individualist approach to social interaction and to the maintenance of socio-political institutions that tend to adequately protect the individual's separate initiatives in order to try out how social coordination will best be achieved bottom up rather than top down.

Equally important is that since in theory and in reality no one is in a position to possess complete knowledge of the social order or to be able to have full control of the consequences of human action, collectivistic top-down approach in determining social interaction is not only rationally unjustifiable; worse still, it is arbitrary, and can only be enforced by prohibiting, by force if necessary, the self-initiatives of the separate individuals, which is a denial of individual freedom as well as a dismissal of the potentially creative and beneficial separate initiatives tried out by the individuals in the process of social interaction.

In developing his social theory to explain the formation of spontaneous social order and to defend individual freedom, Hayek places special emphasis on the coordinating function of the general rules of just conduct which are a means to prevent clashes between conflicting individual actions rather than for the attainment of pre-determined collective ends:

> Our submission to general principles is necessary because we cannot be guided in our practical action by full knowledge and evaluation of all the consequences. So long as men are not omniscient, the only way in which freedom can be given to the individual is by such general rules to delimit the sphere in which the decision is his. There can be no freedom if the government is not limited to particular kinds of action but can use its powers in any ways which serve particular ends. ([1948] 1980, p. 19)

This is how the epistemological thesis of Hayek's idea of true individualism helps to demolish the arrogant claims of Cartesian Rationalism, to appreciate the dispersed, subjective, contextual, and interactive nature of social interaction by the participating individuals, the process of which not only allows each and every individual far more trial-and-error opportunities to discover the more fruitful or productive ways for social coordination and to maximize the chances of the fulfillment of individual choices and preferences, but also to avoid any top-down and often coercive implementation of any arbitrarily determined collective goals by those in power in social action. Hayek's true individualism also requires defensible institutional and political arrangements for the protection of individual freedom and to ensure the smooth functioning of spontaneous social coordination, and Hayek's answer to this is the rule of law and the development of liberal constitutionalism. We shall examine more about this later in Chapter 6 below. Meanwhile, I would like to say that among the post-1949 liberals in Taiwan, I think David Chow and Xia Daoping were the two who understood the Hayekian epistemological insights best (see Xiong 1992, pp. 1–49; Wu Hui-Lin 2015, pp. 201–202). It is to their contributions in this regard that we must now turn.

Economic Liberalism and Dispersed Knowledge of Society

Xiong Zijian is probably right to say that David Chow's contributions to systematically introduce Hayek's thought to post-war Taiwan were the greatest in the last century since he not only was the first one to have published a single author book-length introduction of Hayek's thought (Chow 1975) in Chinese in the 1970s, he was also the first one to have translated Hayek's *The Constitution of Liberty* into Chinese (Chow trans. 1972) with a lot of translator's notes to try to link up Hayek's ideas there with ancient Chinese thought.

Chow's attempt to find affinity between Hayekian liberalism and classical Chinese thought is most remarkable since he was the first Chinese liberal to attempt to do so. I shall examine this interesting topic a bit further in Chapter 5 of this book. However, one may also like to point out that Chow's contributions are not popular reading since his writing style, unlike the passionate approach of Yin Hai-kuang and the fluent and easy-to-read language of Xia Daoping, is both complicated and obscure. This has the unfortunate effect of making Chow's works neglected by the general readers most of the time. This notwithstanding, one must admit that Chow has a good understanding not only of Hayek's sophisticated ideas, but also other leading members of the Austrian School of Economics, particularly Ludwig von Mises's theory of praxeology in explaining human action and defending individualism (Mises [1949] 1966).

In his 1965 article (Chow 2004, pp. 198–217) defending Hayek's idea of true individualism, Chow starts by reiterating the limits of rationality more or less in line with Hayek's critique of constructivism and Cartesian Rationalism, but he also follows in the footsteps of Mises in pointing out that there are two a priori categories embedded in individual human beings that are the prerequisites of purposeful human action: namely, logical reasoning and the individual's subjective desire in striving for happiness (i.e. substituting a more satisfactory state of affairs for a less satisfactory one as evaluated by the individual concerned through some purposeful action to move from the latter to the former). The starting point of the Austrian School of Economics is always that all purposeful human actions are performed by individuals (Mises [1949] 1966, p. 42). All collective actions, understood figuratively and derivatively, are the results, intentionally and unintentionally, of separate individual actions, the meaning of which is attributed by the intent of the participatory individuals concerned. The collective as such does not act, and individual actions are human since they are purposeful and meaningful, trying to bring value to the participatory individuals.

The subjective nature of the individual's striving for happiness does not mean that individual value judgment is necessarily egoistic or self-centered, since the individual concerned may derive his/her value from accepted social norm, convention or through interpersonal consensus; but what cannot be done without is that *ultimately*, so far as we know, it is the individual's personal choice and determination that the end or value of his/her action is chosen after having compared it, implicitly or explicitly, with other possible or competing ends or values. It is in this sense that Mises describes concrete value judgments and definite human actions as an "ultimate given" (ibid., pp. 17–19). The capacity for the individual to reason logically and to establish realistic means-end relations is to facilitate the actor concerned to select the most effective measures to help to achieve the desired end in human action. Social theory, that is the theory in explaining interpersonal interaction, is to explain how social coordination is achieved or fails to achieve under the circumstances given the subjective nature of concrete individual value judgments. When Hayek says that "the differences between socialists and non-socialists ultimately rest on purely intellectual issues capable of a scientific resolution and not on different judgments of value" (Hayek 1973, p. 6), what he means is that the dispute is not about how unjustified the socialist ends are, but the erroneous understanding of the socialists in the possible means to achieve their lofty ends.

To Chow, therefore, true individualism of the Hayekian kind is both a theory to explain human action and social interaction and to appreciate the fact that a proper understanding of human rationality and of the subjective nature of individual concrete value judgments is essential for the nourishment of humanity, and true individualism is therefore also a theory pleading for treating man as man and respecting the separate individuals given the diversity of their respective, subjective preferences (Chow 2004, pp. 200–205).

Xia Daoping was another post-war liberal in Taiwan whose understanding of Hayek's social and economic theory could rival that of Chow. Xia studied in the Economic Department of Wuhan University in the early 1930s, during which he was greatly influenced by the thought of his teacher in economics Ren Kainam (任凱南 1884–1949) who was a student of Edwin Cannan (who was greatly admired by Hayek in his contribution to the study of economics, see Hayek [1948] 1980, p. 9 n. 10) at the London School of Economics (Xia 2013, pp. 226–230). Xia joined the army to fight against the Japanese during the Second Sino-Japanese War (1937–1945), and he became an economic official in the Nationalist government before it was defeated by the Chinese Communist Party led by Mao in the Chinese Civil War. Xia later followed the Nationalist government fleeing to Taiwan and never had the opportunity to return to the mainland again.

Here is not the place to give a full account of the historical context that shaped the intellectual development of Xia (Li 2017). My focus instead is about how Xia's contributions to the then liberal and outspoken journal *Free China* in Taiwan and how his translation of some major works of the Austrian School of Economics have echoed many of Hayek's theoretical insights, making him a leading Chinese Hayekian liberal in post-war Taiwan.

Not long after Yin Haiguang published his selected translation of *The Road to Serfdom* in 1953, Xia wrote an editorial in *Free China*, criticizing the expansion of the state enterprises of Taiwan in taking over many of the private enterprises through buying enough shares to hold a controlling stake in the latter (1989b, pp. 111–112).[4]

The editorial opposed the interpretation of the judiciary over an ordinance governing the management of the state enterprises, fearing that the interpretation would facilitate some industrial sectors being dominated by state monopolies. Under the interpretation, investments made by the state enterprises were regarded as government capital. If a state enterprise used government capital to purchase a controlling stake in any private enterprise, that latter enterprise would be defined as state enterprise even though the minority shares of the enterprise concerned were still in private hands. If this latter enterprise, now being defined as a state enterprise under the interpretation, again managed to hold a controlling stake in another private enterprise, that private enterprise would, in turn, be turned into another state enterprise by law under this interpretation.

In other words, government capital could use this route to turn many private enterprises into state enterprises, putting them under state control even though the majority in the aggregated total shares of these formerly private enterprises could still be in private hands. In the editorial, Xia specifically referred to Hayek's *The Road to Serfdom,* pointing out the domino effect leading to the road to serfdom if the economic arena was increasingly dominated by state monopolies (ibid., p. 112). In another 1956 *Free China* editorial, Xia unambiguously argued that democracy must be based on economic freedom. He contended that whether a state was moving toward democracy or toward totalitarian rule could be detected by observing if the state enterprises sector was expanding or contracting (ibid., p. 125). In other words, some leading Taiwanese liberals now turned increasingly Hayekian and no longer upheld the pre-war Chinese liberal view that state intervention or monopoly in the economic arena is compatible with individual freedom.

Xia was among the first in Taiwan to support the above liberal argument of Hayek. In an article criticizing the inflationary policy of Keynes (Xia 1989a, pp. 119–130), Xia followed the lead of Hayek and pointed out that the nature/artifact dichotomy was misleading if we attributed all natural phenomena to the results of the operation of the laws of nature and all social phenomena to the results of deliberate human design, since the latter included many social practices (such as language, the market, money, morals) that were, as Adam Ferguson said, "the results of human action, but not the execution of any human design." To Xia, these results of non-designed human action, if in the end proven to be sustainable, amounted to a social evolutionary process in which the dispersed and piecemeal efforts of generations of anonymous individuals were spontaneously interacted and accumulated in response to each other and to the social environment, the products of which could not be attributable to any single individual or unit.

As we have referred to above, Hayek argues that in the process of spontaneously evolved interaction, the kind of unorganized and dispersed knowledge plays a crucial role in the subsequent formation of the social order, and he calls it "the knowledge of the particular circumstances of time and place" that cannot exist in "concentrated or integrated from" (Hayek [1948] 1980, p. 80 & p. 77). Many of Xia's essays on free market economics (1989a) are an elaboration of this Hayekian insight. Equally important for the Chinese intellectuals are his translated works of Hayek, Mises, and other liberal economists, since it was through Xia's translated works (which include von Mises' *Human Action* and *The Ultimate Foundation of Economic Science*; Hayek's *Individualism and Economic Order*; Gottfried Haberler's *Economic Growth and Stability*, and Wilhelm Ropke's *Economics of the Free Society*) that many mainland economists had had their first serious encounter with the liberal thoughts of the Austrian School of Economists soon after the Great Proletariat Cultural Revolution when these works in Chinese translation were made available on the mainland. A leading liberal economist in post-Mao China Zhang Shuguang (張曙光), who was Gu Zhun's junior colleague in the Academy of Social Science in Beijing during the Anti-Rightist Movement in the late 1950s, recalled in 2012 that Xia's Chinese translation of Mises's and Hayek's works together with many of Xia's articles on economics were the earliest Chinese sources for him and his colleagues on the communist mainland to learn about economic liberalism (Xia 2013, pp. 2–3).

Perhaps it is also interesting to point out that when Xia rendered Hayek's "The Use of Knowledge in Society" (Hayek [1948] 1980, pp. 77–91) into Chinese, he added the word "dispersed" to the title and made it to read "The Use of Dispersed Knowledge in Society" in Chinese (Xia, trans., 1993). Although Xia's translation here is not strictly in line with Hayek's original title, his insertion of the word "dispersed" shows that he had an excellent grasp of the kind of contextual, circumstantial, and tacit knowledge that is involved in the formation of the spontaneous social order. It is for a better understanding of the nature of this circumstantial knowledge and the mechanism of social coordination that we must now turn.

Knowledge of the Circumstances and Social Coordination

One reason why Hayek's essay "Economics and Knowledge" ([1948] 1980, pp. 33–56) is regarded as transformational (Caldwell 2004, pp. 205–231) is its clear differentiation of the *tautological* nature of the tool of equilibrium analysis in classical economics from the *empirical* nature of those separate and dispersed data possessed by different social actors, the coordination of which is something that needs to be explained instead of assumed away. In other words, if there is an observed tendency of more or less successful social coordination, we will have to explain why such a coordination is empirically achieved without coercive central direction for the sake of certain pre-determined collective purposes.

When human associations have developed beyond the stage of tribal communities, the starting point for successful social interaction must be, given the diverse needs and interests of the human individuals, the coordination of dispersed individual preferences and actions, many of which may be incompatible with each other. Discovering, matching, and utilizing these dispersed data will be one crucial factor determining if a successful coordination can be achieved. These data are not only dispersed, but they are also dynamic—that is, they are changing according to changing circumstances, and they are not being given as something out there. These data are fluid and subject to change, depending on the changing perception and anticipation of the possible outcomes of social interaction by the social actors involved. Steven Horwitz is right to say that these data are "inherently contextual" (2001). As a result, Hayek contends that aggregate and static information like statistics, which by nature disregards the contextual differences existed within the collected data, can never be used to substitute this knowledge of concrete circumstances in the process of social coordination ([1948] 1980, p. 83).

Natural science methods are not applicable to this knowledge of concrete circumstances for another reason: that is, the latter's teleological properties. This means that the data concerned "refer not to some objective properties possessed by the [data]…, but to views which some other person holds about the [data]" (ibid., p. 59). They are what people think they are so long as they can be defined by indicating relations between three terms: "a purpose, somebody who holds that purpose, and an object which that person thinks to be a suitable means for that purpose" (ibid., pp. 59–60). For example, money is money, so long as people attribute certain monetary value to it, irrespective of whether the physical property of the thing concerned is mineral, metal, paper, plastic, or digital.

Furthermore, human interaction involves skill-based activities, the know-how of which cannot all be captured by articulated knowledge. A good chef's skills in making delicious dishes cannot be captured fully by what he has written in cookbooks. Similarly, using circumstantial knowledge requires the exercise of judgment by the actors, and knowledge of this kind is mostly tacit, action-oriented and is often achieved through practice only.

The dispersed, contextual, tacit, and interactive nature of circumstantial knowledge points to the impossibility of centralized direction in social interaction without sacrificing individual free choices and prohibiting individual explorations of new and novel initiatives that do not align with the preconceived central goal. The question is: How spontaneous coordination is achieved under such circumstances? To this, Hayek's explanation of how price signals work in a free market serving as something like a telecommunication system and a discovery process helps to understand how it can register the ever changing and interactive situation of the market and allow individuals to make the necessary and multi-faceted adjustments to these changes.

Allow me to quote the relevant passages from Hayek rather extensively:

> [A]ssume that somewhere in the world a new opportunity for the use of some raw material, say, tin, has arisen, or that one of the sources of supply of tin has been eliminated. It does not matter for our purpose—and it is significant that it does not matter—which of these two causes has made tin more scarce. All that the users of tin need to know is that some of the tin they used to consume is now more profitably employed elsewhere and that, in consequence, they must economize tin (ibid., p. 85).

The point to note here is that in the market, there are suppliers and consumers of tin here and there, who would like to make the best use of their individual circumstances to serve their separate purposes. If coordination is to be achieved by central direction, it is imperative to know exactly where these users of tin are, what quantity they are using, what their respective future plans are, and what possible factors under the circumstances may affect their plans and the plans of other prospective tin users in order to successfully direct the future production and consumption of tin. Here, the dynamic nature of the circumstantial knowledge of existing tin users and prospective tin users is bound to affect the future coordination in the use of tin. But what is crucial in this respect is that this *cannot be known in advance* since knowledge of this kind is fluid and changing, depending upon the evolving circumstances.

For example, some traders who are no producers of tin but with updated knowledge of the tin reserve held in a certain remote location might discover the opportunity of making a profit by acting as middlemen between the potential buyers and the producers when the price signals help them to discover such a need of tin from another part of the globe. Likewise, a producer who are capable of producing various kinds of raw materials (including tin) who initially plans to produce iron may prefer to switch to produce tin once the price signals inform him of greater profit margin in the latter but will switch to iron once that margin has been reduced by competition of greater supply. In other words, these kinds of dispersed skills, information, opportunities, and the like are not only contextual and circumstantial, but they are also dynamic, interactive, fluid, and always changing. Indeed, one producer's signal of opportunity to enter the market can be another producer's signal to exit, depending upon the different circumstances and plans of individual players in the market. All these point to the impossibility of central planning because of the circumstantial nature of the kind of knowledge and skills involved by all. As discussed in Chapter 3 on the issue of economic calculation under central planning, there of course is the fundamental question of on what basis can the central planner determine the price level for tin in cases like this? If there is a need to change the price, how?

But with the price signals determined by spontaneous demand and supply and the freedom to adjust to these signals whenever the users' think fit to do so as long as they are made responsible for the consequences of their respective decisions, all the tin users need to do is this: to detect their own opportunities according to their interpretations of the changing price signals and to make adjustments according to their individual plans and resources available.

Furthermore,

> [T]here is no need of the great majority of [the tin users] even to know where the more urgent need has arisen, or in favor of what other needs they ought to husband the supply. If only some of them know directly of the new demand, and switch resources over to it, and if the people who are aware of the new gap thus created in turn fill it from still other sources, the effect will rapidly spread throughout the whole economic system and influence not only all the users of tin but also those of its substitutes and the substitutes of these substitutes, the supply of all the things made of tin, and their substitutes, and so on; and all this without the great majority of those instrumental in bringing about these substitutions knowing anything at all about the original cause of these changes. (ibid., pp. 85–86)

As a result, "The whole acts as one market…because their limited individual fields of vision sufficiently overlap so that through many intermediaries the relevant information is communicated to all" (ibid., p. 86).

Hayek calls the price mechanism of the free market a "marvel," because,

> [I]n a case like that…without an order being issued…tens of thousands of people whose identity could not be ascertained by months of investigation, are made to use the material or its products more sparingly; that is, they move in the right direction. (ibid., p. 87)

Hayek's social coordination thesis, which in one sense can be interpreted as an excellent explanation of the powerful importance of the division of knowledge in social and economic interaction that is perhaps even more fundamental than the thesis of the division of labor in classical economics, spells out the reason why ignorance in the details of the dispersed knowledge held by other individuals in the market is not a disadvantage, since this does not bar the participating individuals to adjust to the "right direction" of maximizing the utility of their respective resources for free exchange, provided that they can rely on the signals transmitted by the price mechanism to adjust their actions as best they can to achieve their respective aims.

Whether these aims are purely for self-interest or otherwise are not essential to the success or failure of the social coordination concerned. Given their initial ignorance of the overall situation and the vast amount of dispersed, circumstantial knowledge involved, people are in no position to foresee many of the consequences generated by their social or market interactions, many of which will be unintended and form no part of their original plans. Hayek's epistemological explanation helps to avoid the unnecessary psychological and moral assumption of self-centered or self-interest individuals in this regard.

Methodological Individualism

We shall further examine the political and moral implications of Hayek's social theory of true individualism later. From the elaboration of Hayek's epistemological thesis above, it is already clear that in explaining social phenomena and social coordination, the starting point is not the so-called collectives; instead, what is crucial is to start with the separate social actors and their respective subjective data and preferences, the interaction of which will not only produce many of the unintended consequences of social action, but also lead to the question of why some of these consequences eventually have become established and sustainable institutions, which can only be made intelligible if a methodologically individualistic approach is adopted in social explanation.

In *The Counter-Revolution of Science: Studies on the Abuse of Reason* (Hayek [1952] 1979), Hayek keeps on reminding us that students of social sciences must be careful in distinguishing the motivating or constitutive opinions formed or possessed by the individual human agent in social interaction, on the one hand, and the speculative or explanatory views which people have formed about the wholes or unintended consequences of social interaction, on the other, since the former is the starting point of social understanding, the data of which are, as explained above, teleological and intersubjective in nature, while the latter is the theoretical or conceptual reconstruction for social explanation, which is provisional and subject to test and verification.

Social wholes or collectives, in accordance with Hayek's methodological individualism, are not objective or factual entities exist out there in the first place, but falsifiable theories or explanatory models trying to better understand how the separate and individual actors interact with each other leading to the unintended consequences as we can find in social phenomena. If we mistake the provisional, reconstructed social wholes/collectives as given facts, we not only assume away something that need to be explained in the first place, but we also become victims of what Hayek calls "the fallacy of 'conceptual realism'" (ibid., p. 95), which can lead to erroneous social explanation as well as disastrous policy implications since the latter may be totally unfounded in social reality.

The teleological and intersubjective nature of the given data in social explanation, as Hayek argues in *The Counter-Revolution of Science*, distinguishes the study of social sciences from physical science, and one will commit the error of scientism if one applies the method of physical science directly to explain social phenomena. Here is not the place to go into details of Hayek's arguments in this regard, suffice it to say that the contextual and intersubjective nature of our circumstantial knowledge in social interaction implies that human beings can understand the conduct of each other because we have a similar mental order, out of which we can comprehend the meaning of our social interaction and react accordingly, from which we try to come up with social explanation to understand how and why certain unintended consequences are arrived at through social interaction. Our minds can all tell the difference between a blink from a wink, for example. In the case of the former, one can tell that it is being determined by the biological elements of our eyes whose physical attributes are externally related in a certain observable manner to form a certain order; whereas for the latter, it is triggered by human intentions which our mental order somewhat can perceive immediately (though misunderstanding of the intentions cannot be ruled out) whose meaning can be comprehended by our minds on the basis of which people will then react accordingly to their interpretations of the meaning of such human actions. While the social scientists are there to explain the meaning and possible consequences of wink-making conduct by the people in a particular social context, the work of the physical scientists is to start from some given physical phenomena (a blink), from which they try to test and establish the external and causal relationships that may link up the constituting elements (various muscles, the nerve system around a human eye and the like) leading to the resulting phenomena.

Treating Man as Man

The circumstantial and teleological nature of our dispersed knowledge under true individualism also has moral and political implications that go beyond epistemology and methodology. While individual preferences, tastes, commitments, and the like are the starting point of a defensible social theory, the constitutional and circumstantial limits of human reason also point to the fact that there is no such thing as a collective mind that can fully represent all those dispersed individual preferences in society and should therefore direct all members within it to follow the same preference, taste, or commitment in social action. False individualism leads to collectivism precisely because its expensive conception of Rationalism falsely believes that there is such a centralized super Mind that can think, speak, and act for all by rational design, replacing all individual preferences and so on by one supreme plan to pursue perfection for the collective. But for Hayek, this is not only inconsistent and incoherent, but it is also necessarily arbitrary, and is bound to subject the individuals' respective autonomous wills to the coercive will of the centralized authority who insists on its will be done. If, in true individualism, the socially interactive process is a trial-and-error discovery process through which social coordination is achieved with the more successful individual initiatives becoming more widely accepted by the individual judgment of each of the participants without prohibitive interference, no one should be in a position to prejudge or preempt any individual initiatives before the social interaction takes place. Embedded in this theory of true individualism is a conception of the self as a free agent, whose ability to develop and exercise self-consciousness helps to make sense of his own existence and his relationship to the external environment. The free agent's reflective consciousness not only enables him to have self-knowledge, but also to make autonomous choices in relation to his life and existence, through the spontaneous interaction with other free agents of which forms of living, practices, customs, and traditions begin to take place. This self-knowledge of one's free agency also gives rise to the mutual acknowledgment of the autonomy of other free agents, as a result of which the value of respect for the individual is formed, which, according to Hayek, is what Western civilization mainly stands for since the Renaissance:

> [T[he respect for the individual man *qua* man, that is, the recognition of his own views and tastes as supreme in his own sphere…and the belief that it is desirable that men should develop their own individual gifts and bents. (Hayek [1944] 2007, p. 68)

We know that Hayek visited Taiwan three times during his lifetime, which were in 1965, 1966, and 1975, respectively (Wu Hui-Lin 2015, pp. 210–219). By the time when Hayek first visited Taiwan in 1965, some leading liberals in Taiwan had already absorbed Hayek's idea of individualism and classical liberalism and began to incorporate his insights into their own brand of Chinese liberalism. They produced a book entitled *Hayek and His Thought* (《海耶克和他的思 想》), introducing Hayek's thought to the Chinese readers after Hayek's first visit. In the preface of the book (Yin et al. 1968, pp. 1–11), Yin Hai-kuang followed Hayek's epistemological thesis and argued that given man's unavoidable ignorance and the limitations of reason, the protection of individual freedom was required so that the creative powers of civilization could be released. Yin also wrote another article in the book to talk about freedom's ethical basis, in which he introduced many of Hayek's conceptual ideas on classical liberalism. Yin ended his essay with this sentence: "Treating man as man" (ibid., p. 56).

Although Yin did not explore the idea of free agency as the theoretical basis of treating man as man as the ethical foundation of individual freedom in these two articles, by linking the creative powers of freedom with the ethical principle of respect for the individual man *qua* man, he in fact tried to demonstrate that individualism or respect for the individual and creativity and progress were mutually constitutive. In other words, the former were not a means to national salvation or nation building per se. Instead, this conception of individualism contends that treating man as man creates the conditions for the release of the individual's initiated creative powers in social interaction, and it believes that individual freedom and the creative powers of a society are mutually reinforcing rather than being dichotomous, they are not, strictly speaking, engaged in a means-end relationship. In the preface to *Hayek and His Thought*, Yin referred to Hayek's talk in the National Taiwan University on October 8, 1965, in which Hayek cited Michael Oakeshott's idea of nomocratic society as best to illustrate the political relationship of a free people consistent with his idea of true individualism. While it is true to say that there are a lot of affinities between Hayek and Oakeshott in their respective ideas of nomocracy or civil association, Oakeshott, in his *On Human Conduct* ([1975] 1991), premises his discussion of civil association with the philosophical postulate of free agency in human conduct before exploring into the required institutional conditions for nomocracy or civil association. To this extent, we can find in Oakeshott a very rich conception of the self as a free agent is developed in his theory of human conduct and the civil condition, and the readers can find my detailed discussion of Oakeshott's contribution in this regard in the Appendix of this book when I am examining how relevant Oakeshott's theory of civil association is to Chinese liberalism.

As regards Hayek, however, while, as I said earlier, I think that a conception of the self as a free agent is also embedded in his social theory of true individualism, Hayek's focus is far more social and institutional in this connection. To him, the important point is that nomocracy indicates that the political association is constituted by a set of common, non-instrumental, and abstract rules of just conduct demarcating and determining the freedoms, rights, and responsibilities of citizens and officials alike within the association. These rules not only help to define citizenship and distribute public powers and responsibilities, but they also protect a sphere for each individual where he can enjoy his freedoms and to act in accordance with his individual initiatives, together with others as and when appropriate, in a voluntary manner. While these rules do not in any way directly help to achieve the individual's separate aims and preferences, they are there to prevent the collision of all the individuals' personal pursuits and pay equal respect to all their self-initiated endeavors so long as there is no breach of the rules governing their interaction. Common, pre-determined purposes for all have limited place in a nomocracy, though a state constituted and governed by such a set of rules is governed by the rule of law. (Cheung 2014a).

In the light of this, one can find that Hayekian liberals in post-war China tend not to explore the philosophical conception of free agency in their discussion of the important ethical thesis of treating man as man in their liberal thought; instead, they follow Hayek in focusing on the social and institutional conditions for the protection and promotion of respect for the individual in their liberalism, leaving other Chinese liberals to develop a conception of the self that presupposes free agency. For a detailed discussion on this interesting topic related to Chinese liberalism, please refer to the Appendix of this book.

Yin's colleague Xia Daoping was another post-war Taiwan liberal who placed treating man as man as his central value in liberalism (Cheung 2017a). In the preface to his translation of Hayek's *Individualism and Economic Order*, he said that after very careful consideration, he finally decided not to use "individuality/個體主義" in Chinese to translate Hayek's idea of individualism since, to him, the word "man/人" was so important in the translation to signify the centrality of the value of man/the individual over any so-called pre-determined common purposes. He therefore preferred to use "individualism/個人主義" as the proper translation in Chinese, even though such a translation might still have some derogatory connotation in the sense of self-centeredness in the common usage of the Chinese language (Xia trans 1993, pp. 9–10). This again shows that post-war Chinese liberals have increasingly sided with the Kantian value of respect for the individual and individual dignity (see Kateb 2011) in the development of Chinese liberalism and are prepared not to be trapped by the dichotomy of individual freedom versus national salvation like the pre-war liberals in China. For these post-war Chinese liberals under the influence of Hayek's idea of true individualism, what is crucial is not national salvation in the sense of pursuing a pre-determined common purpose (be it wealth and power, national unification, the revolutionary goal of the abolition of class exploitation, revival of the greatness of the Chinese nation and so on), but to create the necessary institutional and political conditions that are conducive to the maintenance of the equal respect of the individual together with releasing the creative powers of the individuals in spontaneous social interaction in a liberal and democratic society.

In this regard, post-war Chinese liberals, following in Hayek's footsteps in institutional development for a liberal society that would facilitate and protect spontaneous social coordination, have begun to pay attention to the need of building liberal institutions and the rule of law (see Yao 2012) and have superseded the efforts of their predecessors (such as the new culture liberals, see Lubot 1982) who were mostly concentrated on using education, moral teaching and rational discussion to promote their idea of liberalism in pre-war China.

Furthermore, the appeal to tradition, established social practices, and the appreciation of the unintended consequences of social interaction in Hayek's social theory also make it clear that it is wrong to assume that individualism cannot but postulate the existence of isolated or self-contained individuals. Hayek's individualism requires no atomistic individuals. Instead, men's "whole nature and character is determined by their existence in society" (Hayek [1948] 1980, p. 6). This theoretical insight not only helps the post-war Chinese liberals to develop a conception of the individual that is sensitive to the social context, it also starts what I shall call the conservative turn of Chinese liberalism in the sense that Hayekian liberals in China have since abandoned the radical iconoclastic and wholesale attack on the Chinese tradition, and they begin to appreciate that if they really want this Western and modern idea of individual freedom to have a chance to be accepted as a core political value in China, they will need to revisit their critique of the traditional culture of China. One important theoretical proposal in this regard is suggested by Hayek's last student in Chicago in the early 1960s Lin Yu-sheng, who calls for "the creative transformation of the Chinese tradition" for liberalism (Lin 1998). In the next chapter of this book, I am going to examine the conservative turn of post-war Chinese liberalism, after which Chapter 6 of this book will analyze the problems and prospects of developing liberal constitutionalism in mainland China as proposed by some leading contemporary Chinese liberals.

Notes

1. My analysis in this section follows many of my arguments made in Cheung (2007, pp. 55–61).
2. For a full description of the mental order and how it classifies external stimuli in relation to its experience, see Hayek ([1952] 1976, pp. 127–131). See also Cheung (2011) for my detailed discussion of Hayek's *The Sensory Order: An Inquiry to the Foundations of Theoretical Psychology*.
3. "Whenever a *type* of situation evokes in an individual a *disposition* towards a certain *pattern* of response, that basic relation which is described as 'abstract' is present" (Hayek 1973, p. 30, emphasis in the original).
4. From 1949 till *Free China* was banned by the Nationalist government in 1960, Xia published 116 quality editorials in the journal. He also contributed commentaries to it, many of which were critical reviews of government policies.

5

The Conservative Turn of Post-War Chinese Liberalism

Rationalism and Chinese Liberalism

Hayek's epistemological thesis in support of his idea of true individualism, his division of knowledge theorization, and his critique of scientism, as shown in the last chapter, together constitute the core of his critique of constructivism of the Cartesian kind of modern social and political thought. Closely related to Hayek's critique of constructivism is Michael Oakeshott's critique of modern rationalism in politics, and they both were towering figures of the twentieth century in social and political philosophy, who had contributed a lot to the defense of individual liberty.

Oakeshott's criticism of the sovereignty of technique in modern rationalism is premised on his claim of the inseparable partnership of technical knowledge and practical knowledge in all human cognition and action. While the former is demonstrable and explicit, the latter is by nature tacit, contextual, and exists mainly through practice. This,

The arguments and analysis in some parts of this chapter follow quite closely my previous work in Cheung (2017b, pp. 160–180), though some important additions have been made to the current chapter.

C. Cheung, *Hayek and Post-War Chinese Liberalism*, Palgrave Studies in Classical Liberalism, https://doi.org/10.1007/978-3-031-64888-5_5

together with his recognition of the poetic character of all human activity, allows Oakeshott to develop a critique of rationalism that is in full appreciation of the importance of the uniqueness of individual style, meaning, and freedom (Oakeshott 1991, also see Coats and Cheung 2012). The affinity between Hayek's and Oakeshott's respective critiques of rationalism notwithstanding, there are important philosophical differences between the two in this regard. I have elsewhere critically assessed these differences (see Cheung 2014b), but I am not prepared to repeat my analysis here since it is their affinity that is instructive in our study of post-war Chinese liberalism. In what follows, I intend to argue that Oakeshott's and Hayek's respective critiques help to shed light on the problems of rationalism in Chinese liberalism. I also contend that their critical thoughts have helped to trigger a conservative turn in post-war Chinese liberalism.

Professor Zhang Rulun (張汝倫 1953–) of Fudan University, as far as I know, is the first scholar who reflects on Oakeshott's relevance to Chinese liberalism. At the inaugural Michael Oakeshott Association conference held in 2002 at London School of Economics, he presented a paper entitled "Oakeshott and Chinese Liberalism," a revised Chinese version of which was subsequently published in his *Conscience and Theory* (《良知與理論》) (Zhang 2003).

In that paper, Zhang observes that judging from Oakeshott's critique of modern rationalism, Chinese liberalism is rationalist through and through. Zhang argues that there are clear family resemblances between Chinese liberalism and modern rationalist's insistence on the sovereignty of technical knowledge. Citing Yin Haiguang's critical study of Chinese liberalism and the Chinese culture, Zhang refers to the six positions that are identified by Yin as commonly adopted by post May Fourth Chinese liberals, and these positions are: (1) against Confucianism; (2) promoting science; (3) pursuing democracy; (4) advocating freedom; (5) believing in progress; and, (6) using the vernacular language to replace classical Chinese (see Yin 2009, pp. 275–352). Like the modern rationalist, Chinese liberals, according to Zhang, acknowledge the sovereignty of technical knowledge over traditional practices, and they believe in the authority of reason and radical doubt over rationally unexamined experience and prefer things that are eternal and universal to things that are traditional and partial.

In other words, according to Zhang, Chinese liberals, when confronted with the political and cultural challenges from Western imperial powers forcing China to modernize, believe that what is required is a rational blueprint to help to revive the greatness of China. In particular, they think that there must be a comprehensive plan to revitalize China's national strengths, and the key to that is to develop a scientific culture and to establish democracy in the modern Chinese state.

To the Chinese liberals, the traditional Chinese culture, with its emphasis on feudalistic, hierarchical, and collectivist values, resistance to change, and aversion to modern and scientific scholarship, is more a fundamental barrier than a pool of resources for China to achieve those modernization goals. In his early years, Yin Haiguang already drew the conclusion that China as a nation could only be revitalized if and only if she adopted science and democracy (Yin 1982, Volume 1, p. 176). In his 1955 essay criticizing the backwardness of the Chinese culture, Yin lamented that democracy was nowhere to be found in traditional China. Yin further pointed out that although scientific knowledge was introduced to China at least since Matteo Ricci's visit to China in the late Ming Dynasty in the sixteenth century, ancient Chinese were mostly interested in some of the applied aspects of science without really paying much attention to the development of theoretical science in the West (ibid., p. 178). In modern China, while post May Fourth Chinese liberalism is not as successful as Chinese communism in wielding political power to implement its modernization programs, it is culturally no less radical in believing that the outdated Chinese tradition must be replaced in a wholesale manner by the "universal" culture of modernity, and the key to this is to use scientific knowledge and a rational, albeit somewhat gradual, plan to help to transform China both politically, economically, technologically and culturally, and the model to follow is the modern culture of the West, not the intimations of the conventional practices within China's own tradition (see, e.g. Hu 1926).

Oakeshott's relevance to Chinese liberalism in this regard, therefore, is that his philosophical insights can help us to understand the follies of the rationalistic pretension of Chinese liberalism if one finds Oakeshott's analysis persuasive. Or, conversely, what amounts to the same logic, though with an opposite substantive conclusion from the above position, for the Chinese liberals who have yet to appreciate why the wholesale rejection of one's tradition is unlikely to help one to nurture the development of liberal institutions in one's community, Oakeshott is totally irrelevant and unconvincing, since they strongly disagree with his claim that "political crisis (even when it seems to be imposed upon a society by changes beyond its control) always appears *within* a tradition of political activity; and 'salvation' comes from the unimpaired resources of the tradition itself" (Oakeshott 1991, p. 59, emphasis in the original).

More recently, Zhang has revisited some of the issues he raised in his 2002 paper in "Oakeshott in China" (Zhang 2015). In this 2015 published article, Zhang further observes that since the Chinese liberals very much like to import constitutional democracy to China to save her from the tyrannical rule of totalitarianism under the party-state regime or despotism under the traditional dynastic emperors, Oakeshott's stricture over the illusion of putting abstract theory into practice without regard to one's traditional context makes it difficult for the Chinese liberals to use his understanding of the civil condition (see Oakeshott [1975] 1991 and the Appendix to this book) as a guide to convert China into a liberal state. Oakeshott's emphasis on the importance of the authority of the state as a postulate in his philosophical idea of the rule of law also puzzles the ideological liberals in China since they have already put freedom and democracy as pre-mediated purposes for the construction of a legitimate state for a modern China. Freedom, therefore, must be protected by human rights, which are more or less universal. Laws are instruments to constrain the government from infringement against the rights of the citizens, and the model of separation of powers must be accepted as a prime principle for constitutional democracy in China.

In a nutshell, what Zhang is saying is that while the Chinese liberals' plan to resist the socialists' central planning or totalitarian rule is laudable, they nevertheless are not skeptics but rationalists, holding a highly ideological view of a liberal state, the style of which is the same as the socialists or even similar to the advocates of totalitarianism. Their difference, as a matter of fact, is more a matter of degree rather than of substance. Chinese liberals in the end believe that the way to introduce constitutional democracy to China is by technical reason and rational design, with tradition playing little part in this undertaking.

Zhang's Oakeshottian arguments against Chinese liberalism are powerful and illuminating, and one cannot deny that there is much truth in his critique if this critique is applied to the May Fourth and many of the pre-war liberals. However, this is not the whole story. The relationship between tradition and Chinese liberalism is richer than what Zhang has described in his two essays discussed above, and a closer look at the development of post-war Chinese liberalism reveals that more and more Chinese liberals increasingly come to realize that to cope with the challenges of modernity, "even the help we may get from the traditions of another society (or from a tradition of a vaguer sort which is shared by a number of societies) is conditional upon our being able to assimilate them to our own arrangements and our own manner of attending to our arrangements" (Oakeshott 1991, p. 59). But before some Chinese liberals came to appreciate Oakeshott's insights in the early part of the twenty-first century (see Qiu 2014), Hayek's critique of constructivism and his classical liberalism had already helped post-war Chinese liberalism in Taiwan to whittle down the arrogance of synoptic rationalism, with emphasis on the role performed by traditional practices in the spontaneous development of a liberal society. In this regard, the cases of two leading liberals in post-war Taiwan David Chow and Yin Haiguang are perhaps most illustrative.

In the case of Chow, his attempt to try to demonstrate that in fact the philosophy of freedom of the Hayekian kind was quite compatible with many of the insights embedded in classical Chinese thought, including the thoughts of Confucius (孔子 551–479 BCE), Mozi (墨子470–391 BCE) and Xunzi (荀子 310–238? BCE) respectively, is quite exceptional in Chinese liberalism. In the case of Yin, his turning from supporting in his earlier years logical empiricism, which is highly critical of the metaphysical nature of the traditional Chinese culture and aspiring to unify all branches of genuine knowledge under the scientific approach, to his increasingly receptive attitude in his later life toward the Chinese tradition within which "a viable creative reformism" should be explored (Yin and Lin [1981] 1984, p. 150), indicates that Yin has changed from an anti-traditionalist (ibid., p. 154) to one who thinks that there is a need to maintain one's identity with traditional practices in order to engage in an internal renewal of one's culture for the development of freedom (ibid., p. 150). These two cases, in my view, clearly show that there has been a conservative turn of post-war liberalism in the Chinese speaking world at least since the 1960s.

David Chow: The Philosophy of Freedom and Classical Chinese Thought

I think there is no exaggeration to say that David Chow occupies a unique place among the Chinese liberals for at least two reasons. Firstly, he was one of a handful of leading Chinese liberals who since the pre-war period never subscribed to any form of wholesale Westernization or anti-traditionalism in China.[1] Chow in fact made a further step by claiming that there was close affinity between the philosophy of freedom of the West and some classical Chinese thought, especially those ideas deriving from Confucius, Mozi, and Xunzi (Chow 2004, pp. 1–117). I shall say more on this shortly.

Secondly, as Hayek's first Chinese student at the London School of Economics in 1933, Chow was not only instrumental in introducing Hayek's liberal philosophy to China as I explained in Chapter 2 of this book, he, unlike most pre-war Chinese liberals who believed then that socialism would be the logical consequence of liberalism, was busy criticizing central planning, socialism and Marxism and promoting ideas from classical liberalism as articulated by Adam Smith, Mises, Hayek and Gottfried Haberler in a journal called *China's Path* (《中國之路》)[2] during the Second Sino-Japanese War after he had returned to China and taught at Hunan University (Chow 2011, pp. 431–449). In other words, Chow did not subscribe to the then consensus among most Chinese liberals about what Edmund S. K. Fung calls the statist and revisionist liberalism of pre-war China (Fung 2008/2009). Based on the above reasons, I believe that Chow deserves more acknowledgment of his contributions to the development of Chinese liberal thought even though, as I said, for various reasons (such as his difficult writing style and his being a high-ranking official in the Nationalist government not playing an active part in academic and current affairs discussions), his works and his translation of Hayek's *The Constitution of Liberty* are not widely read not only by the general public, but even by scholars in the academia in the Chinese speaking world unless one is quite an expert in the study of modern Chinese liberal thought.

In an essay exploring the affinity between what Chow calls the philosophy of freedom of the West and classical Confucianism in China (2004, pp. 1–41), Chow highlights three aspects of the thought of Confucius as most compatible with the philosophy of freedom of the West. The first comes from *The Doctrine of the Mean* (《中庸》) where Confucius aspires to a situation where "all living creatures grow together without harming each other, and different Ways run in parallel without in conflict with each other." The second is a famous saying in *The Analects* (《論語》) where Confucius counsels that knowledge and wisdom comprise not only what is known, but also the awareness of what is not known. The third also comes from *The Analects* where Confucius says that if one wishes to establish oneself, one should, to be consistent, also wish others to be established. And if one wishes to be allowed to make achievements, the same allowance should be granted for others to make their achievements. This, in effect, is like what is said in the West: "do to others as you would have them do to you."

To Chow, classical Confucianism is fundamentally a kind of universal learning, in which man tries to develop an overall and consistent understanding of the principles behind the relationships of the myriad of things, including the principles behind the relationships between man, heaven, and the external environment, as well as the principles behind human action and social interaction, with a view to achieving a kind of social order that can ensure universal peace and prosperity (ibid., 2004, pp. 2–3). Chow also credits Confucius as the great thinker in China who first promotes an understanding of the world and of man mainly from a human perspective. Although it is true that Confucius has given extremely high regards to those mythical sage kings in pre-historic China, Chow says that Confucius nevertheless refrains from making comments on affairs related to the other worldly or the mythical realm. Not only that Confucius never resorts to God or deity to explain the origin or creation of the world and human society, but he also explicitly says that while the way of heaven is vague and remote, the way of people is concrete and close (ibid., p. 48). In understanding social rules and rituals of the ancient time that regulate and coordinate social interaction and relationships, Confucius also stresses elements of continuity from one era to another, and he says that by studying the historical and empirical evidences that are still available to us at the time, if those evidences are more or less adequate, we should be in a position to explain and understand how such rules and rituals have been evolved from one era to another (ibid., p. 25 & pp. 29–30).

Chow sees a lot of parallels between classical Confucianism as understood above and classical liberalism. To start with, classical liberalism's emphasis on the protection and promotion of individual liberty and the establishment of nomocratic institutions and practices to allow maximal space for each and every individual to engage in their respective individual pursuits is very much consistent with Confucius's idea of allowing different Ways to run parallel with each other according to some beneficent and common rules and rituals. Hayek's critique of constructivistic rationalism and his emphasis on the limits of rationality also echo well with Confucius's insight that admission of our ignorance is a constitutive part of human wisdom. Although Confucius does not appear to have a theory similar to Adam Ferguson's idea of the development of social institutions as the result of human action but not human design, Confucius's emphasis on the evolutionary and empirical approach in understanding the changes and development of social rituals in ancient China is certainly no design theory of the rationalistic kind. As regards the principle of "do to others as you would have them do to you," there is no doubt that Confucius and the Bible both arrive at such a moral conclusion independently, which arguably can be said that such a principle perhaps underlines man's understanding of a common humanity from which the value of equal respect for the individual is to be derived.

While Chow's efforts in finding affinity between classical Chinese thought and Western liberalism have the merits of not only avoiding the excess of radical anti-traditionalism in Chinese liberalism, but also allowing Chinese liberals to constructively and sympathetically look at traditional practices and identify agreeable elements from within that may be conducive to the development of liberal values in the Chinese context, one may suspect that perhaps Chow's understanding of classical Chinese thought is colored too much by his adoption of some Hayekian liberal lens. In other words, he may have been retrospectively reading too much Western classical liberalism into his interpretation of Confucianism. For example, by selectively concentrating on some of the classical texts of the ancient time in his interpretation of Confucianism and by denying neo-Confucianism of the Song Dynasty representing the high-water mark of the development of orthodox Confucianism (ibid., p. 3), Chow perhaps may not be able to command much assent within the mainstream scholarship of Confucianism for his interpretation of Chinese classical thought. As a result, he may be regarded as having papered many of the incompatible elements in Confucianism, such as its hierarchical and collective presuppositions, over liberalism.

Even from the classical liberal's perspective, if civilization and values evolve concurrently as argued by Hayek, the more convincing approach to demonstrate this in the Chinese context is not to rely mainly on some selected classical texts in Confucianism and then to develop an ahistoric interpretation of them that is conducive to some Western liberal values; rather, what is required is a more detailed historical explanation of how certain practices and institutions that may be found conducive to individual freedom having in reality been emerged, developed, and grown in the Chinese context. Equally important in this regard is the need to show to what extent these practices and institutions are well embedded in the tradition of China and what is the potential for them to be turned into constructive and meaningful resources facilitating the further development of liberal practices. Otherwise, the selective textual analysis approach looks more like an intellectual exercise in the abstract. Such an analysis may be suggestive, but it is far from establishing a genuine link between tradition and liberty in the Chinese context.

In fact, Chow himself admits that while in the thought of the classical Chinese thinker Mozi, we can find in some of his writings where he advocates a conception of the law the application of which shall go beyond the familial context, the scholarly gentlemen context, and even the princely government context on the ground that only the universal and impartial application of the law (i.e. all are equal before the law) can ensure that it is beneficent and genuinely fair to all (ibid., p. 114), Chow admits that in fact, Mozi's idea remains at the abstract level, and he has not developed any adequate theory of the rule of law jurisprudence from his idea, not to say to help to develop in practice a system of laws and institutions in China that are consistent with the nomocratic practices in the West. In fact, China's conception of law in practice has still very much been dominated by the traditional Legalist thinking, where laws are regarded as instruments for the ruler to help control both the officials and the people to ensure that they are subordinate to the will of the ruler in their action and interaction (ibid.). All these point to the conclusion that the gap between tradition and freedom is indeed still wide even though one cannot deny that Chow is exceptional among Chinese liberals whose ideas have been consistently shown to be having a lot of sympathetic understanding toward classical Chinese thought.

Yin Haiguang and Post-War Chinese Liberalism

Yin Haiguang, who was born in the May Fourth year of 1919, always regarded himself as belonging to the post May Fourth generation of the Chinese intellectuals who had inherited the challenges and burden of the May Fourth Movement without inheriting its fame and glory (Chen ed. 2020, p. 51). In previous chapters of this book, I have already mentioned how after having learned from Hayek's classical liberalism, Yin has abandoned his statist understanding of liberalism and clearly recognized that economic equality through state redistribution may hugely undermine the protection of individual liberty. While Yin always supports the development of freedom and democracy in China, Hayek's social and political thought reminds Yin the importance of adhering to what Hayek calls "true individualism" where, "to be free" for the individual, is not the same as "to be liberated," for the latter may only be applied to a collective entity where individual freedom may not be guaranteed (Yin & Lin [1981] 1984), p. 151). The understanding of true individualism and the recognition of the spontaneous evolution of social practices in human associations also helps Yin to appreciate that the pursuit of freedom and democracy cannot be made in the abstract, how this pursuit is to be aligned with those conventional and moral practices that are taken for granted by the people in a society is equally important (Yin 1982, Volume 2, p. 999).

As regards science, Yin in the 1950s still contended that all knowledge must be derived from scientific knowledge (Yin 1982, Volume 1, p. 189) and the unity of knowledge could be achieved by logical empiricism (Chen ed. 2020, p. 36). Yin at that time also believed that the Cartesian method was crucial to science, thinking that Descartes's method of systematic, universal, and radical doubt is the basis of certain knowledge since only those premises that can survive the critical scrutiny of the radical doubt approach are reliable or verifiable knowledge, on which scientific knowledge can be built (Yin 1982, Volume 1, p. 190). This is exactly what is criticized by Hayek as rationalistic arrogance and is fundamentally erroneous. Although Yin's subsequent change of mind cannot all be attributed to the influence of Hayek, it is clear that just before Yin's unfortunately early death at the age of 50, he no longer subscribed to this kind of conception of scientific knowledge, saying that logical empiricism's ambition of unifying all branches of knowledge was in fact a kind of "knowledge totalitarianism," and logical empiricism's claim that the questions of mind (as distinguished from the questions of the brain) are "pseudo-problems" is baseless because humanity cannot do without emotions and sentiments, and the questions of mind are therefore "genuine problems" (Chen ed. 2020, pp. 36–37).

Yin said in a letter to his student Lin Yu-sheng in 1968 that before 1963, he regarded himself as an "anti-traditionalist"; but now, all he could say was that he was a "non-traditionalist" (Yin and Lin [1981] 1984, p. 154). The reason for this was that while Yin now admitted that in terms of science, mathematics, logic, and other "cognitive knowledge," the West was far ahead of China, it was not clear that in terms of social mores, rituals, outlook on life or one's world view, in the absence of a set of universal criteria for the evaluation of our common humanity, one can meaningfully assert whether the West was necessarily better than the East or vice versa (ibid., pp. 154–155). To be fair to Yin, even when he was an anti-traditionalist, he did not go all the way to support the claim of wholesale Westernization. Although Yin agreed that only science and democracy could save China and yet science and democracy were nowhere to be found in the Chinese tradition, he still believed that one should not totally discard one's tradition even under such circumstances since in doing so, it might create new problems and make it even more difficult to help science and democracy to take root in China. The real question was how to introduce science and democracy into the Chinese context without destroying the Chinese tradition (Yin 1982, Volume 1, pp. 165–185).

Translating and examining Hayek's works had certainly helped Yin Haiguang to begin to be mindful of the danger of turning science into scientism and the potential totalitarian horrors of synoptic rational social planning. Yin was also aware of the role of the rule of law as a bulwark for democracy after studying Hayek. More importantly, Hayek's emphasis on the importance of traditional practices and evolutionary rationality had convinced Yin and other Chinese liberals in Taiwan that a modern China could not be developed without revitalizing her own tradition, and from that time (i.e. in the mid-1960s) onward, we can see that Chinese liberalism, at least in Taiwan, has started to lose its wholesale radical rejection of the Chinese traditional culture. Since then, the proper relationship between liberty and tradition in China's pursuit of modernization has accordingly become an unavoidable question to be reflected on by Chinese liberals.

I have elsewhere examined this transition in Chinese liberalism and criticized Yin Haiguang as a leading post-war Chinese liberal who still failed adequately to assimilate Hayek's complicated theoretical insights into his Chinese liberalism, since the former's adherence to the radicalism and rationalism of the May Fourth Movement was perhaps too strong for him to make a smooth U-turn to Hayek's classical liberalism (Cheung 2018, pp. 187–212). It was unfortunate that Yin died at a relatively young age of 50 in 1969 and was thus deprived of the possibility of further developing his more tradition-sensitive kind of Chinese liberalism. But his student Lin Yu-Sheng, who went to Chicago to study under Hayek in 1960, has continued this intellectual pilgrimage in Chinese liberalism and has since contributed to a more profound and convincing reflection on the proper relationship between liberty and tradition under Chinese liberalism.

Liberalism and the Creative Transformation of Chinese Tradition

Lin, in my view, is one of the more profound Hayekian Chinese liberals whose ideas are immune from many of the Oakeshottian criticisms against Chinese liberalism raised by Zhang Rulun. In the limited space of this chapter, I will not be able to do justice to many of Lin's carefully considered and nuanced arguments, nor to give a systematic critical overview of his liberal thought. What I can manage to do here is to briefly examine how, through the influence of Hayek and other classical liberals, Lin comes to appreciate the limits of reason, the mutual dependence of freedom and authority, and the need to creatively transform those unimpaired resources of Chinese tradition to help to provide a moral foundation allowing democracy and the rule of law, which are foreign to traditional Chinese culture, to take root in China as she faces the challenges of modernity.

First of all, it is of interest to stress again that in his devastating critique of the May Fourth's anti-traditional intellectual radicalism, Lin finds that despite the fact that leading radical intellectuals of the May Fourth like Hu Shih, Chen Duxiu and Lu Xun, all adopted an explicit totalistic rejection stance against the Chinese cultural heritage (Lin calls this "totalistic iconoclasm"), their frame of mind ultimately was powerfully though unconsciously influenced by the deep-rooted traditional Chinese mode of holistic thinking, which assigns primary responsibility to cultural and intellectual ideas in social and moral changes, though this time round the "ideas" concerned was a wholesale adoption of science and democracy from the West (Lin 1979, pp. 10–55). This should remind us of Oakeshott's observation that "The Russian Revolution (what actually happened in Russia) was not the implementation of an abstract design worked out by Lenin and others in Switzerland: it was a modification of *Russian* circumstances. And the French Revolution was far more closely connected with the *ancien regime* than with Locke or America" (Oakeshott 1991a, p. 59, emphasis in the original). If Oakeshott were in a position to reflect on the May Fourth era, he probably would agree that the radical intellectuals' "totalistic iconoclasm" was largely a modification of the dominant traditional Chinese mode of holistic thinking, the emphasis of which is more on abstract ideas than on actual concrete practices. To Oakeshott, this is very much in line with the nature of ancient Confucian thought:

> *Ren* [仁] in the Confucian morality was an abstraction from the filial piety and respect for elders which constituted the ancient Chinese habit of moral behavior. The activity of the Sages, who (according to Zhuangzi [莊子 369-286 BEC]) *invented* goodness, duty and the rules and ideals of moral conduct, was one in which a concrete morality of habitual behavior was sifted and refined; but, like too critical anthologies, they threw out the imperfect approximations of their material and what remained was not the reflection of a literature but merely a collection of masterpiece. (Oakeshott 1991, p. 480, n. 2, emphasis in the original)[3]

I do not think that Lin arrives at the above conclusion under the influence of Oakeshott, but the conclusion nevertheless is in line with one important common ground shared by the respective critiques of rationalism by Hayek and Oakeshott: that the abstract Cartesian type of reason is wrong to think that one can go beyond one's traditional practices to start afresh *in toto* for rational planning for reform or revolution (see Cheung 2014b).

Hayek's critique of Cartesian rationalism is based on his sophisticated theory of knowledge, in which the mind is characterized as essentially a mechanism of classification in which external stimuli one has perceived are related to other stimuli, or to one's past experience remembered within the classificatory structure of one's mental order, in relation to which one makes sense of human interaction and the external environment, and also in relation to which one derives meanings and values which guide one's actions. Like all classificatory structures, the mind cannot classify itself and it is therefore logically impossible for it to fully explain itself or to go outside itself to give a full and synoptic view of the mind. That is why Hayek contends that "The mind can never foresee its own advance" (Hayek 1960, p. 24).

Furthermore, in a market or a society, there exists numerous, diverse, and dispersed "knowledge of particular circumstances of time and place" (I have discussed this in detail in Chapter 4 above), the contents and possible use of which are only known to each and every participatory individual. Also, the nature of this type of knowledge (such as personal preferences) is contextual and fleeting, changeable in accordance with the anticipated or perceived results of the interaction among the participating individuals, whose respective perceptions and decisions made under the circumstances will not be known in advance by any single mind. With these logical and circumstantial limitations in mind, it is absurd to assume that rationality can be based purely on certain, abstract, clear, and distinct premises which have survived the test of universal doubt and are therefore conceptually certain in the absolute sense, from which one can deduce a system of certain knowledge to design the most rational result for all. That is why Hayek says,

> Man did not simply impose upon the world a pattern created by his mind. His mind is itself a system that constantly changes as a result of his endeavor to adapt himself to his surroundings...[T]he growth of the human mind is part of the growth of civilization; it is the state of civilization at any given moment that determines the scope and the possibilities of human ends and values. (Hayek 1960, pp. 23–24)

In a number of essays written in the 1980s (Lin 1988, pp. 43–64, pp. 65–75, & pp. 76–87) to examine what rationality was and what the relationship between freedom and authority was, Lin essentially adopted the above Hayekian understanding of rationality. In these essays, following in the footsteps of Hayek, he also cites Polanyi's ideas of "focal awareness" and "subsidiary awareness" (Polanyi 1962, Chapters 4–5) to argue that in every rational thinking process, both types of awareness are needed since subsidiary awareness provides us with the context to make sense of our focal attention (e.g. the meaning of a particular word in a text depends on the sentence the word is in as its context, and the meaning of the sentence or the full text depends on certain general grammatical and linguistic rules and practices and so on) even though we are not fully conscious of the former or able to articulate it in full.

The concurrent development of mind and civilization not only points to the implausibility of the Cartesian understanding of rationality, but it also draws Lin's attention to the importance of existing and accepted institutions and practices embedded in a stable but evolving civilization for the possible growth of knowledge. Lin calls these institutions and practices "authorities" and only when we subscribe to these "authorities" can we learn the skills and acquire the necessary knowledge for those practices or ways of doing things. This of course does not mean that "authorities" are fixed once and for all, since we as individuals and civilization as a whole always face new challenges and the environment we are in is changing all the time. But innovations or new ways of doing things to cope with these new challenges will not come from the void, they must come as improvements or modifications of existing and accepted rules and practices, be they scientific, social, political, cultural, or aesthetical, which proven to be more effective, agreeable, or desirable and hence have become new authorities. Naturally, without freedom, people cannot explore new possibilities to discover innovative solutions and to make mistakes. Equally, without subscribing to these established practices or authorities in the first place, people simply cannot act at all, not to say inventing new measures. In the light of this, Zhang Rulun's criticism of Chinese liberalism in his "Oakeshott in China" (Zhang 2015) is not completely applicable to Lin's liberalism to say the least, since the latter does not think that freedom and authority are antithetical; instead, properly understood, they are mutually reinforcing.

One fundamental problem facing Chinese liberals like Lin is that since democracy and the rule of law are largely foreign to the Chinese tradition, how can they subscribe to accepted institutions and conventional practices that are conducive to the protection and enhancement of liberal values, yet at the same time preserve their identification with the Chinese culture? To Lin, the only way to go about this is by the creative transformation of Confucian humanism such that a moral foundation can be created out of the unimpaired resources of Chinese tradition to support the political and legal institutions of democracy and the rule of law in the Chinese context.

Lin accepts that democracy and the rule of law cannot be found in the tradition of China, but this does not entail that the liberal values these institutions support, such as respect for the intrinsic worth of the individual, are necessarily incompatible with certain core Confucian values such as *ren,* which still command respect and acceptance by the Chinese. To Lin, while institutions and cultural values are mutually reinforcing, they are also mutually irreducible in the sense that each sphere has its own relatively autonomous status. "One can reject all the evils in Chinese traditional society" says Lin, "without necessarily attacking traditional Chinese culture as a whole." To him, "It does not seem far-fetched to say that the formal structure of classical Confucianism is quite compatible with liberal humanism. The concept of *ren* is not identical with the belief in the worth of the individual. But…in a creative re-interpretation of Confucianism…there is plenty of room for creative integration of Confucian moral idealism and Western liberal humanism' (Lin 1973, p. 57 and p. 58). Lin is of the view that a creative re-understanding of Confucian core humanist values may lend support to liberal and democratic institutions in modern China.

In this respect, Edward Shils is in agreement with Lin. Like Lin, Shils argues that while "Confucianism…does not have a concept of civil society [understood as a society of the rule of law] as a complex of institutions and patterns of activities different from those of the family and the state" (Shils 1996, p. 46), there are nevertheless elements of civil society in ancient Chinese philosophy because, for example, Confucius' idea of *ren* contains important virtues like "Moderation, serenity, tranquility, modesty, equanimity, courtesy, resistance to any impulse toward anger" that are "required in a civil society if the individualism, ambition, and acquisitiveness in the economic sphere are to be held in check' (ibid., p. 67). Nevertheless, we should be reminded of Lin's qualification in this respect: "One cannot foretell what the outcome of this integration will be; but only on such an integration…can liberal individualism take root in the consciousness of the Chinese intellectuals. This new liberal individualism will certainly not be the same as that of the West. But it will converge with Western liberal individualism on many important points. Working for this new synthesis may…discover a new sense of identity [for the Chinese intellectuals]" (Lin 1973, p. 58).

Of course, to Oakeshott, the claim that one must create a "moral foundation" for the adoption of Western institutions in the process of creative transformation of Chinese culture is still too much for a skeptic to endorse, since that is a symptom of the politics of the "felt need" rather than the politics of continuity and practical reason. But a sympathetic reader of Lin's proposal may argue that this is no transcendental foundation of any sort. It simply acts as a cultural compass or anchor for assimilation in the Chinese context. At one point, Lin compares his proposed creative transformation of Chinese tradition as analogous to Weber's *The Protestant Ethic and the Spirit of Capitalism* (Lin 1988, p. 64). I take this to mean that like the Protestant ethic, Confucian humanism, as a kind of traditional value, must be developed during the transformation process so that it can help to sustain the emergence of a new kind of liberal, social institution, or practice, the exact outcome of which cannot be foretold. However, one should remember that Weber's classical work is a masterpiece of *explanation*, not a practical *guide* to transform Middle Ages Christian Europe into capitalism. In the case of Lin's creative transformation proposal, however, it acts more like a plan, albeit one that is immune from the arrogance of Cartesian rationalism and is mindful of the role played by tradition, with a clearly pre-mediated purpose.

Tradition, "Guided Pursuit of Intimations," and Conservative Liberalism in China

Theoretical contributions to Chinese liberalism made by people like Lin are one reason that helps the Chinese intellectuals to become receptive to the kind of conservative liberalism they have encountered since China has adopted Deng Xiaoping's "reform and opening" policy from the 1980s onward. Hayek's influence, of course, has been significant. In addition to *The Road to Serfdom,* his life-long critique of socialism of various kinds turned out to be hugely vindicated by the collapse of the USSR and her eastern bloc socialist allies in 1989/1990. China's own failed socialist experiment since 1949 played a dominant role in the conservative turn of the Chinese intellectuals too. By the time when Liu Junning (劉軍寧 1961–), a leading conservative liberal in China, published his article "Classical Liberalism Catches On in China" in 2000 (Liu 2000), he could claim that "Classical liberalism now dominates China's intellectual landscape. No other school of political thought enjoys greater popularity in the Chinese intellectual community."[4]

Of course, it will be wrong to think that classical liberalism is now the only brand of liberalism that is influential in China. However, here is not the place to give a comprehensive account of the development of liberalism in China since the Chinese government has loosened its ideological control in late 1970s and early 1980s. We must also be mindful of the fact that since Xi Jinping (習近平) has assumed supreme power in 2012 in the Chinese Communist Party and enforced what appears to be a life-long tenure of personal dictatorship under political/party-state capitalism in China (Yadav 2023, *The Economist*, 2023.12.02–08, pp. 65–66), there are new and significant challenges facing the Chinese liberals in their attempts to transform China into a liberal association. I shall briefly deal with this latest development in China in the conclusion chapter of this book later. In the meantime, however, for the purpose of this chapter, I intend to briefly examine the works of two leading conservative liberals in present-day China Liu Junning and Qiu Feng (秋風 also known as Yao Zhongqiu 姚中秋 1966–)[5] to see how they have benefited from the insights of classical liberalism and Western conservatism to further develop a kind of Chinese liberalism that pays due regard to traditional practices in its pursuit of freedom and constitutionalism in the Chinese context.

Unlike their fellow liberals during the May Fourth era, Chinese conservative liberals like Liu and Qiu have a far more nuanced and positive view of tradition. In his book *Conservatism* (《保守主義》) (Liu 2014), Liu argues that, properly understood, tradition is open, evolving not static, covering past, present and future and is structurally pluralistic with possible internal tensions. Tradition is necessarily ambiguous but concrete, and our attitude to tradition must be selective since no one can embrace tradition as a whole. With these attributes, tradition, to Liu, is capable of self-correction, and the richer and more complex a tradition is, the more it may have internal conflicts yet at the same time the more resources it may be absorbed to be used for assimilation or adaptation (Liu 2014, pp. 264–272). While Liu has not cited Oakeshott for this account of tradition, it seems to me clear that it shares many of the characteristics of Oakeshott's conception of a tradition of behavior. Allow me here to quote Oakeshott's superb analysis of what a tradition of behavior (1991a, pp. 61–62) is:

> [A] tradition of behavior is a tricky thing to get to know. Indeed, it may even appear to be essentially unintelligible. It is neither fixed nor finished; it has no changeless centre to which understanding can anchor itself; there is no sovereign purpose to be perceived or invariable direction to be detected; there is no model to be copied, idea to be realized, or rule to be followed. Some parts of it may change more slowly than others, but none is immune from change. Everything is temporary. Nevertheless, though a tradition of behavior is flimsy and elusive, it is not without identity, and what makes it a possible object of knowledge is the fact that all its parts do not change at the same time and that the changes it undergoes are potential within it. Its principle is a principle of *continuity*: authority is diffused between past, present, and future; between the old, the new, and what is to come. It is steady because, though it moves, it is never wholly in motion; and though it is tranquil, it is never wholly at rest. Nothing that ever belonged to it is completely lost; we are always swerving back to recover and make something topical out of even its remotest moments: and nothing for long remains unmodified. Everything is temporary, but nothing is arbitrary. Everything figures by comparison, not with what stands next to it, but with the whole. And since a tradition of behavior is not susceptible of the distinction between essence and accident, knowledge of it is unavoidably knowledge of its detail: to know only the gist is to know nothing. What has to be learned is not an abstract idea, or a set of tricks, not even a ritual, but a concrete, coherent manner of living in all its intricateness. (1991a, pp. 61–62, emphasis in the original)

With such an understanding of tradition, Liu argues that although in the mainstream of the Chinese tradition, it does appear that there is a lack of strong elements which would lend support to liberal values and institutions, it does not follow that we cannot select those elements within the tradition that may be conducive to the development of freedom and civility in order to nurture and enrich the liberality of the Chinese culture. As Edward Shils says, "Tradition is not the dead hand of the past but rather the hand of the gardener, which nourishes and elicits tendencies of judgment which would otherwise not be strong enough to emerge on their own' (Shils 1997, p. 107).

Two points, however, need to be made here. Unlike Oakeshottian conservatives, conservative Chinese liberals like Liu, while having developed a far more amiable conception of tradition than their forebears, still regard freedom as a *sovereign* ideal that needs to be promoted. Indeed, Liu tries to distinguish his conservatism from traditionalism in China by his contention that traditionalism maintains tradition for its own sake even if it is not liberal, whereas conservative liberalism is conservative because it is there to maintain and conserve the value of freedom in tradition (Liu 2014, pp. 258–260). Liu also explicitly says that if tradition is in conflict with freedom, his conservatism will always stand on the side of freedom, not tradition (ibid., p. 263). While I am sure that Liu will no doubt endorse Shils's gardener metaphor in selecting and nourishing liberal elements to enrich the Chinese culture, an inevitable dose of rationalism has imbued his conservatism since an invariable commitment to freedom is fundamental to his concept of tradition.

Secondly, as Oakeshott says, to learn from a tradition of behavior is never just to learn about the gist, but to learn about a concrete and coherent manner of living. As Oakeshott has famously argued, learning always involves the partnership of the two aspects of knowledge: the technical aspect and the practical aspect, with the technical part being demonstrable and, in a sense, acting as the gist, while the practical aspect is the detailed and concrete part which normally exists only in doing/acting (Oakeshott 1991, pp. 6–42). In the light of this, two questions immediately come to mind. First, if, as Liu and other Chinese liberals readily admit, liberal elements within Chinese tradition are far from strong, is the gardener in the Chinese garden skillful or experienced enough to nourish freedom in Chinese culture? Even with the benefit of cross-cultural experience, it will be highly inadequate for the gardener to rely entirely on foreign books on gardening in his/her attempt to transplant liberal flowers from foreign gardens to his/her own without firsthand concrete knowledge. Second, if to know the gist is to know nothing at all in a tradition of behavior, then even the best theoretical efforts by Chinese liberals to explicate the kind of conservatism or liberalism most compatible with tradition are all half-baked at best, since without practically engaging in a concrete way of living, one can learn and nourish little from abstract principles or arguments alone. In the light of this, will it not be better if we direct more of our attention to learn about the actual, practical, and detailed experience of the Chinese in places like Hong Kong (at least up to the time when the common law tradition was still prevalent there before the enactment of the Hong Kong National Security Law in 2020 and thereafter) and Taiwan (after democracy has been entrenched from 1996 onward) in order to see how the former managed to become the most liberal and open society within a Chinese context and how the latter has become the most democratic?[6]

Qiu Feng is perhaps the Chinese Confucian liberal most mindful of the need to have practical knowledge that is conducive to the nourishment of liberal values in Chinese tradition. He also readily admits that non-rational and non-demonstrable knowledge of this kind can only be learned through doing and acting in contexts in which practical skills of this kind are already embedded. Therefore, he acknowledges that in the process of learning from the liberal West, the Chinese have learned most at the abstract level of ideological and cultural values like freedom and democracy, on the one hand, and institutional arrangements like the separation of powers, a parliamentary system, and an independent judiciary, etc., on the other. What the Chinese have learned least is the kind of practical and circumstantial knowledge that can only be imparted through doing in the right context (Qiu 2014, pp. 231–306). However, he further observes that in modern China's political history, it is wrong to just concentrate on the increasing radicalization of Chinese politics since the late nineteenth century. This is because after every stage of radicalization or even revolution from the late Qing era to the republican and subsequent communist regimes, it was followed by a conservative turn for constitutional reform in China. Though most of these conservative turns did not succeed in establishing meaningful constitutionalism in China, the Nationalist government's constitutional enactment in 1946–1947 for the Republic of China eventually brought that constitution to Taiwan after the Nationalist government fled there in 1949. It is based on that constitution that Taiwan has developed its democratic institutions and practices since 1996 when its president was first returned by universal suffrage. Qiu therefore believes that in fact, there is an emerging, though far from prevalent, tradition of constitutional politics in the context of Chinese culture which is understudied, and that a better and more thorough understanding of this kind of experience will not only help Chinese liberals to enrich their knowledge of constitutional principles, but also their knowledge of the strengths and limits of Chinese practical experience in intimating the politics of constitutionalism in the pursuit of democracy (ibid., pp. 173–229).

Qiu, like other Chinese liberals, admits that the elements of liberal values in Chinese tradition are weak. But he shares Liu's idea of tradition, believing that tradition is open-ended and can be self-correcting, and that the more liberal elements within tradition can be nourished and enriched in ways that assist the development of democracy and freedom in China in a practical and concrete manner, the better. As such, more studies of Chinese's practices in constitutionalism may help in this regard. Also, unlike pre-war Chinese liberals, Qiu argues that since most contemporary Chinese liberals now get their inspirations from classical liberalism instead of from that of the French Enlightenment (or what Hayek calls "false individualism"), it is to be hoped that this combination can provide a better chance of success in pursuing the intimations of freedom and democracy in the Chinese culture. It is true that Qiu's and Liu's suggested approaches are perhaps still treating freedom and democracy as independently premeditated sovereign purposes, pre-determined for the evolution of Chinese tradition, but by ameliorating the arrogance of technical reason and putting more emphasis on the need for practical reason in the development of traditional behavior toward freedom and civility, what their proposals amount to are possible ways to have a "guided" pursuit of intimations in order to help China to overcome her challenges of modernity.

As a theorist of civil association, Hayek is distinguished by the fact that he is never short of a plan. For example, near the end of his career, he proposed a new model constitution for Western democracies, which aims at rectifying democracy's past failings. Though he thinks that one should not expect that this model can be transplanted into a state which lacks a well-entrenched tradition of the rule of law, he nevertheless believes that it can serve as a *reserved guide* for the improvement of the nomocratic order of future democracies (Hayek 1979, Chapter 17). For Chinese liberals who are experiencing a "felt need" created by the political crises in China and the challenges of modernity, Hayek is naturally easier to understand and to follow than the skeptical Oakeshott, whose advice for political activity "to keep afloat on an even keel" and to use "the resources of a traditional manner of behavior in order to make a friend of every hostile occasion" (Oakeshott 1991a, p. 60) is a sober but illusive reminder. However, I hope that this chapter has shown that the theoretical insights of Hayek and Oakeshott are both relevant to Chinese liberalism, and that the conservative turn of the Chinese liberalism owes not a small debt to these two Western political thinkers. Although no one can foretell what the outcome of this conservative turn will be, it looks like that the Chinese liberals are determined to continue their intellectual journey to enrich the civil elements of the Chinese tradition, hoping that in the end they may transform this great traditional culture into a liberal one.

Notes

1. Another Chinese liberal who probably can be grouped under this category is Kung-chuan Hsiao (蕭公權/Xiao Gongquan 1897–1981).
2. I have yet had the opportunity to find out if copies of this journal still exist. If they do, they will be an important source of materials for the study of history of political thought in China to ascertain the influence of classical liberalism of the West on the development of Chinese liberal thought in the late 1930s. I am not, however, aware of any references being made to the articles published in this journal other than references made from Chow's autobiography (Chow 2011).
3. I have discussed Oakeshott and classical Chinese thinking in "Skepticism, Poetic Imagination, and the Art of Non-Instrumentality: Oakeshott and Zhuangzi" and "Learning and Conversation: Oakeshott and Confucius," both in Coats and Cheung (2012, pp. 19–40 & pp. 57–78) respectively.
4. I should also mention that the late Deng Zhenglai (鄧正來 1956–2013) spent eight years in China translating Hayek's works into Chinese and writing many in-depth commentaries on Hayek, which have helped to promote Hayek's social and political philosophy to the Chinese intellectual community. See Deng (2004) as an example. Unfortunately, Deng died in 2013 at the relatively early

age of 57. Chapter 6 of this book will contain a fuller discussion of the spread of Hayekian scholarship in mainland China in the 1990s to the first decade of the twenty-first century.

5. Qiu has since embraced Confucianism instead of classical liberalism when he comes to develop his idea of constitutionalism in China, though he acknowledges his intellectual debt to Hayek in developing his idea of Confucian constitutionalism. See Yao (2016). Please note that Qiu is also known as Yao Zhongqiu (姚中秋).
6. Of course, Hong Kong did have the benefit of being part of the British Empire (1842–1997) where the rule of law was not only exported to it as a set of abstract principles but was accompanied by skillful practitioners from the UK for over 150 years with amble practical firsthand experience in doing and implementing it in a community. However, the open conflicts between the democratic protestors in Hong Kong and the authorities in Hong Kong and Beijing in 2019 had led to the imposition of the Hong Kong National Security Law by Beijing on Hong Kong in 2020. Such an imposition, in my view, has undermined the rule of law in Hong Kong since. See Cheung (2022) for some relevant discussion on this. The enactment of Hong Kong's own national security law in accordance with Article 23 of Hong Kong's Basic Law in March 2024 was another important step along the same direction.

6

The Rule of Law, Liberal Constitutionalism, and China: Problems and Prospects

Hayek's Ideas and Post-1989 China

The death of Mao and the end of the Great Proletariat Cultural Revolution not only led to the national policy of China shifting from political struggle to fundamental economic reform and opening to the outside world under Deng Xiaoping, but it also left a big ideological vacuum on the Chinese mainland since the orthodox communist ideology no longer held much water, at least for many intellectuals in the People's Republic of China. In the late 1970s and throughout the 1980s, China once again was keen to seek theoretical and ideological inspiration of the more liberal kind from the West, even though the Deng leadership of the Chinese Communist Party remained determined to maintain its authoritarian control over the regime. While the People's Liberation Army's bloody suppression of the student-led democracy movement in Beijing in 1989 demonstrated the failure of the quest for democratic reform in China, liberal ideas, particularly of the market-oriented kind, survived on the mainland after the Tiananmen Square crackdown when Deng revived the Chinese Communist Party's market reform zeal by his Southern Tour

C. Cheung, *Hayek and Post-War Chinese Liberalism*, Palgrave Studies in Classical Liberalism, https://doi.org/10.1007/978-3-031-64888-5_6

to the special economic zone Shenzhen in 1992, which had paved the way for China's relatively sustainable economic growth to become the second largest economy in the world decades after Deng passed away in 1997 and before the current leader Xi Jinping has assumed supreme, personal political power in the party-state of China in 2012.[1]

It is in this context that Hayekian liberalism had emerged as the most prevalent liberal thought in the People's Republic of China among the intellectuals and the reading public (Liu 2000; Gao 2017, pp. 217–251; Li et al. 2017). A leading liberal thinker in China Gao Quanxi claims that from the late 1980s to the first decade of the twenty-first century China, Hayek's thought had at least influenced a whole generation of Chinese intellectuals. Writing in 2000, Liu Junning claimed that "Classical liberalism now dominates China's intellectual landscape" (Liu 2000, p. 54). Even recently, according to Gao, whether one agrees with Hayek or not, he is one major Western thinker that no contemporary Chinese intellectuals who care about China's social and political development can ignore (Gao 2017, pp. 218–220). Later in this chapter, I am going to introduce some leading ideas of Gao on how to develop liberal constitutionalism in China and show that Hayek's classical liberalism is an important source of inspiration behind Gao's works, even though Gao believes that one will have to go beyond Hayekian liberalism if one wants to further develop liberalism in the Chinese context.

According to one preliminary counting before 2017, 24 of Hayek's major works in English and German have been translated and published in Chinese. Even for secondary materials on Hayek, no less than seven biographies of or monographs on Hayek written by Western authors have been translated and published in China. In this regard, one must mention the mainland scholar Deng Zhenglai's (see also note 5 of Chapter 5) remarkable contribution to Hayek scholarship in China. Deng was so determined to thoroughly study Hayek's theory and to transmit Hayek's major ideas to the Chinese reading public that he, starting from 1994, endeavored to translate many of Hayek's major publications into Chinese, to the extent that out of the eight to nine years (1994–2003) of his undertaking in this regard, five (1998–2003) of which were spent in a kind of self-imposed academic seclusion, declining any participation in non-Hayek-related works and social engagements in order to totally concentrating on this intellectual endeavor to produce a translation workload of over 2.2 million Chinese characters of Hayek's major works on top of his own monographs on Hayek's ideas on liberty and order, social theory and jurisprudential theory (Deng 2004, pp. 564–572). I think Li, Feng, and Sun are right to say that Deng, who sadly passed away at the age of 57 in 2013, should be regarded as "the top contributor" (2017, p. 225) in China in helping to spread Hayek scholarship to the Chinese reading public on the mainland so far.

Furthermore, the same 2017 preliminary counting says that in the prestigious Chinese Academy of Social Science Press, three of its 18 published monographs in its Modern Western Thought Series are on Hayek (ibid., pp. 226–231). Likewise, among the 15 monographs of Peking University Press's Series of Political and Legal Thoughts published in the first decade of twenty-first century, two are directly on Hayek, with most of the remaining monographs on Hayekian themes like constitutionalism, classical liberalism, the rule of law, economic development and the like. In 2005, a Hayek Association of Chinese Scholars (華人哈耶克學會) was set up in Beijing by mainland Chinese liberal intellectuals, which provided a platform for like-minded Hayek scholars in China, Taiwan, and Hong Kong to gather together on an annual basis for academic exchanges, mostly in the format of conferences alternately held in these three places respectively. The Association lasted for over a decade (Xia 2017), and it is understood that in recent years, the title of the Association has been amended to avoid political sensitivity on the mainland as the Chinese Communist Party under the current leader Xi Jinping has tightened political control again.[2]

It is not difficult to understand why Hayek's ideas became attractive to China soon after the Great Proletariat Cultural Revolution. As I said in Chapter 2 of this book, Hayek's critique of totalitarianism and Rationalism was very persuasive to the Chinese intellectuals when they were given access to read Hayek after China had opened in the late 1970s, since they could find a lot of echoes from Hayek's critique from their personal catastrophic experiences before and during the Great Proletariat Cultural Revolution. Similarly, Hayek's critique of economic central planning and his explanation of the massively powerful coordination function of the price mechanism in market allocation has become useful to the Chinese Communist Party since Deng Xiaoping started pushing China toward market reform. As I said in an endnote to Chapter 3 of this book, a key economic advisor of Deng during the period of "reform and opening" was Sun Yefang, and Sun was famous for being the first Chinese mainland economist who advocated the indispensability of the law of value and the market mechanism in socialist economy (Sun 1979, pp. 1–14). In this respect, Sun personally acknowledged to his colleagues and students that he was then influenced by Gu Zhun (who is deemed by some as China's Hayek) while developing this idea (Zhang 1993, in Luo ed. 2017, pp. 24–25). That is why many observers believe that to a certain extent, liberal ideas of the Hayekian version, particularly those related to the market economy, had been tolerated by the political establishment of the Chinese Communist Party even though they could not openly support Hayek or abandon orthodox socialist ideas (Gao 2017, pp. 232–233; Li et al. 2017, p. 224).

To the Chinese liberals in post-Mao China, however, the importance of Hayek's ideas in China goes beyond the critique of totalitarianism and the support for market mechanism. To them, the exodus of the Chinese intellectuals from the then orthodox socialist ideology, firstly after the death of Mao in 1976 and subsequently after the 1989 Tiananmen Square bloody crackdown, created a big ideological vacuum for China in transition, and Hayekian liberalism, being quite a systematic and comprehensive social and political theory, had provided them with an intellectual framework of the liberal kind which was not only independent of and distinguished from the former Maoist official socialist doctrine or discourse, it was also pertinent enough to address many of the pressing problems of transition in China when she was facing the socio-economic challenges created by the "reform and opening" policy.

As an early advocate of classical liberalism in post-Mao China (Liu 1998), Liu Junning was certainly too optimistic to say in 2000 that "Since the process of marketization in China is irrevocable, liberalism's triumph is inevitable" (Liu 2000, p. 55). Nevertheless Hayekian liberalism has not only helped the Chinese liberals to face many of the intellectual issues confronting China's economic reform, Hayek's theoretical conviction that a good functioning market and liberal order must be presupposed by the rule of law and liberal constitutional government, and that the social order shall be embedded with the kind of negative values (freedom, justice and peace) that are largely rule-based, evolutionary rather than rationally designed or innate continues to inform the Chinese liberals, leading them to develop some theoretically more and more mature liberal social and political thought in China since Yan Fu first introduced this modern Western ideology in the late 19st century to this old nation. In this chapter, I am going to examine how some leading Chinese liberals have been inspired by Hayek's ideas of the rule of law and constitutionalism in their attempts to offer a cogent answer to the perplexing question of what is to be done after the revolutions in China, though as we will see in the next section, promoting and understanding the core importance of rule of law when modernizing and liberalizing China is not an easy task in China.

The Rule of Law and Modern China

It is generally agreed that the rule of law was absent in traditional China, and the school of classical Legalism in ancient China was no rule of law as understood in modern Western jurisprudence, since the former was about how to help the emperors in ancient China to enact laws to exert absolute political control on the officials, who were tasked with the responsibility of implementing the laws for the people to comply. The emperors themselves, however, were above the laws for that matter (Liang 1998; Luo 1931; Lin 1989, pp. 99–117; Chow 2004, pp. 118–125; Zhang 2021). Although the first major but failed attempt after China's defeat in the first Sino-Japanese War of 1894 to reform the political regime of the late Qing Dynasty was Liang Qichao and Kang Yuwei's proposals for constitutional monarchy under Emperor Guangxu (光緒), it was the more radical revolutionary movement under the leadership of Dr. Sun Yat-sen that succeeded in ending the rule of the Qing Dynasty and established the first republic in China (i.e. Republic of China) in 1911–1912. Although the constitutionalists in the late Qing Dynasty would like to introduce constitutional government to China, even Liang Qichao, a leading first-generation constitutionalist in the late Qing era and the early republican period, admitted that there was a lack of public spiritedness among the then Chinese people since no modern public sphere existed under China's traditional family-centered ethos to nurture the development of citizenship there. As a result, to develop the virtue of civic rule-abiding habit of the Chinese people under the rule of law was very difficult (Liang 1903/1904). Subsequent generations of the Chinese liberals in the pre-war period agreed that not only the Chinese people found it difficult to develop the habit of procedurally focused law-abiding behavior, political elites, and leaders in China used to rule by commands to impose their political will and judgment onto the people, and hence it would be equally, if not more, difficult for those in power in China to respect the requirement of equality before the law by all and to practice procedural fairness under the rule of law (Lou 1931).

The 1911 Chinese Revolution did not establish constitutionalism to modern China, even though in Sun Yat-sen's Three Principles of the People, the principle of the rights of the people is one important component of them (Sun 1924). Instead, the post-1911 era in China was firstly dominated by the warlords, in which two of them even tried to revive monarchial rule in Beijing though the attempts ultimately failed miserably (Lin 1979, pp. 19–25). In order to try to unify China and to end the political chaos of the rule of the warlords after the Revolution, Sun started to reform his revolutionary Chinese Nationalist Party along the Leninist party-state model in the early 1920s, dropping the requirements of constitutionalism in the beginning of the republic and advocating instead a period of military rule, followed by a period of political tutelage under party dictatorship before constitutional government might be established in China in an unspecified future.

Hu Shih, the leading post-May Fourth liberal in modern China, criticized the party dictatorship of the Chinese Nationalist Party in the Republic of China after it had eliminated the rule of the warlords in its Northern Expedition in 1927, saying that the mistrust of the Chinese people's ability to practice constitutional rule was unwarranted since one could only learn about constitutionalism through the practice of constitutional politics (Hu 1929). However, even many of Hu's liberal friends had reservations about constitutional rule in China when the threat of military invasion by the Japanese became both imminent and probable in the 1930s, leading to the famous national debate among

Chinese liberals on whether China should adopt democracy or dictatorship under the then Nationalist government (Zhi 2010). In that debate, Hu found himself probably in the minority in supporting democracy in an unfailing manner, since many of his liberal friends believed that a strong and charismatic dictatorship was needed in such a crisis situation to modernize China and to save her from political collapse. On top of all these, many Chinese intellectuals also agree that the traditional Chinese political culture in general favors resolution of social and political disputes either by appealing to moral considerations, the accepted will of the community, or the command of the superior in accordance with the hierarchy of the existing social/political structure. Chinese people are not used to follow those mutually applicable rules of just conduct governing personal behavior and regulating interpersonal relations in a formal and legal manner, nor are they very confident in seeking impartial adjudication from a judiciary which is far from independent when disputes arise (Lin 1989, pp. 99–117).

As will be shown in the next and subsequent sections of this chapter, Hayek has developed a very sophisticated idea of the rule of law in his classical liberalism, and his defense of the market and price mechanism as well as the smooth functioning of the spontaneous social order in a liberal society is very much premised on this idea of the rule of law. In the development of Hayekian liberalism in post-war China, given the incompatibility between the Western idea of the rule of law and China's traditional cultural and political context, we may have reason to expect that it is not easy for intellectuals in China to absorb and develop Hayek's idea of the rule of law into the liberal thought of post-war China. In this connection, the case of Yin Hai-kuang, a leading Hayekian liberal in post-war Taiwan, is perhaps the most revealing. Even Yin misunderstood Hayek's idea of the rule of law, and this perhaps was a good example to show how difficult it could be for a proper cross-cultural understanding to take root when some new and unfamiliar core values of one culture were first being introduced to the other.

Yin was the first Chinese liberal who translated Hayek's *The Road to Serfdom* into Chinese in the early 1950s (Yin trans. [1944] 2011). However, a careful reading of Yin's translation, particularly in his translator's comments on Hayek's original work there, shows that Yin in fact had either mistranslated or misunderstood quite a few important points regarding Hayek's idea of the rule of law as found in *The Road to Serfdom.* One serious misunderstanding is this.

In Chapter 6 ("Planning and the Rule of Law") of *The Road to Serfdom*, Hayek refers to a quote from Kant,[3] which is this: "Man is free if he needs to obey no person but solely the law" (Hayek [1944] 2007, p. 119). In his translator's comment to this quote, Yin says, "if the law is enacted not in accordance with a single person's will or likes and dislikes, but with the will or likes and dislikes of the people, the man obeying such a law is a free man" (Yin trans. [1944] 2011, p. 92). Such a comment has obviously ignored the words "no person" in the quotation, which appears to be an attempt to make a contrast between the rule of *man* (whether it is one, a few, or many) and the rule of *law*. In fact, it is strange to find the approving remark made by Yin on enacting the law in accordance with the "will" or "likes and dislikes" of "the people" in his translator's comment. Nowhere in the text of *The Road to Serfdom* can we find any indication from Hayek to approve anything like that. This translator's comment shows that Yin has failed to understand Hayek's insistence on the abstract, formal, and non-instrumental nature of the law in his idea of the rule of law, which is inconsistent with the nature of command, will or any pre-determined, substantive collective purpose, whether any of these is attached to a rule or not. It is also not the case that if the "law" reflects the will of the majority of the people or the so-called General Will, it is consistent with the rule of law. Hayek in this respect is far more influenced by Hume rather than by Rousseau, and Yin's comment here, I think, clearly shows that theoretically, he is confused about Hayek's idea of the rule of law as explained in *The Road to Serfdom.*

Of course, not all leading post-war Chinese liberals have misunderstood Hayek in this regard. Lin Yu-sheng, Yin's student in Taiwan in the 1950s and Hayek's student at Chicago before his retirement there from 1960, has a far more accurate understanding of what the rule of law entails in Hayek's ideas (Lin 1989, pp. 99–117). But Lin's main contribution in developing Hayekian liberalism in China is not in the field of Hayekian political thought and liberal constitutionalism, but in his idea of creative transformation of the Chinese tradition, which is an attempt to entrench liberal moral values and practices into the Chinese culture, a topic we have briefly discussed in Chapter 5 of this book. David Chow, Hayek's first Chinese student at London School of Economics in the early 1930s, is exceptional among Chinese liberals since he, under the influence of Hayek's classical liberalism, was probably the only one who favored a kind of conservative liberalism in pre-war China when all the others were either adopting an anti-traditionalist interpretation of liberalism in China or, following Laski's approach, favored an interpretation of liberalism along the line of the left-wing ideology of social democracy. Chow also came up with the first Chinese translation of Hayek's *The Constitution of Liberty* (Chow trans. 1973) in Taiwan in 1973, but even he admits that all along, historic China failed to develop laws and institutions to protect human rights due to the overall low level of state capacity in centralized political control in ancient China and its lack of institutional protection of rights in its traditional thinking (Chow 2004, pp. 151–156).

Only in the early twenty-first century did we find some serious attempts by post-war Chinese thinkers who have been influenced by Hayek's classical liberalism to come up with theoretical discourses on the development of liberal constitutionalism in China (Gao 2003, 2016, 2017; Yao 2016; Xu 2017; Zhang 2021), though it must be mentioned that the twentieth century Confucian thinker Carsun Chang (Zhang Junmai/張君勱 1887–1969) (Guo 2017) was the leading contemporary Confucian thinker in the last century who helped draft the 1947 Constitution for the Republic of China (Nie 2017), and Taiwan's current democratic constitution is inherited from the 1947 Constitution initiated by the then Nationalist government before they fled to Taiwan after their defeat in the civil war in 1949. Later in this chapter, I will examine Gao's contribution to the development of liberal constitutional thinking in China. But before that, it is to a better understanding of Hayek's idea of the rule of law that we shall now turn.

Hayek's Idea of the Rule of Law

In offering a systematic articulation of his understanding of the tradition of the rule of law in the West in *The Constitution of Liberty*, Hayek first focuses on contrasting the different nature between laws and commands (1960, pp. 149–151). To Hayek, while both laws and commands, properly understood, are normative or imperative rather than factual statements regulating human relationship and interpersonal behavior, they differ in at least three fundamental respects. Firstly, while commands are mostly specific in their orders and particular in their applicable actual circumstances, laws are in the main far more general in their conditional requirements and abstracted from most time and space or other circumstantial specifications.

Secondly, commands always presuppose a personal commander who issues the instruction to someone under his/her order to achieve a specific purpose or to realize a particular end-result. Laws, on the other hand, do not have such a personal commander presupposition and are in theory applicable to everyone equally and generally who falls within their respective jurisdictions all the time. Thirdly, while commands will exhaust themselves after issuance and implementation, laws are long-standing until being amended or repealed. As such, commands presuppose a superior-subordinate relationship, while laws create general conditions that facilitate coordination of social interaction (such as traffic laws facilitating law-abiding drivers to drive without collision) when social actors either observe or refrain from violating those conditions while engaging in their respective individual pursuits.

In a sense, one can say that the generality of laws and the specificity of commands are, strictly speaking, a matter of degree. Commands can be more or less general, just as laws can be more or less specific. However, there is a limit to both. If commands have become so general to the extent that they fail to include an intent that will lead to a specified, positive, end-result by the issuer; or, if laws are so specific that they will be exhausted after one implementation, it will not be right to call them commands or laws respectively.

The rule of law is therefore different from the rule of command. From the distinction made in the above paragraphs in this section, it is not difficult to understand that the rule of command is closely related to the rule of man, whereas the rule of law does not have such a presupposition. While the general, abstract, and potentially coordinating nature of laws are clearly spelt out in Hayek's idea of the rule of law, there are additional important attributes identified by Hayek to help to distinguish the kind of rules that should be properly called laws in the political tradition of the West.

First, laws are obligatory rules, or rules of just conduct as Hayek likes to call them in *Law, Legislation and Liberty* (1973–1979). Although not all rules are conducive to the formation of a sustainable social order, "only the observance of common rules makes the peaceful existence of individuals in society possible" (Hayek 1973, p. 72). These rules are commonly observed because they embody accepted, general conditions that define and protect legitimate and reasonable expectations (ibid., p. 98) of the members of the society. Failure to honor these expectations from any party concerned in social interaction might be a legitimate cause for complaints that will require redress in the name of justice. In other words, under a regime of the rule of law, while the obligatory rules of conduct do not specify or require any members of the society to perform any substantive action to achieve a pre-determined result, they do delimit, through past experiences or common beliefs and practices, general conditions defining or protecting legitimate expectations of the members concerned in social interaction in regulating how members shall behave so that no one will intrude into the other's protected domain in violation of his/her legitimate expectation.

To maintain the integrity and stability of the social order concerned in this respect, sometimes there is a need to enforce those obligatory rules that are conducive to the preservation of the social order when for some reason adequate compliance is in question. If maintenance is proven to be successful, the community concerned will have become a viable and sustainable one, and these enforced obligatory rules will be accorded a more important status in the community and hence the emergence of the practice of law. Hayek believes that "Law in the sense of enforced rules of conduct is undoubtedly coeval with society," (ibid.) and human beings, as rule-following social animals (Hayek 1967, p. 43), had long been able to conform to these obligatory rules in early, pre-historic societies, and failure to conform to these rules might not be accepted as a member of the community concerned in primitive tribes and so on (Hayek 1973, pp. 72–73).

Furthermore, Hayek argues that the practice of obligatory rules emerged at the same time as a sustainable social order was evolved, even though most of these rules were observed only in practice rather than in articulated or conscious form in the first place. To Hayek, it is therefore wrong to believe that in the first instance, obligatory social rules were products of deliberative human design, since "from 'knowing how' to act, or from being able to recognize that the acts of another did or did not conform to accepted practices, it is still a long way to being able to state such rules in words" (ibid., p. 72).

When society became more complex and its size continued to grow, the task of obligatory rules enforcement could become more and more a complex and sophisticated job, and the need to articulate the meaning or requirements of the legitimate expectations and general conditions embedded in these rules in more accurate and consistent form was on the rise, both in rule adjudication as well as in a more coherent and systematic development of these rules to regulate social interaction as and when required (ibid., pp. 88–89). Those communities that managed to give rise to an effective political authority to be tasked with the responsibility of obligatory rules enforcement could help to better sustain the social order of these communities. To Hayek, law, in the sense of enforced rules of conduct (both in the sense of actively observing the rules and in the sense of ascertaining/recognizing the meaning or requirements of the rules concerned) is therefore always older than legislative enactment and the deliberative exercise of obligatory rules making. Likewise, society is older and more than government in the sense of a well-organized, centralized political authority, and Hayek reminds us that the stress on the law being prior to the state goes back at least to David Hume (Hayek 1960, p. 452), and most of these obligatory rules of just conduct in a rule of law society are, according to Hayek, mostly elaboration of what Hume called the "three fundamental laws of nature, *that of the stability of possession, of transference by consent, and of the performance of promises*" (quoted in ibid., p. 158, emphasis in the original), which are rooted in the moral tradition of the society concerned (ibid., p. 206).

Hayek continues to point out that "a group of men can form a society capable of making laws because they already share common beliefs which make discussion and persuasion possible and to which the articulated rules must conform in order to be accepted as legitimate" (ibid., p. 181). In this understanding of the idea of the rule of law, since law is prior to government and older than legislation, the public articulation and determination of the meaning of the obligatory rules, governmental legislation, and the exercise of public power will be accepted as legitimate only if they are consistent with the shared values and beliefs embedded in the obligatory rules of conduct themselves that help to constitute the social order, which has made the peaceful co-existence of the individuals possible. In other words, from this evolutionary understanding of law as enforced rules of just conduct, one can distinguish two types of laws, namely private laws defining and maintaining general conditions of legitimate expectations for individual social actors engaging in social interaction, and public laws for the enforcement, articulation, adjudication, and legislation for the public authorities to carry out their service duties to maintain the rule of law in a society (Hayek 1973, pp. 131–134).

Strictly speaking, therefore, private law, understood as rules of just conduct, is mostly not legislation and is fundamentally different from government's executive commands or policy enactment, for the latter are to achieve particular ends and their legitimation is very much dependent on their consistency with the requirements of the former, which, in the common laws system developed in the United Kingdom, is also called the laws of the land. Likewise, under the rule of law, the function of the judge, an independent, impartial, and knowledgeable party to adjudicate legal disputes, is not to serve any particular, extra-legal purposes, but to try his/her best to resolve the legal ambiguities or controversies given rise to the disputed parties in a faithful and fair manner to protect legitimate expectations as provided for in the general rules of conduct so as to prevent the recurrence of such conflicts in the future in order to protect and to improve the integrity of the overall legal order (ibid., pp. 94–101). These points are emphatically stressed by Hayek in *Law, Legislation and Liberty* though only occasionally touched upon in *The Constitution of Liberty* (Hayek 1973, p. 3. See also Deng 2004, pp. 182–367; Gao 2003, pp. 198–219).[4] The rule of law, in this understanding, is not the rule of man since the law concerned is the result of mutual and evolutionary acceptance of the common obligatory rules by all rather than the result of rational design or the result of imposition of the will or preference of any separate group(s) or individual onto the social order. Individual members of the society under the rule of law are free to pursue their own chosen undertakings so long as they are not in breach of those general conditions protecting everybody's legitimate expectations embedded in the rules of just conduct, and each and every one of them is free to act within the legitimate condition defined and protected by the obligatory rules, though whether one can achieve his/her individual end in practice also depends on factors other than just compliance of the obligatory rules of conduct, just like a free transaction may not lead to a final result that satisfies both parties if there is a miscalculation from one of the parties, for example.

The Rule of Law vs. the Sage King[5]

Before we further explore Hayek's idea in this area, I think it will be instructive at this point to compare some fundamental differences between the Western tradition of the rule of law as understood by Hayek and one pivotal and supreme Chinese political institution—universal kingship—which had already been in place since the beginning of the Chinese civilization in the Shang Dynasty (17th BCE–11th BCE). This institution lasted more or less continuously and influentially throughout the political history of China until the end of the dynastic era in 1912 when the Republic of China was established after the 1911 Revolution.

To start with, the institution and notion of universal kingship in ancient China concentrates mainly on the unique figure of the king/emperor who is entrusted with the Mandate of Heaven to govern the land under Heaven. Scholars of sinology always refer to the evidence as found in the earliest written records of China in the Shang oracle inscriptions to say that the notion of universal kingship had taken shape since then when the king of the Shang started to call himself "I, the One Man" to signify the uniqueness and supremacy of the king under

Heaven who was blessed by the supreme deity of the Shang, Di (i.e. the Heavenly Emperor). Di, in turn, made His will known by His approval and assistance of the king in person in his activities of governance, of course indirectly through revelation as interpreted in the oracle or in allowing the king to achieve harmonious and prosperous social and political condition in the kingdom or the like.

Although Di, or the Heavenly Emperor, can in theory withdraw His approval and Mandate from the king and pass it on to another king, leading to the change of the Mandate of Heaven to a new dynasty (Chang 1990, p. 20), until then the mandated king was given the supreme power to govern the land under Heaven universally, who was the proprietor of all territories and the highest authority of all people, wielding both temporal as well as religious-spiritual power (Lin 1979, pp. 12–13). This notion of universal kingship did not just pass on from the Shang Dynasty to the Zhou Dynasty (11th BCE–3rd BEC), it is said that among the leading classical schools of thought in ancient China, including Confucianism, Mohism, Legalism, and even Daoism, they all more or less subscribed to such a notion, though with different emphasis. As Lin Yu-sheng says, "Clearly, the idea of universal kingship had roots deep within classical Chinese culture. It survived challenges presented by the political divisions and intellectual diversities of the late Chou [Zhou] period. Reinforced by the establishment of the Chinese empire in 221 B.C. [221 BCE], it remained intact throughout later period of barbarian assaults, political divisions, and the cultural dominance of Buddhism" (ibid., p. 14).

Citing Benjamin Schwartz, Lin further argues that the notion of universal kingship was given a firmer religious-cosmological base in the Han Dynasty (206 BCE to 220 BCE) with the metaphysical arguments developed by Han's great Confucian thinker Dong Zhongshu (董仲舒 179 BCE–104 BCE), who incorporated the idea of a cosmos comprising *yin-yang* and five elements in its natural and spiritual orders and patterns, with the universal king being regarded as the *yang* (the dominant component) and exists always in the cosmos and the world, while the people being the *yin* (the passive component) subject to the political and spiritual leadership of the king. Through the supreme and unique figure of the king, the institution of universal kingship provided the link between the supposedly perfect and divine cosmic order and the earthly social order, bringing moral and religious values from Heaven and imparting them onto a harmonious social order constituted by the Three Bonds where the ministers were there to faithfully and loyally serve the king, the sons to serve the fathers and the wives to serve their husbands (ibid., p. 15).

While here is not the place to discuss in detail ancient Chinese political theory and institution, a quote from Dong's writing on the notion of universal kingship will help us to better understand why the king (written in Chinese as王) was regarded as so important in occupying the pivotal position on earth as well as in Heaven:

> Those who in ancient times invented writing drew three [horizontal] lines which they connected through the center [by a vertical stroke], and then called this "King" [王]. These three lines represent the [king's] penetration of their [interrelated] principles. Who, indeed, if not a [true] king, could take the central position between Heaven, Earth and man, so as to act as the connecting link between them? Therefore the king models himself on Heaven. He takes its seasons as his model and gives them completeness. He models himself on its numerical [categories] and uses them when initiating affairs. He models himself on its course and thereby brings his administration into operation. He models himself on its will and with it attaches himself to *jen* [*ren*, beneficence]. (quoted in ibid., p. 15, n.11)

The first point to note when comparing Hayek's understanding of the rule of law and the ancient Chinese notion of universal kingship is that while the former is law (in the sense of general, abstract and coordinating rules of conduct) or abstract rules of just conduct, the latter is pivot to the supreme importance of the personal king as "I, the One Man" to link up the divine cosmic order and the earth in bringing about a moral but hierarchical order to human society. In other words, while the rule of law is qualitatively different from the rule of man, universal kingship is dependent upon the rule of the king who is mandated to occupy the pivotal position of translating the divine cosmic order into an earthly moral order to the state, and this kingship is the key to good governance on earth.

In this connection, the notion of universal kingship in theory is rather compatible with the rule of man so long as the king has been conferred the mandate from Heaven and occupies the pivotal position to translate, through the cultivation of his inner moral strengths and the practice of rites and customs (Chang 1989, pp. 20–21), the divine cosmic order into a moral and socio-political order for the governance of the people under his jurisdiction. Although the institution of universal kingship collapsed as a result of the success of the 1911 Revolution that attempted to turn China into a modern republican state, this does not mean that the institution's affinity to the conception of the rule of man through transcendental moral idealism has also collapsed without a trace in China's modern political practice and thinking, since the presumed pivotal position used to be occupied by the personal king could be transferred, in a subtle manner, to other entities, such as the vanguard revolutionary party like the Chinese Nationalist Party or the Chinese Communist Party in the case of the successful establishment of a party-state in China; or, in the case of aspiring for democracy, the entity could be "the people" as such if the will of the majority is preferred under popular sovereignty. Old habits may die hard. This perhaps explains why even a post-war liberal like Yin Huang-kuang could have misunderstood Hayek's idea of the rule of law as the same as the rule of the majority will in his fight against dictatorial rule of the party-state when he was translating Hayek's work as we have explained above.

From a more theoretical perspective, it is clear that Hayek's idea of the rule of law is based upon a modern, liberal, social theory (Hayek [1948] 1980, p. 6), whereas the Chinese classical notion of universal kingship is derived from a cosmological-religious worldview that is rich in metaphysical assumptions.

When Hayek argues that enforced rules of conduct must be coeval with the emergence of society, he is referring to the successful social coordinating function of certain general rules of conduct that makes social interaction possible and sustainable in human communities. Subscription to the obligatory rules of the group by social actors and fair enforcement of these rules by the recognized public authority concerned demonstrate that these rules are regarded as important, with certain common beliefs and values embodied in the general conditional requirements and practices of the rules to regulate social interaction and to define the relationships, legitimate expectations, and identities of the actors of that community. In this regard, one can say that inherent in the regime of the rule of law is the negative but enabling values of peace, justice, and freedom (Hayek 1979, pp. 132–133), since subscription to these obligatory rules of just conduct facilitates the peaceful co-existence of the members of the society concerned to engage in social interaction to their respective individual pursuits, though what positive results will come out from such interaction is always an open and trial and error process.

Hayek's social theory further contends that this social coordinating process is largely evolutionary, in which groups that have chosen the more successful practices through trial and error are likely to turn out to outperform other groups, and their success may be imitated by others if the latter do not want to be left behind, even though people may not in the first place consciously know why certain rules and practices are more successful. The articulation and conscious understanding of these rules and practices normally only come after reflective deliberation at a later stage, and that is why Hayek says that in the social evolutionary process, law is older than legislation and society is prior to the state. When society becomes increasingly complex, diverse, and extended (both in size and in population), the need to have more effective and acceptable general and abstract rules of conduct to regulate interpersonal interaction successfully and mutually among members of the society also becomes more acute, and this is a process of continuous and spontaneous adjustment to the changing and evolving circumstances. A social order so developed is rule-based, nomocratic (Cheung 2014a), with the enforced rules of conduct acknowledged and practiced by most and applicable to all as far as possible. There may be social and economic inequality, but as far as the laws are concerned, there is, to a large extent, equality before the laws. Articulation and legislation of obligatory rules in such a social order takes place every now and then as and when necessary, such as in resolving disputes and adjudication, in delimiting the powers of the authorities in enforcing the rules, and in determining the due process and so on. All these must be carried out in a fair and just manner in order to maintain the integrity of the rule of law system. Given Hayek's evolutionary epistemology and his anti-Cartesian psychology (Cheung 2011), such conscious articulation and enactment of laws may help to make the obligatory rules consistent, more effectively administered, or in a better position to satisfy the test of universalizability in the system of laws (Hayek 1976, pp. 24–49) when needed. But this system of laws can never be synoptic to the extent that a society can create a complete system of laws by a purely rational plan deriving from some first-order, pre-determined principles from afresh. That is why Hayek insists that while one can reconstruct the practice of the rule of law by abstracting certain underlying principles, or what he calls meta-legal doctrine in *The Constitution of Liberty*, deriving from our experience in our subscription to the obligatory rules of just conduct to guide us to better understand the legitimate nature of the laws, these principles nevertheless must be rooted in the moral tradition of the society, which constitutes part of our common beliefs and values (Hayek 1960, p. 206).

As regards the Chinese classical notion of universal kingship, apart from the pivotal position occupied by the king between Heaven and earth, what is remarkable is the kind of transcendental, moral-cum-religious assumptions built into this institution of sage king as the key to good government. If Hayek's rule of law idea is very much premised on the embodiment of many of the negative but enabling values of individual freedom, justice, and peace that can accommodate a large degree of social diversity through the coordinating function of the abstract rules of just conduct, the notion of universal kingship is founded on a perfectionist and expensive moral metaphysics. In explaining and evaluating the ancient Chinese notion of universal kingship and classical Confucianism's idea of sage king, that is, the supreme political ruler possesses inner sainthood and outer kingship at the same time, Hao Chang has made the following observations and argues that its theoretical orientation is therefore largely incommensurable with liberalism (Chang 1990).

Firstly, Chang points out that the idea of sage king comprises the unity of politics and religious faith by combining "the roles of political leader and chief shaman" into the cosmological kingship (ibid., p. 18). The king, who is called Son of Heaven, occupies the sacral center linking

Heaven and earth to flow the virtues and values embedded in the divine cosmic order onto the land under Heaven for good government. The king can manage to do so by two means. One is by inner transcendental moral cultivation through the ethical personality of the king himself for moral perfection and exemplary deeds to set the example for and to motivate the people to become good. The second is to use outer moral-ritual propriety *li* to educate the upper-class and learned people and to regulate their behavior so as to bring them in line with proper, moral conduct for compliance. As for those poor or unruly people who are not up to moral-ritual instructions, then punishment by laws (like those advocated by classical Legalism) will be the answer for them.

Secondly, the unity of politics and religious faith above also presupposes that there is the unity of Heaven and man at his best (i.e. the gentleman becoming a saint when his moral self is developed to the fullest). Just like the sage king, he could fuse the divine cosmic order into his ethical personality to achieve a kind of transcendental moral idealism for himself as well as for the secular world. Such a morally optimistic assumption has induced a tendency of utopianism into the idea of sage king in China.

Thirdly, this utopianism in Chinese thought is further buttressed by Confucianism's belief in the underlying inner moral orientation in the cultivation of man's inherently noble nature as spelt out in the Confucian classic *The Great Learning*. Such a belief leads to the reliance of the sage king's top-down, paternalistic/authoritarian rule to impart exemplary moral instructions to the people for good government of the whole kingdom. The following text from *The Great Learning* captures this point nicely:

> What the Great Learning teaches, is---to illustrate illustrious virtue; to renovate the people; and to rest in the highest excellence…Things have their root and their branches. Affairs have their end and their beginning. To know what is first and what is last will lead near to what is taught *in the Great Learning*…The ancients who wished to illustrate illustrious virtue throughout the kingdom, first ordered well their own states. Wishing to order well their states, they first regulated their families. Wishing to

> regulate their families, they first cultivated their person. Wishing to cultivate their persons, they first rectified their hearts. Wishing to rectify their hearts, they first sought to be sincere in their thoughts. Wishing to be sincere in their thoughts, they first extended to the utmost their knowledge. Such extension of knowledge lay in the investigation of things. Things being investigated, knowledge became complete. Their knowledge being complete, their thoughts were sincere. Their thoughts being sincere, their hearts were then rectified. Their hearts being rectified, their person cultivated, their families were regulated. Their families being regulated, their states were rightly governed. Their states being rightly governed, the whole kingdom was made tranquil and happy...From the Son of Heaven down to the mass of the people, all must consider the cultivation of the person the root of everything besides. (Legge trans., pp. 308–313)

Fourthly, when the transcendental moral idealism of classical Confucianism confronts the often poor, imperfect, and even corrupt political and moral reality on earth, the former may serve as a critical, evaluative consciousness to assess the latter so as to trigger fundamental, socio-political or spiritual reform to address issues related to man's dark consciousness. The moral optimism in China's transcendental moral thinking, however, has limited the influence of this kind of critical consciousness, making it, as Chang contends, biased toward the approach of trumping up more spiritual efforts to realize transcendental, moral idealism within the state by the sage king, or to centralized more political power by the Son of Heaven to fight against the corruption of the people, rather than to develop institutional check and balance for limited government to avoid personal abuse of power, or to put more emphasis on toleration for moral diversity (Chang 1989, pp. 33–78).

I hope that the above contrast between the Hayekian liberal idea of the rule of law and China's classical understanding of the notion of universal kingship is clear enough to bring out some salient but fundamental differences between the nature of these two important moral and political practices and their embedded values and orientations.

While the idea of sage king presupposes the unity of politics and religious faith in China, the success of modern liberalism in the West is very much dependent on the separation of the secular from the ecclesiastical, as the crisis of secularization in European history in view of the vicissitudes in the development of Christianity has demonstrated (Watkins 1957). Such a separation not only endows liberalism with pluralism in value, toleration in faith, and the politics of imperfection, but also empiricism in method since the results of men's social and political endeavors in the secular realm are the unintended consequences of social interaction, not pre-ordained, transcendental, and spiritual fulfillment of religious telos. Hayek's social theory-based rule of law understanding is evolutionary and empirical in nature and is largely devoid of presuppositions of expensive moral metaphysics. The unity of politics and religious faith in China has instead led to a kind of transcendental moral idealism in China's political tradition that encourages not only the top-down approach of the sage king to bring about good governance to the people, but also assumes that political leadership on earth is about bringing the kind of sacred, perfectionist, and harmonious cosmic order to the kingdom under Heaven. In other words, good government is about bringing a pre-existing divine cosmic order (a kind of moral-religious telos) via the political and spiritual leadership of the sage king to the people. The collapse of the institution of universal kingship in China after 1911 has largely discredited the perfectionist, monistic, metaphysical foundation of the ideal of sage king in China. This has brought a crisis of order and a fundamental disruption of the traditional universe of meaning to China's political and moral values and thought (Chang 1989; Chang 1990 and Lin 1979, pp. 10–25), though this does not mean that this traditional worldview has lost all its impacts on the modern Chinese mentality.

Notwithstanding the above, the question I would like to ask is: given the relatively secular and rule-based nature of the rule of law and the moral-spiritual and telos-based nature of the sage king conception, how the Chinese liberals can make Hayek's idea of liberal constitutionalism relevant in theorizing a liberal turn of modern Chinese political thought? Before we examine this question and its implications, we need to take a closer look at Hayek's understanding of the two kinds of constitutional order, one rule-based and the other telos-based, from which he comes up with an ambitious, political proposal for a model liberal constitution to cope with the crisis of Western democracy in the twentieth century.

Nomocracy and Teleocracy[6]

Hayek uses the ancient Greek term *nomos* to describe an abstract and end-independent universal rule of just conduct (Hayek 1973, p. 94), and nomocracy is the kind of political order formed not by deliberate design, but by the adjustment and interaction of a body of *nomoi* that members of the same political entity are obliged to follow.

It is important to note that to Hayek, while the order of the physical environment is given to us independently of human will, the order of our social environment is at most only partly the result of human design (Hayek [1978] 1990, p. 73). This is so because in any complex society, there are numerous individuals making different but simultaneous decisions all the time. Each and every decision of these is made in the context of a particular circumstance, the knowledge of which is known by or useful to the individual concerned, and other people might not necessarily know or find this knowledge useful in their social interaction. Therefore, no authority facing such dispersed circumstantial knowledge can gather all the fragmented knowledge therein to come up with a centralized plan and make a better use of it for all (Hayek 1973, p. 14, see also Chapter 4 of this book and Cheung 2007, pp. 55–61). More fundamentally, a Cartesian mind that can start from scratch and model the society in *toto* according to its own rational design is impossible according to Hayek. This is so because mind and society or civilization can only develop concurrently (Hayek 1973, pp. 8–34; [1978] 1990, pp. 3–22). The mind, being essentially a mental classificatory mechanism, cannot foresee its own advance and its ability to manipulate the environment is far from perfect. Therefore, there is no guarantee that the individual's self-determining efforts will necessarily achieve their intended results (Hayek [1952] 1976; Cheung 2011).

In other words, a nomocracy to Hayek is no designed order deriving from the human will. Although it is the result of human interaction, it is not deliberately made in a synoptic manner and thus serves no common and substantive purposes for all those involved in it. Its orderly relations help to define the identities, not the relative positions, of the members of the nomocracy concerned. The same relations also help to provide stability and to maintain a peaceful environment for all to pursue their separate and different purposes of their own. While there is no guarantee that all these individual and separate purposes can be achieved in the nomocracy (since human reason cannot pre-empt unintended consequences in social interaction), the orderly relations and *nomoi*, whether articulated or not, within a nomocracy help the individuals to cope with any new and unanticipated circumstances and to continue to adjust to the emergent order, or what Hayek also calls cosmos (Hayek [1978] 1990, pp. 76–80), in the light of new experiences and development. One of the most important practices of this kind that makes us human is our language, which does not direct us to *what* to say but only *how* to say it; and the individual's ability to command a language is essential for human communication and understanding. Other equally important social practices include the price mechanism of the market, moral rules and convention, the rule of law and so on. These rules and practices, whether articulated or not, can be followed by us all. They are essential in coordinating human interaction and in the maintenance of social order, even though we may not be aware of them or totally understand the logic behind them.

On the contrary, if a political order is deliberately designed to help to achieve some common and pre-determined goals or hierarchy of ends, it corresponds to an organizational order, or, as Hayek calls it, taxis (Hayek [1978] 1990, pp. 76–80). Within this order, the individual elements obtain their positions in it in accordance with their relative merit or utility in helping to achieve those goals or ends pre-determined by the order and its telos, and the rules or orderly relations in taxis ultimately must be instrumental and end-dependent in nature, specifying, directly or indirectly, the concrete requirements or condition for the realization of those pre-determined goals and ends.

Hayek describes such a political order teleocratic since telos signify the particular and pre-determined ends to which all the elements and rules within the order must be directed. There is a common purpose for such an order, which is the realization of its pre-determined ends. The rules within such an order can be said to have embodied the common good in so far as they are instrumental to the realization of the pre-determined ends. Likewise, the relative merits of the individual members or groups of individual members are dependent on how useful they are in helping to realize the same pre-determined ends. As such, a teleocracy presupposes that there must be some given concrete and indisputable political ends in the form of a hierarchy binding a political community together, to which all those within the community must pay allegiance. It is further assumed that there is a way to determine how far and how good the rules within the teleocracy can help to fulfil its telos, and how and what every individual element within that order could help in the same endeavor. With the influence of Constructivistic Rationalism "whose criterion of rationality is a recognizable concrete order serving known particular purposes" (ibid., p. 89), Hayek believes that teleocracy becomes equivalent to a centrally planned political order of the organizational kind, which assumes that human reason is good enough to help us to devise some coherent and systematic strategies to create a political order for the achievement of a common hierarchy of pre-determined ends through comprehensive and rational design. The nature of teleocracy is therefore not only qualitatively distinct from nomocracy, the consistent application of such organizational logic in a comprehensive manner will certainly ruin a nomocracy.

Nomocracy and Teleocracy: Are They Mutually Exclusive in Practice?

While Hayek is right to point out the qualitative distinction between nomocracy and teleocracy, I think he at times pushes his logic too far in saying that the consistent and comprehensive application of the organizational approach to a nomocracy "must" (ibid.) lead to the replacement of its cosmos order by a teleocracy. If Hayek's criticisms of Cartesian Rationalism or Constructivism are correct and his claim of the fragmentation of circumstantial knowledge is plausible, it is impossible to apply the so-called organizational logic consistently in *toto* for long.

Any political authority that tries to consistently implement the organizational logic in a comprehensive manner to a nomocracy is self-defeating, since doing so is most likely to bring chaos, disasters, confusion, and even total collapse to the political order instead. In other words, what Hayek should have said is that as ideal types, nomocracy and teleocracy are qualitatively distinct, pushing teleocracy to its logical extreme is self-defeating, since it will create intellectual confusion, political disasters, defeating the teleocratic attempt in the end.

But what about nomocracy? Can a nomocratic order do without any organizational approach? The Hayekian answer to this latter question is also "no" since Hayek is no anarchist (Hayek 1960, p. 62), and he is of the view that government is needed in any nomocracy. Government, by nature, is necessarily an organization according to Hayek. All along, Hayek contends that the spontaneous order of society is made up of individuals *and* organizations (Hayek 1973, pp. 46–48).

Contrary to common perception, Hayek is not an advocate of laissez-faire government or night watchman state either. Instead, he argues that so long as the government in an advanced country acts outside the free market and in compliance with the abstract and end-independent rules of just conduct, the government, through its organizational efforts and policies, can provide various services to the people through the public resources at its disposal. For example, Hayek thinks that it is morally acceptable for the government in an affluent society to provide basic decent necessities such as food and shelter for all those who are incapable of securing these provisions by themselves (Hayek 1960, pp. 300–301; Hayek 1976, p. 139). Another example is that although Hayek is not in favor of universal free medical service, he does not disagree with compulsory medical insurance coverage for all if the coverage is not to be provided by one single scheme of state insurance alone (Hayek 1960, pp. 297–300). It seems that what Hayek is suggesting is that while the spontaneous order of society is made up of individuals and organizations (including the government as an organization), the cosmos order of a nomocracy will not be undermined if the organizations within that political order only apply their organizational logic either outside the free market, or in compliance with the abstract and end-independent rules of just conduct.

But a closer look at the above two examples cited by Hayek seems to reveal a more complicated relationship between nomocracy and teleocracy. While the government can certainly make provision for basic necessities for all those in need outside the free market, it will have to do so by public money, part of which at least must come from taxation, which is a kind of mandatory, legal measure for the citizens to pay, failing which they are liable to be coerced to comply with the requirements. Likewise, if the government makes universal medical insurance coverage compulsory, no individual citizen can take exception to this, though they are free to opt for a scheme that is not provided by the government. Even if we put aside the interesting question of how the government who possesses legislative power can be a neutral player in the market when it is competing with other insurance providers for business,[7] the fact that Hayek is prepared to accept taxation and other compulsory measures to make provision for some specific, social necessities means that he thinks it permissible for certain non-abstract and non-end-independent logic to get into the market or the laws of a nomocracy for the purpose of some limited, specific social good. Perhaps Hayek is no dogmatic advocate of pure nomocracy after all.

I therefore think that the following comment made by Andrew Gamble when he compares Hayek and Keynes is interesting but only partially correct: "the real disagreement between Keynes and Hayek was…the question of knowing where to draw the line between intervention and non-intervention. Keynes's criticism of Hayek was that he accepted that the logical extreme of no intervention at all was not possible, but gave no guidance in *The Road to Serfdom* as to where the line should be drawn…[Keynes] argued that since Hayek accepted that a line had to be drawn, it was disingenuous of him to imply that 'so soon as one moves an inch in the planned direction you are necessarily launched on the slippery path which will lead you in due course over the precipice.'" (Gamble 1996, pp. 159–160) It is interesting because it is right to point out that pure nomocracy is inadequate even for Hayek, but it is incorrect to say that Hayek fails to give any guidance as to where to draw the line for some teleocratic policy to be allowed, even though one may disagree with him on the exact line to be drawn. In addition, I think Hayek is right to point out that if teleocracy has become the order of the day in government, the *logical* consequence will be requiring total government control even though in practice the teleocratic government may be forced to make compromises in views of opposition or the government's attempts have resulted in chaos undermining the fulfillment of the teleocratic end-results as intended.

Why is the logical extreme of a purely nomocratic order not possible? I think a more detailed analysis on Hayek's difficulty in maintaining the state as *simply* one organization among many others within a nomocratic society will help to illuminate this.

State, Government, Nomocracy, and Political Determination

Apparently, Hayek does not like to admit that nomocracy is a form of state (Hayek [1978] 1990, p. 89, n. 19). Whenever possible, he equates nomocracy as the kind of society that embodies a spontaneous order (Hayek 1976, p. 15). Hayek argues that it is misleading to contrast the *state* with the *society* within one country to indicate that the former is an organization and the latter a spontaneous order. Instead, Hayek prefers to put this as a contrast between *government* and *society*. This is so because it is always the government as an organization that acts or pursues policy within the broader context of a spontaneous society, whereas the term "state" is not only metaphysically charged (Hayek 1973, p. 48), but its status as a spontaneous order is also ambiguous.

However, when it comes to international politics, contrary to his own explicit preference, Hayek is forced to use the term "state" to contrast it with "society" (ibid., p. 48, Hayek 1976, p. 61). Presumably, this is the case because in international exchanges, a state does not simply refer to a government or any organization within that political entity, but also the nation, the territory, sovereignty, the society, and so on of that recognized independent entity. It is through the state that these latter units can acquire a political form and their political meaning defined. It is also through the state that these units are coherently represented in the international arena. In other words, Hayek's disregard of the state and his emphasis on the government instead as only one of the organizations within a nomocratic spontaneous order is plausible only if we can assume away the political pre-conditions presupposed by a viable idea of nomocracy in the first place.

Moving beyond the context of international politics, a similar criticism against Hayek's failure to take note of the political pre-conditions presupposed by nomocracy can be found in Roger Scruton's discussion of membership of a political community. Scruton thinks that Hayek fails to take proper note of the accepted identity, emotions, and motives that are presupposed by the political form that embodies Hayek's spontaneous association, because "Classical liberalism of Hayek's kind begins from the assumption that society exists, and that the distinction between the member and the non-member is securely established in the thoughts and emotions of those who are facing the future together—so securely established that it need not be mentioned" (Scruton 2006, p. 237).

The case for distinguishing between state and government becomes more compelling in the case of war and peace. When war is declared, it is the state that defines, on behalf of society, who its friends and enemies are. A government minister can quit the government if he disagrees with the declaration of war against another state made by that government. But that state, like it or not, is still that ex-minister's enemy politically speaking so long as the declaration is still valid. It is in the light of this that Adam Ferguson's acute observation that "without the rivalship of nations, and the practice of war, civil society itself could scarcely have found an object, or a form" can be readily understood (Ferguson 1995, p. 28). In other words, while the government is certainly an organization in a state, the fundamental political decisions made by the government or by the people for that matter (e.g. in a revolution against the government of the day), if effective, could define the limits and possibilities of the society even if the society concerned is understood as essentially a spontaneous order or nomocracy.

In his discussion of emergency powers under a model constitution for the protection of the spontaneous order, Hayek says, "when an external enemy threatens, when rebellion or lawless violence has broken out, or a natural catastrophe requires quick action by whatever means can be secured, powers of compulsory organization...must be granted to somebody." (Hayek 1979, p. 124) Clearly, apart from the threat of an external enemy, the other incidents which require powers of compulsory organization to be granted are internal matters. In those cases of the exceptional, Hayek does not hesitate to admit that somebody must assume emergency powers, he even goes so far as to admit that "whoever has the power to proclaim an emergency and on this ground to suspend any part of the constitution is the true sovereign" (ibid., p. 125). It appears that in the case of the politics of the exception, Hayek is moving closer to the position of Carl Schmitt of the concept of the political (Schmitt 1996).

This is in great contrast to the other claim stressed by Hayek, which is that sovereignty, understood in the sense of unlimited power, has no place at all in constitutional government, since the latter denotes a limited government in which the supreme power must be negative in nature by restricting subordinate powers in accordance with the general rules of just conduct rather than exercising omnipotent control (ibid., p. 123). This contrast here, however, lies not so much in the fact that the sovereign holding emergency powers is claiming unlimited power. Rather, it is in recognition that in the end, the authority to declare a state of emergency and to decide what powers, whether assertive or passive, are necessary to cope with the situation rests with the sovereign, whose power can never be *just* passive or negative a priori.

The same logic applies to normal situation too, though in a less apparent manner, since the same political entity (i.e. the state) "is required to provide *an effective external framework within which self-generating orders can form*" (ibid., p. 140, emphasis added), and the decision about the nature and parameters of this framework is again a *positively* political one that the state has to take in order to facilitate the society to operate. In other words, while nomocracy is qualitatively distinct from teleocracy, the cosmos within nomocracy is not a standalone, self-sufficient entity. It presupposes the political determination of a certain kind, such as a nation, a community, an idea of citizenship, each of which helps to define membership and non-membership, friends and enemies, war and peace, acceptable and prohibitive mores, the reasonable levels of various social provisions, and so on. As a result, like teleocracy, the spontaneous character of nomocracy cannot be pushed to the extreme to exclude all other things, since even the negative tasks ascribed to the state under a spontaneous order are to be determined and sustained by the positive action or political determination of the state. As Renato Cristi aptly says, "It was thus positively and actively that the state ought to restrict and limit its action to a merely negative one, so that the depoliticization of civil society could turn dialectically into the state's active preservation of its monopoly over the political as such" (Cristi 1998, p. 167). In this regard, I would suggest that Hayek's bold design for a model constitution to save modern democracies from bargaining politics and the scramble for particularistic interests by organized coalitions of fleeting majorities is politically a very positive and gallant attempt to try to restore the nomocratic order through constitutional reform to save the democratic ideal in the West gone astray. Such an attempt, successful or not, certainly goes beyond the negative values normally stressed under the internal rules of just conduct in a nomocracy.

Hayek's Model Constitution

In Hayek's view, the great democratic experiment since the American revolution of 1776 has failed to adequately secure the prevalence of the spontaneous order in modern democracies. The reasons for this are of course complicated and diverse. But the main ones, in his view, include the mistaken idea of popular sovereignty, which equates majority rule with unlimited power (Hayek 1979); the rationalistic belief in human's ability to use synoptic planning to achieve whatever policy result we aspire to, including the hollow conception of "social justice" (Hayek 1976); the positivist error in translating whatever the majority will prefer into legislation, including the transformation of private law into public law by the so-called social legislation (Hayek 1973); and the need to bargain with different pressure groups or parties by partisan politicians to form temporary majorities in fleeting coalitions to push through government policy in the legislature aiming at particularistic interests; and the delusion to favor government intervention over the spontaneous adjustment of the market for a more rational and effective use and distribution of resources.

In order to rescue the democratic and nomocratic ideal, Hayek dismisses the idea of sovereignty as unlimited power; instead supreme political power must be based on disinterested majority opinion (not majority will, see Hayek [1978] 1990, pp. 82–88) of what is right and what is wrong in the form of abstract and end-independent rules of just conduct, many of which are the results of social evolution over time to restrict arbitrary powers. In this connection, Hayek proposes to draw up a constitution that spells out the general attributes, not the substantive contents, of the enforceable universal rules of just conduct with which government policy must not in breach of. To avoid the government-controlled legislature to transform particularistic policy decision into rationalistic social legislation, Hayek thinks it imperative to create a separate, elected, second legislative assembly for genuine separation of powers at the constitutional level. This assembly is to be tasked with the responsibility of looking after and articulating the general and end-independent rules of conduct for all to follow to ensure the spontaneous *nomoi* or the rule of law (not social legislation) to prevail. Such an arrangement is essential to halt the contemporary trend of making whatever the majority will into "law" and ensuring the real separation of powers (i.e. private law making vs. public policy decision and execution) in a liberal constitution. Members of this legislative assembly must be independent from the government and political parties to free them from bargaining for sectoral interests and partisan politics. To further protect the independence and quality of the members of this second legislative chamber, Hayek proposes a 15-year tenure period for each and every elected member, and they should be elected once in a life time at the age of 45 to sit in the chamber by their peers who, generally speaking, are the best judges of the candidates' quality and ability for this important public and constitutional duty.

Within this nomocratic model, Hayek believes that an elected governmental assembly is still required to form a government supported by the majority of the electorate. Party line is allowed in this assembly in determining government policy and public service, so long as the enforceable decisions of the governmental assembly do not contradict the *nomoi* as upheld by the second, non-partisan legislative assembly. The government or the executive arm of the governmental assembly is to be supported by an administrative bureaucracy to implement its policy and decision in the actual governance of the society. Hayek further suggests that a constitutional court is required to settle any disputes in the respective jurisdictions of the second legislative assembly and the governmental assembly in accordance with the constitution (Hayek 1979, pp. 105–127).

Here, in spelling out the principles and the main outline of his constitutional blueprint for nomocracy, Hayek in fact is trying to *organize* a viable political framework to create the right kinds of constitutional conditions that can nurture all kinds of self-generating orders to flourish from within. The basis of his five-tier model constitution (i.e. the constitution itself, the constitutional court, the second legislative assembly, the governmental assembly, and the administrative bureaucracy) is twofold: his clear understanding of the qualitative difference between a nomocratic order and a teleocratic order, and the deliberate, positive and political design of a constitution, which "ought to consist wholly of organizational rules" (ibid., p. 122) to allocate and restrict powers. In other words, *a nomocracy requires the right kind of organizational rules or public laws to help to create the political pre-conditions for it to sustain and to flourish.*

In this connection, one cannot but feel that every now and then, Hayek the bold theorist makes too sharp a contrast between nomocracy and teleocracy, creating the impression that they are always and necessarily mutually exclusive. For example, when Hayek says, "For [nomocracy] the 'public good' or 'general welfare' consists solely in the preservation of that abstract and end-independent order which is secured by obedience to abstract rules of just conduct" (Hayek [1978] 1990, p. 89), it appears that he has left little room for the important organizational rules of the model constitution as suggested by himself to play in preserving a spontaneous order. To me, a more profound and consistent reading of Hayek's arguments in this area should be that while nomocracy and teleocracy are qualitatively and conceptually different, a nomocratic order nevertheless requires certain organizational logic and positive political determination as its infrastructure in order to endure. In this regard, perhaps Oakeshott is a thinker with better clarity of mind when he describes nomocracy and teleocracy as "sweet enemies," in which "each is a historic character and a character on the wing continuously exposed to modification in intercourse with the other" ([1975] 1991, p. 326, see also Oakeshott 1996).

Hayekian Constitutionalism and Its Relevance to China

To Hayek, the aim of liberal constitutions "has been to prevent all arbitrary action" (Hayek 1979, p. 36). A constitution, as a political document, is the basic law of a state laying out the organizational rules to regulate the rightful exercise of powers by different branches of the government so that the obligatory rules of just conduct of the state can best be enforced, practiced and maintained in accordance with the commonly accepted principles, values, and beliefs of the society concerned. Constitutionalism or constitutional politics is the political determination in favor of limited government since unlimited government does not require constitutionalism. Constitutional law making could be deliberate, like the case of the United States after her War of Independence in 1776. Alternatively, it could be tacit and evolutionary, like the case of the unwritten constitution of the common law system in England (Hayek 1960, pp. 162–192).

As the basic law of a state, the constitution and its implementation are meant to be regulating the politics of the normal time. But this does not mean that there is no constitutional innovation in constitutional politics. Furthermore, if and when necessary, when there arises in a political association the so-called constitutional moment at a time of crisis or critical situation, political determination needs to be called for to make some fundamental political decisions for a new or revised framework for constitutional politics. I would say that Hayek's gallant attempt to design a model constitution is a most impressive intellectual effort to prepare a set of revised institutional-constitutional arrangements for a possible constitutional moment in the future to restore the spirit of the rule of law in Western democracies that, in his view, have gone astray. This could also be used as a kind of intellectual reserve instruments of democratic government when there is a need to create new supra-national democratic institutions (Hayek 1979, pp. 107–109).

Perhaps one can call Hayek's theoretical effort in this regard amounts to adopting a political and deliberative approach to nomocratic constitutionalism. The subtitle of Hayek's 3-volume *Law, Legislation and Liberty* is "a new statement of the liberal principles of justice and political economy." The intention of Hayek is clear. He is trying to revive and to further develop the set of liberal principles implicit in many Western and Christian political traditions to cope with the political challenges facing liberal constitutionalism in the twentieth century and beyond, a theoretical ambition that can already be found in Hayek's earlier major works such as *The Road to Serfdom* ([1944] 2007) and "Individualism: True and False" ([1948] 1980, pp. 1–32). Hayek comes up with a liberal constitutional blueprint in response to his perceived crisis of democracy in the West. He believes that Western democracies have by and large become unlimited democracy, allowing social legislation to pursue particularistic and even partisan interests arbitrarily, overriding constitutional politics and the rule of law in populist democracies, making governmental power almost omnipotent and dangerous. In order to reset the ideal of nomocratic constitutionalism in the crisis-ridden political reality of Western democracies, some teleocratic and institutional-organizational approach for liberal political determination is called for in order to better secure individual liberty for all.

Of course, Hayek is keenly aware of the fact that given the entrenchment of vested interests and the political reality of contemporary democracies, his proposed model constitution is not meant for "present application" (ibid., p. 107). He certainly does not think that any state without an established tradition and a prevalent belief in the rule of law or spontaneous order can just transplant his proposed blueprint into its constitutional settings for immediate use. In this connection then, to what extent is Hayek's thought on constitutionalism relevant to the contemporary Chinese political context?

In my view, a leading mainland constitutionalist liberal Gao Quanxi has perhaps learned most from Hayek and contributed a lot in developing our understanding in this area, and I intend to make reference to some of Gao's most relevant historical and theoretical observations in this regard to offer an answer to this question in this concluding section.

For constitutionalist liberal in contemporary China like Gao, Hayek's liberal ideas are relevant at least for the following reasons.

Firstly, Gao believes that after more than one and a half century of imperial invasions, political radicalism, utopian movements, and revolutionary politics in China from the late Qing Dynasty up to the early twenty-first century, the time has come for China to ask the question Gu Zhun asked in the 1970s (see Chapter 3): what happens after the Revolution? With all the political upheavals passed and radical politics gradually subsided, could the People's Republic of China manage to return to normal politics and maintain a peaceful and sustainable political environment for development? Without constitutional politics of the liberal kind, how can China prevent arbitrary and totalitarian rule, which has plagued Chinese politics for decades, in the future? Under what circumstances can the party-state of the People's Republic of China make a fundamental, political determination to gather the fruits of the revolution and to start constitutional building so that the rule of law can prevail for the long term?

While Gao knows well that Hayek did not come up with his idea of constitutionalism with China in mind, he thinks that the Chinese liberals can learn from Hayek's theory to help the Chinese to better understand what the rule of law is, the qualitative difference between nomocracy and teleocracy, and the contrast between constitutionalism and radical revolutionism, so that conceptual confusion and categorial mistakes can be avoided, and the appreciation of the nature of and the need for liberal constitutionalism enhanced.

To Gao, Hayek's proposed model constitution is in fact political through and through, amounting to a theoretical attempt to secure the rule of law in a liberal state by making a political determination of the constitutional kind for nomocracy (Gao 2017, pp. 68–157, especially p. 112 and p. 142). Learning constitutionalism through Hayek would enable the Chinese liberals to recognize the importance of differentiating the conceptual and theoretical distinction between nomocracy and teleocracy, this might also inspire them to develop some similar but essential intellectual reserved instruments of the nomocratic kind appropriate to China's political experience that could facilitate, should the appropriate constitutional moment arise, some future liberal constitution-building endeavors to take place in the Chinese context. This in effect is to continue the more than a century long effort of introducing constitutional politics to China to help her to modernize when Kang and Liang first introduced their constitutional thinking and proposed reform to Emperor Guangxu of the late Qing Dynasty. (ibid., p. 237).

Secondly, Gao thinks that Hayek's classical liberalism is particularly useful for the Chinese liberals not only because of his critique of totalitarian politics, Gao is of the view that Hayek's return to the Old Whig tradition (Hayek 1960, pp. 395–411), to the insights of the Scottish Enlightenment, to John Locke and those early modern experience in Western Europe, and his efforts in distinguishing true individualism from false individualism (see Chapter 4 of this book) are all highly relevant to the Chinese context.

For Gao, he believes that China in essence is a late developing state in the modern world, the social and political challenges facing China are therefore more akin to the early modern era of the seventeenth and eighteenth centuries Europe in terms of nation building, like how to transform China from a traditional empire to a modern state, and to turn political China from an ancient metaphysical paradigm to a paradigm of a secular, liberal, and emerging market-oriented kind. One should not forget that the important traditional notion and institution of universal kingship as explained in this chapter collapsed only a little bit over 100 years ago in China. This speaks volumes of how recent China was forced to start to take up her path to modern transformation.

However, since the May Fourth Movement, Chinese intellectuals have been subject to the influence of the more Rationalistic new liberalism as well as to all kind of radical ideological teachings (such as socialism and communism) made popular in the nineteenth century Europe. This deprived the then China the opportunity to chart its road to modernity via the more moderate, classical liberal path like the Glorious Revolution of the seventeenth century England and the eighteenth century War of Independence of the US. The discovery of Hayekian liberalism in the 1990s and the early twenty-first century in the People's Republic of China therefore acted as a timely reminder to the Chinese intellectuals that there is an alternative, or even more relevant, intellectual reference point of the early modern era in the West for China to refer to in her road to modernity and modernization, and Hayek is a profound reference point in this regard (Gao 2003, pp. 380–382; Qui 2014). Indeed, Hayek's emphasis on constitutionalism and the rule of law instead of democracy as such is particularly interesting, since the so-called Chinese Enlightenment in the political realm since the May Fourth is always linked to the aspiration of radical democracy and revolution (Li 1987), the former of which, as Hayek has argued, has gone astray as a political ideal in the West, and a political determination to recreate the conditions for nomocracy is required. For the Chinese liberals, while the republican 1911 Revolution and the Chinese Communist Party's socialist revolution were indeed political determinations of the Chinese elites made at the time to opt for a radical departure of the past that aimed to overthrow the traditional political order, the need to make a political determination of the liberal kind after the radical revolutions is required if China wants to avoid permanent revolution or the repeat of the Great Proletariat Cultural Revolution, and returns to normal politics to achieve long term stability to fulfil the revolutions' original ideals of modernizing the nation as well as to liberating individual citizens.

Thirdly, as explained in Chapter 5 above, Hayekian liberalism helps Chinese liberalism to take a conservative but constructive turn in post-war China. Given the systematic and profound nature of Hayek's system of ideas and his social-scientific approach, it helps Chinese liberalism to return to a sympathetic and serious re-examination of the Chinese tradition. Hayek's anti-Rationalism epistemology certainly does not favor synoptic constitutional planning, but his ideas of making a political determination for the establishment of liberal constitutionalism in a modern state, his proposed model constitution, his idea of the rule of law, and his social theory in general are all powerful intellectual reserve tools for the Chinese liberals to make reference to when they try to chart the road to develop a clear, theoretical and even practical approach for social and constitutional reform in China toward liberal and normal politics (Gao 2003, pp. 236–240).

The need to take tradition seriously has also helped Gao to engage in some important historical and analytical examination of the Chinese tradition of constitutionalism since the late Qing Dynasty. Gao argues that closer scrutiny indicates that China in fact has developed quite an important moderate constitutionalism tradition over the past 100 years or so. Gao believes that after the outbreak of the 1911 Revolution, the fact that the Qing Emperor was willing to abdicate peacefully and to pass his mandate to the republic in order to avoid further bloodshed in return for the preservation of the royal privileges enjoyed by the royal family in the Forbidden City after China had become a republic, and the fact that revolutionary armies accepted these terms to end the revolution is a very important constitutional development of the moderate kind in modern China. The Abdication Edict further specifies that the citizens of the republic shall from now on include all the major ethnic groups (i.e. the Hans, the Manchus, the Mongols, the Huis, and the Tibetans) in China. To Gao, all these are not only of great historic significance, and the Abdication Edict should be regarded as an important constitutional document in modern China, illustrating the adoption of the constitutional politics of moderation and compromise to complete the revolution. Gao even describes this as "China's Glorious Revolution" (Gao 2016, pp. 248–278; 2022, Volume 1, pp. 186–192).

Another example given by Gao is the Nationalist government's proclamation of the relatively liberal 1947 constitution to the then Republic of China, which has been effective only in Taiwan after the Chinese Nationalist Party fled to Taiwan after their defeat in the Chinese Civil War since 1949. Although many of the democratic elements of this constitution were suspended and martial law put into place soon after its proclamation because of the Civil War and the political division and confrontation between the mainland and Taiwan, Taiwan started to abolish the martial law measures in 1991 and has managed to make her democratic transition a success since its direct presidential election held in 1996. This successful experience of political transition from party-state rule to democratic constitutionalism again has proved that the hope of liberal constitutionalism being put into practice in the Chinese context (though only restricted to Taiwan in this case) is not an absolute pipe dream after all (Gao 2022, Volume 2, pp. 162–191).

As regards the mainland, although Mao's China was largely the antithesis of constitutionalism, particularly during the Great Proletariat Cultural Revolution from 1966–1976, the death of Mao eventually brought the policy of "reform and opening" to China by Deng, and its 1982 constitution, while upholding the political leadership of the Chinese Communist Party and insisting on the Marxian ideology in the Preamble, has started to provide the baseline for China to move to liberalize its economy and to practice marketization. Article 31 of this constitution even empowers Beijing to establish special administrative regions like Hong Kong (after 1997) and Macau (after 1999) where capitalism is practiced with a high degree of autonomy (including maintaining the common law system in the case of the Hong Kong Special Administrative Region) so that the mainland's modernization efforts can be benefitted from these regions, which, by providing know-how and foreign capital, could facilitate the mainland to open its doors and to gradually emerge into the global market.

Gao also puts special emphasis on the first four amendments (1988, 1993, 1999, 2004) made to the 1982 constitution, which characterizes China as in the preliminary stage of socialism, practicing socialism with Chinese characteristics, with socialist market economy, the protection of the private sector in the economy, the protection of private property rights and human rights acknowledged, and pledging to govern the state according to the rule of law. From these amendments, Gao detects a new constitutional spirit moving from the politics of the revolution to normal constitutional politics, though the way ahead is still long and uncertain to say the least (Gao 2016, pp. 321–355).[8] In other words, while it is true that modern Chinese political experience is dominated by revolutionary radicalism, one should not forget that there is also a parallel, though secondary, tradition of moderate constitutionalism being pursued in China every now and then in her modern political experience.

While all the above may not be terribly favorable to the Chinese liberals in their conviction to turn China liberal, they are not going to admit defeat either, because, to them, both from an empirical and from a theoretical point of view, radical revolutionism and totalitarian politics are no answers to China's future either (Gao 2022, p. 231).

There are, of course, difficult theoretical problems facing the application of Hayekian liberalism in the Chinese context. Since the rule of law, constitutionalism and all these liberal values and practices are largely deriving from the Western tradition and are absent in the Chinese tradition, it is not clear how these foreign values can effectively be nurtured and developed in the Chinese context. Even Hayek himself dares not to hope that his proposed model constitution can be transplanted to China where no tradition of constitutionalism existed before. That is why some

Chinese leading intellectuals, such as Yao Zhongqui (also known as Qui Feng), after having influenced by Hayek in the late 1990s, started to change to Confucian constitutionalism instead since according to the teaching of Hayek, the rule of law is a tradition-bound practice and system and in China, the tradition must be Confucian if we take the past seriously. Introducing constitutionalism to China without taking the Confucian tradition seriously is ultimately not taking Hayek's insights seriously, one could argue (Yao 2016). Can the relatively new and thin tradition of modern China's constitutionalism as specified by Gao above good enough to guide the way forward?

Furthermore, even Gao appears to agree with people like Roger Scruton in saying that Hayek's system of thought appears to have taken the issue of nation and identity for granted (Scruton 2006). That is why Gao argues that while nation building is still important and the question of citizenship and political identity is still very much a central issue in the People's Republic of China, one will have to go beyond Hayek in order to strengthen the liberals' efforts in enriching their understanding in these political areas in China (Gao 2016, pp. 49–70; 2017, pp. 242–251). Likewise, how to develop a persuasive historical-cum-theoretical narrative to enrich the liberal account of China's transformation from the classical era to the modern era, and whether Hayekian liberalism's largely thin and negative conception of values embedded in its political association is adequate to tackle the question of political theology and moral metaphysics in modern China remain to be seen, given the fact that traditional Chinese political thought was very rich in the latter and their lingering influence on the Chinese modern mind may still be something that the Chinese liberals cannot ignore. At the present moment, I myself do not have answers to all these problems, but they are outstanding and important issues and challenges facing the Chinese liberals and they for sure form parts of the agenda for the further development of Chinese liberalism in the long and tortuous path toward modernity by the Chinese people.

Notes

1. Steve Tsang and Olivia Cheung claim in Tsang and Cheung (2024) that Xi has succeeded in centralizing supreme power of the Chinese Communist Party into himself since all other members of the party's Politburo are now made directly accountable to him. Tsang and Cheung, however, are of the view that Xi, unlike Mao during the Great Proletariat Cultural Revolution, is using the enhanced, even more centralized party as the main vehicle and platform for his governance in China.
2. Personal communication with a founding member of the Association. It seems that even Hayek's name is regarded as politically sensitive under Xi Jinping's regime now.
3. Bruce Caldwell said in a note to this quote that he was unable to locate the source of the quotation attributed to Kant here by Hayek. See Hayek ([1944] 2007, p. 119, n. 6).
4. That is why many (e.g. Deng and Gao as cited in the main text of this chapter) claim that there is a change of emphasis of Hayek's idea of the rule of law from *The Constitution of Liberty* to *Law, Legislation and Liberty*. While the former is more statue law oriented, the latter is more common law oriented.
5. For some good discussion on the concept of universal kingship in traditional political theory of China, see Ching (1997) and Liu (2006).
6. I follow many of the arguments I have used in Cheung (2014a) in my analysis in this and the subsequent 3 sections of this chapter.
7. Ernest Gellner believes that "the most effective modern economies are those which practice a loose state-economy co-operation, working on the basis of informal networks and pressures, without depriving productive units of their autonomy and liberty of movement, but frankly recognizing the significance of the state as weather-maker, and the inevitably political nature of major economic decisions." Gellner (1994, p. 92) As a result, Gellner thinks that we are not dealing with a genuinely neutral market situation under modern capitalism.

8. The fifth amendment to the 1982 constitution was made by Xi in 2018, which was a major regressive move away from Gao's so called "new constitutional spirit" for further "reform and opening." I shall briefly discuss this in Chapter 7, the conclusion of this book.

7
Conclusion

The Vicissitude of the Development of Chinese Liberalism

Since Yan Fu introduced Western liberal thought to China in the late nineteenth century, there has not been a lack of leading Chinese intellectuals in each generation since to advocate Chinese liberalism for the sake of liberalizing and modernizing the Chinese nation. Chinese liberalism, however, has never been the dominant ideology in the political history of modern China. While the constitutional monarchists of the late Qing Dynasty like Kang Yuwei and Liang Qichao managed to persuade the Emperor Guangxu to institute constitutional reform in 1898, it was soon crushed by the conservative faction in the Qing court led by the Empress Dowager Cixi (慈禧 1835–1908), who undid almost all the proposed institutional reform measures introduced by the constitutionalists. Those who were disenchanted of the Qing Dynasty then opted for the more radical approach of revolution under the leadership of Dr. Sun Yat-sen who believed that the pre-conditions of liberal constitutionalism in China were military rule and party-state tutelage of the people before democracy could be practiced.

C. Cheung, *Hayek and Post-War Chinese Liberalism*, Palgrave Studies in Classical Liberalism, https://doi.org/10.1007/978-3-031-64888-5_7

The 1911 Revolution failed to set up constitutional government in the Republic of China (Price 1990). Instead, it brough warlordism and two occasions of failed attempts to revive monarchical rule in China (Lin 1979). The May Fourth Movement heralded the pursuit of democracy and science by the Chinese intellectuals in China, and Chinese liberalism under the leadership of Hu Shih did flourish for some time then, but it was the party-state doctrine of Lenin that eventually helped China to become more or less unified, first under the "reformed" (along the line of Leninism) Chinese Nationalist Party, and later, under the more disciplined and powerful Chinese Communist Party under Mao Tse-tung when the latter won the Chinese Civil War after the Japanese were defeated in the Second World War. The People's Republic of China under Mao regarded liberalism as capitalistic and hostile, what was practiced then was Mao's utopian socialism and totalitarian politics (Lin 2020, pp. 3–61). Even after the defeated Chinese Nationalist Party fled to Taiwan after the Civil War, its leadership continued to practice party-state governance until the early 1990s.

Perhaps what is remarkable under such unfavorable circumstances is the fact that Chinese liberalism has survived and continued to develop. I think the most extraordinary example to demonstrate Chinese liberalism's resilience and perseverance is the case of Gu Zhun during the Great Leap Forward and the Great Proletariat Cultural Revolution, which we have covered in Chapter 3 of this book. The sufferings brough by Mao's utopianism and totalitarian politics, in a sense, not only showed the cogency of Hayek's classical liberalism against socialism, they also triggered Deng Xiaoping's determination to abandon radical revolutionism and to return to normal and developmental politics under his "reform and opening" policy, which created conditions for the Chinese intellectuals to learn from the West again, and Hayekian liberalism, as we saw in Chapter 6 above, had once become a most important reference point for the Chinese intellectuals to explore how China should develop into a more civilized and liberal society. Post-war Taiwan in fact was also under the party rule of the Chinese Nationalist Party until the early 1990s, and the moral and political courage of the Chinese liberals such as Yin Haiguang in Taiwan were crucial in continuing the development of Chinese liberal thought, where Hayek's theoretical influence started to be felt at this juncture.

The success of Taiwan's democratization since the 1990s has at least partially demonstrated that liberal democracy is not incompatible with the Chinese culture. However, the People's Republic of China under Xi Jinping's centralized strongman leadership now regards liberal democracy as the leading "false ideological trend" prevalent in China that the Chinese Communist Party must proactively and vigorously fight against (Tsang and Cheung 2024, p. 81).

Mainland Chinese liberals under the strengthened party rule of Xi Jinping have had a very difficult time (Gao 2017, pp. xv–xviii) with Xi's attempt to restore "the party leads everything" doctrine again (Tsang and Cheung 2024, Chapter 3). In the last chapter of this book, I discussed Gao's historical review of the 4 relatively liberal amendments (1988, 1993, 1999, and 2004) made to the People's Republic of China's 1982 Constitution where Gao argued that these might signal the return of normal politics to China in which liberal constitutionalism may have more room to develop. However, Xi's 2018 amendments to the 1982 Constitution have not only made the requirement to uphold the leadership of the Chinese Communist Party even more entrenched in the Constitution by moving this requirement from the Preamble of the Constitution to Article 1 of the Constitution, the abolition of the term-limit requirement of the posts of the State President and State Vice President has signaled the intention of Xi to hold together in his own person the supreme position of the Secretary General of the Chinese Communist Party and the supreme state position of state presidency (together with the position as Chairman of the party's Military Commission of the People's Liberation Army) for life.

The entrenchment of these measures and the re-emphasis of the party leading the state and everything under the People's Republic of China amount to the establishment of a personal, centralized authoritarian rule by Xi via the strengthened party-state (Tsang and Cheung 2024). In the light of these developments, even a not unsympathetic legal scholar studying laws and constitution of the People's Republic of China under the political leadership of the Chinese Communist Party notes that this "would take China further away from liberal constitutionalism, and probably make a gradual and non-revolutionary transition to liberal constitutionalism in the future more difficult" (Chen 2022, p. 31). One must also not forget that as Vikash Yadav reminds us, the party-state of China is now practicing a kind of political or party-state *capitalism* which is very different from what was practiced under Mao before (2023). All these call for a new agenda for the development of liberal thought in the Chinese context.

The Continuing Relevance of Hayekian Liberalism in the Chinese Context

While Hayek's critique of totalitarianism and his criticism of the impossibility of social calculation are both profound and devastating to orthodox socialism, Chinese liberal thought needs to move on to tackle the new phenomenon of party-state capitalism. If Hayek is right about the superior social coordinating function of the spontaneous order ([1948] 1980, 1973) and the creative powers of a free civilization (1960, Chapter 2), Hayekian liberals should be able to develop powerful theoretical and empirical critique of the inherent instability of party-state capitalism since a social and political framework meant to facilitate the social coordinating function of the market for the maximal fulfilment of the separate and respective pursuits of the individuals are not the same as a social and political framework that requires the market, among other things, to serve the party-state's political missions in which "the party leads everything." This is an area that the Chinese liberals are in a position to come up with critical analysis and explanation both at the level of theoretical critique as well as at the level of comparative policy analysis to demonstrate the possible superior performance of Hayekian spontaneous order.

The social, moral, and political implications of the thesis of the superiority of the social coordinating function of the spontaneous order is another area that can be further developed in Hayekian liberalism. If "treating man as man" has been entrenched as a core value of Chinese liberalism, the Chinese liberals should further enrich their understanding of free agency in their social and political theory. While Chinese liberals have been here and there talking about this in a relatively unsystematic manner (see Appendix of this book), a fuller and more profound treatise of this topic will certainly help to make Chinese liberalism more mature and persuasive in the future. How can the development of a conception of the liberal self in the Chinese context be benefited from the traditional Confucian conception of the moral self (Lin 1973) is an area that may have a lot of theoretical potential for modern Chinese liberalism to build a link to traditional Chinese moral and political thought, though how to make the traditional hierarchical and collective Confucian social order agreeable with the egalitarian and individualist orientation of the modern liberal self will be a tall order for the Chinese liberals to tackle in this respect.

As we have discussed in Chapter 5 of this book, Chinese liberalism cannot develop without paying due regard to the Chinese tradition, and how Chinese liberalism manages to tap into the civil and liberal elements of the Chinese culture and to use them to strengthen the appeal of Chinese liberalism is one important task for the Chinese liberals. Indeed, unlike Mao whose political campaigns had been anti-traditionalist and anti-Confucian through and through, Xi Jinping's "socialism with Chinese Characteristics for the new era" claims having established continuity with the Chinese tradition. One example is the Chinese Communist Party's recent effort in building an amiable dialogue between Marx and Confucius (*The Economist*, 2023.11.04–10, pp. 54–55) where the party claims that both these thinkers have a shared ideal of bringing great harmony to the people and the society. Apparently, Xi wants to use this as a basis to make amend with the tradition and to use it as one reason to claim traditional legitimacy for his party-state rule. In this regard, whether the Chinese liberals can develop a kind of synergy between liberalism and Confucianism that is both convincing and free from the authoritarian and hierarchical overtone or inclination of traditional Confucianism is crucial in developing a theoretical response to the Chinese Communist Party's ideological discourse.

As Hayek (1973, 1976, 1979) and Oakeshott ([1975] 1991) have demonstrated, the protection of free agents in the political realm requires the establishment of a constitutional order that gives priority to nomocratic rules rather than to teleocratic purposes. How this can be theorized in the context of the Chinese culture requires a lot of historical and theoretical examination of issues related to constitutional and political practice in the greater China region. In this regard, Gao Quanxi's pathbreaking works on political constitutionalism of the liberal kind (2003, 2016, 2017, 2022) are most relevant and inspiring, but how liberal constitutionalism can be further developed in the light of the enhanced authoritarian rule of Xi Jinping's party-state is no small matter for the Chinese liberals. If the Chinese liberals, inspired by Hayek's theoretical effort in developing a model constitution for the future of liberal democracy (1979, Chapter 17), can develop some intellectual and institutional reserved instruments that may suit the Chinese context, this will not only enhance the theoretical clarity of what liberal constitutionalism may involve, but also may help to bring a liberal democratic transition in the Chinese context easier to be realized should opportunity of that kind arise. I believe that in this respect, Chinese liberals should pay close theoretical and empirical attention to the liberal constitutional experience (such as constitutional and institutional innovations, check and balance in political powers, liberal and democratic policy making, liberal governance and professional bureaucracy, citizen participation, the importance of civil society, media, professionalism and democratic development, moral conviction and democratic virtues and so on) as practiced in Taiwan in its democratic and transitional politics when they try to better understand the quality of democracy there. This may also provide lessons to be learned in the greater Chinese context for the future development of liberal democracy.

I have no intention to come up with an exhaustive list of issues that the Chinese liberals will have to tackle in their further development of liberal thought in the Chinese context. I doubt very much if such a list can be developed at all. However, even with the limited number of issues I have identified above, I believe there are already a lot of theoretical and empirical works for the Chinese liberals to carry on, and I think that Hayek's theoretical framework is still a good enough major reference point to continue to inspire them to come up with more systematic and profound understanding of the tasks at hand.

Whatever shortcomings this work on Hayek and Chinese liberalism have, I cannot but feel that since Yan Fu's introduction of Western liberal thought to China in the late nineteenth century, Chinese liberalism has come a long and tortuous way. While national salvation and scientific enlightenment may no longer be the prime concerns for the present-day liberals in the greater China region, their theoretical pursuit for a better understanding of what liberty is about and how to realize it in the Chinese context remains as important as ever after all these intervening years. Although liberal thought is still quite new to many of the general public of the Chinese people, I hope my humble effort in this book has demonstrated both the complexity, difficulty and fascination of this intellectual undertaking that has attracted so many first-rate Chinese thinkers over the years to make their intellectual pilgrimage to better understand the question "why liberty for China?". I believe that this pilgrimage will be continued despite all the theoretical, political, and practical difficulties the Chinese liberals will face in the future.

Appendix

Theorizing the Civil Condition: Oakeshott and Chinese Liberalism

The appendix explores the relevance of Oakeshott's philosophical politics to Chinese liberalism. Although Oakeshott is seldom mentioned by Chinese liberals, his clear-headed theorization of human conduct and the civil condition, his prudent skeptical realism in understanding politics not only can help the Chinese liberals to avoid the traps of political Rationalism, but also to achieve better clarity in understanding the postulates regarding free agency, the morality of individuality, the rule of law that are presupposed by the liberally oriented civil condition. The appendix examines how leading liberals like Hu Shih, Luo Longji, and Zhang Fo-chuan have made important contributions to develop the idea of treating man as man in this regard.

C. Cheung, *Hayek and Post-War Chinese Liberalism*, Palgrave Studies in Classical Liberalism, https://doi.org/10.1007/978-3-031-64888-5

Introduction

Oakeshott is perhaps one of the more profound theorists of civil association of the twentieth century.

Oakeshott's philosophical reflection on the postulates of human conduct, such as free agents, reflective intelligence, choice, deliberation, transactional and practical interactions among free agents, practices as vernacular languages, moral conduct as self-disclosure and self-enactment of free agents, is, in my view, an excellent exposition of a modern, philosophical conception of the morality of individuality, which puts the human individual at the center of an intellectual inquiry on conduct *inter homines* ([1975] 1991, pp. 1–107; 1991, pp. 295–350).

In theorizing the civil condition as a distinctive mode of human association, Oakeshott's identification of the centrality of the rule of law in civil association, which is being composed entirely of civil, non-instrumental rules or *lex*, with authoritative prescriptions constituting various ruling offices (the judiciary, the legislature, and the executive), their respective procedures and the rights and obligations of the citizens concerned ([1975] 1991, pp. 108–184), is a most clear-headed account of why governing, at least theoretically, can be "recognized as a specific and limited activity;...its business is to keep its subjects at peace with one another in the activities in which they have chosen to seek their happiness" (1991, pp. 429–430).

Furthermore, his historical and theoretical discourse on the ambivalent nature of a modern European state ([1975] 1991, pp. 185–326), comprising two irreconcilable, "sweet enemies" (ibid., p. 326) type of characteristics (i.e. the civil, rule-based component, and the enterprise, common purpose dominated component) "contingently joined by the choices of human beings" (ibid., p. 323), is, as Terry Nardin aptly points out, both skeptical and realist, since Oakeshott recognizes that although principles and outcomes are both important in politics, the vicissitude of our political experience is such that it is never certain that the former should be privileged over the latter whatever the consequences (Nardin 2015, pp. 34–35).

How relevant is such a theory of civil association to Chinese liberalism?

Judging from the lack of discussion of Oakeshott's philosophical politics among the Chinese liberals, the answer appears to be that there is little relevance of Oakeshott's theory of civil association to the liberal thought of the Chinese-speaking world.

The more sophisticated readers of Oakeshott, however, detect that Oakeshott's ideas can play a critical role against modern Chinese liberalism. Among the few Chinese scholars who take Oakeshott's thought seriously, Zhang Rulun is the first to point out that if one is to examine Chinese liberalism from an Oakeshottian perspective, one will find that many of the Chinese liberals' understanding of politics are both ideological and Rationalist. "Chinese discourse reflects not only a simplistic liberalism," says Zhang, "but also, and primarily, what Oakeshott called 'Rationalism'" (2015, p. 146). This observation is based largely on a careful reading of Oakeshott's critique of modern Rationalism and the politics of the felt need (1991, pp. 5–42), and I think there are good arguments to support such an observation.

According to Zhang, when confronted with the political and cultural invasions from Western imperial powers, forcing the then Qing Dynasty to open the doors of China after a series of military defeats since the 1840s, many of the Chinese intellectuals inspired by Western liberal thought have come to believe that what is required is a rational blueprint importing the success of the West to help China to modernize. Also, the traditional Chinese culture, with its emphasis on feudalistic, hierarchical, and collectivist values resistance to change and aversion to modern and scientific scholarship, is regarded more as a fundamental barrier than a pool of resources for China to achieve its national salvation goals.

Moreover, after the tyrannical rule of totalitarianism under Mao's China since 1949, the Chinese liberals have become even more determined in their conviction that what China needs is the import of liberal democracy with the power of the government restrained for the protection of fundamental, universal human rights, and the way to do so is for a transplant of the Western model of constitutionalism rather than intimating the authoritarian oriented Chinese tradition.

All the above are symptomatic of the Rationalist politics of the felt need, and Oakeshott will not be surprised to learn that as a result, liberal values and democratic practices are far from being entrenched in China.

Inspired by Zhang's Oakeshottian critique of Chinese liberalism, I, in an earlier paper entitled "Oakeshott, Hayek, and the Conservative Turn of Chinese Liberalism" (Cheung 2017b, pp. 160–180), try to supplement Zhang's observation. I argued that as time goes by, some more nuanced Chinese liberal thinkers had started to appreciate Oakeshott's insight and initiated a conservative turn of their political and theoretical thinking, realizing that like a tradition of behavior, the activity of governing is never the result of the application of some abstract, demonstrable, general principles to the political association, but involves a concrete, a more or less coherent manner of acting, and making choices and decisions that can sustain the loyalty of the members of the association concerned. The activity of governing in a constitutional democracy is no exception. Though general principles can always be abstracted from such a concrete context, they are but abridgements, not the flesh and blood of the actual activity of governing in a political association. The Chinese liberals, therefore, will have to make rapport with the more open elements found in the concrete Chinese traditional practices if they wish constitutional democracy to be entrenched in their political association. As Oakeshott famously said, "political crisis (even when it seems to be imposed upon a society by changes beyond its control) always appears *within* a tradition of political activity; and "salvation" comes from the unimpaired resources of the tradition itself. Those societies which retain, in changing circumstances, a lively sense of their own identity and continuity (which are without that hatred of their own experience which makes them desire to efface it) are to be counted fortunate, not because they possess what others lack, but because they have already mobilized what none is without and all, in fact, rely upon" (1991, pp. 59–60, emphasis in the original).

In my (2017b) paper, I pointed out that while some tradition sensitive Chinese liberals had proposed the approach of initiating a creative transformation of the Chinese tradition so that it could be made more compatible with liberal and democratic values of the modern world (ibid., pp. 166–172), other constitutionalist liberals in China also noted that in response to the challenges of the West since the late Qing Dynasty, there was a growing body of practical experience built up in China for the introduction of constitutional politics in its activity of governing, and the opening up for political reform (albeit limited) in the post-Mao era on the Chinese mainland and the successful adoption of democracy in Taiwan since 1996 might form parts of the "unimpaired resources" or transformed materials for the further development of liberal values and practices in the Chinese context.

The current paper intends to further explore the relevance of Oakeshott's philosophical politics to Chinese liberalism. I am going to argue that although Oakeshott is seldom mentioned by leading Chinese liberals when they are developing their liberalism in the Chinese context, his clear-headed theorization of human conduct and the civil condition, together with his prudent skeptical realism in understanding politics may not only help the Chinese liberals to avoid the traps of political Rationalism and the politics of the felt need, but also to achieve better clarity in understanding the postulates regarding free agency, the morality of individuality, the rule of law, and so on that are presupposed by the liberally oriented civil condition.

While Oakeshott's philosophical politics can never be applied, not to say giving direct instructions, to the development of Chinese politics, it is hoped that it may nevertheless help to inform the further pursuit of liberal values in the Chinese context and avoid some misconceived approaches in the pursuit.

From the Politics of the Felt Need to the Primacy of the Individual

In China's traditional, centralized, and hierarchical order, individualism, if literally and straightforwardly translated into Chinese, is not often having a good reputation. Cultures are complex entities. When two distinctive cultures meet, a lot might be lost in translation in their respective attempts to understand the complexity of each other, particularly in areas where there are few overlaps between the two. Even as late as the early 1980s, a leading sinologist in the United States John K. Fairbank could still make the following observation:

> To say that liberalism rests on individualism under the supremacy of law is more sensible and gratifying than to say, as one does in Chinese, that the doctrines of spontaneous license rest on the doctrine of self-centeredness under the supremacy of administrative regulation. (quoted in Pye 1985, p. 192)

It is not just the traditionalists or reactionaries in China who fault individualism as selfish or self-centered. Revolutionaries like Mao Tse-tung also view individualism and liberalism with hostility. For example, in his 1937 essay "Combat Liberalism" (Mao 1961, pp. 31–33), Mao denounced liberalism as opportunistic, arguing that the liberal ideology rooted in petty bourgeoisie's selfishness and always placed personal interest above the interest of the revolution. He called for the elimination of liberalism in the ranks of the revolution.

In his "The Development of Individualism in Modern China" (Chow 1995), William C. L. Chow argues that since China was exposed to the challenges of the West in the mid-nineteenth century, "the lack of an individualistic concept of man is doubtless the most obvious point that distinguishes Eastern from Western culture" (ibid., p. 78).

While Confucius was a great educator who did not make any class distinction when it came to learning, and his idea of Confucian personality may be interpreted as consistent with the values of moral autonomy of the self, self-cultivation and self-development, the elitist, hierarchical ethos, and the socio-political structures of pre-modern China were such that only the educated and cultivated gentlemen (*junzi*) were supposed to be leading the way to social harmony and moral and political excellence. However, these gentlemen, even in Confucius's own teaching, were to be sharply distinguished from the ordinary folks who were regarded as little men (*xiaoren*). William Theodore de Bary has made a valid point when he examines the lack of individualism in China:

> For one thing we should distinguish between individualism and "individuality." The existence of the latter does not always imply the presence of the former. Many flourishing cultures have recognized individuality in arts and letters, for instance, without affirming an equal right to individuality of expression in other fields of endeavour or among all classes of society. Aristocratic societies have often encouraged more individuality

> among the elite than the democracies have tolerated among the masses. (quoted in Chow 1995, p. 79)

Even the commitment to individualism by liberal-minded Chinese intellectuals who were pioneers in introducing liberalism to modern China in the late Qing era is always being questioned. In his authoritative study of the father of Chinese liberalism Yan Fu (a student of the old Royal Naval College in Greenwich of England in the 1870s who first seriously and systematically introduced modern liberalism to China in the late nineteenth century), Benjamin Schwartz puts forward the following argument: Yan was so preoccupied with the need for national salvation in the face of scrambling for concessions of China by Western imperial powers that he altered John Stuart Mill's original conception of liberty in his translation of *On Liberty* by fitting it into a framework of Herbert Spencer's categories of energy and "survival of the fittest," which had effectively turned individualism into a means of national salvation (Schwartz 1964. See also Chow 1995, p. 84). Although Schwartz's thesis of Yan deliberately mistranslating Mill out of the concern for national salvation has been powerfully challenged by subsequent scholarship on Yan Fu, what appears not to be disputed is the fact that because of Confucianism's influence, Yan's advocacy of liberalism in the Chinese context was at best vacillating between individualism and collectivism (see, for example, Huang 2008; Liu et al. eds. 1999; Zhou 2017).

Likewise, there is general agreement by students of modern Chinese political thought that the famous constitutionalist reformer of the late Qing Dynasty and the early republican era Liang Qichao had by and large premised his idea of new and active citizens in China on the need to adopt a collective approach in modern nation building (Chang 1971; Lubot 1982; Chow 1995; Yang 2009; Qiu 2019). The following paragraph from Liang on new citizenship is one good example to illustrate this point:

> It is not merely to have rulers, officials, students, farmers, laborers, merchants, and soldiers, but to have ten thousand eyes with one sight, ten thousand hands and feet with only one mind, ten thousand ears with one hearing, ten thousand powers with only one purpose of life; then

> the state is established ten-thousand fold strong...When mind touches mind, when power is linked to power, cog to cog, strand around strand, and ten thousands roads meet in one center, this will be a state. (quoted from Chang 1971, p. 100)

However, once the modern concepts of liberty and citizen have been introduced to China and, since the collapse of the Qing Dynasty and the establishment of the Republic of China after the 1911 Revolution, the idea of the individual has been severed from the traditional relationship of Master and Slave with the demise of the traditionally predominant institution and understanding of universal kingship (Liu 2006, pp. 224–240), subsequent Chinese liberals have, in different ways, been trying to enrich the ideas of individualism and liberty as they come to better understand the different strands of Western political thought, even though the need for national salvation and national revival is still thought to be there.

For example, Hu Shih, the leading Chinese liberal since the May Fourth Movement of 1919 (a movement that brought democracy, science, and nationalism to the forefront as indispensable values for modern China), introduced the works and ideas of the Norwegian playwright Henrik Ibsen to China in 1918, arguing that collectivism tended to destroy individuality and independent thinking. To Hu, what was required in China at that time was a genuine, pure form of self-centered-cum-cultivated ideology to develop one's talent and ability, which was the best method to contribute to society (Hu 1918, pp. 196–220). In addition, in citing the US philosopher John Dewey's idea on the individual in the May Fourth period, Hu distinguished two kinds of individualisms as introduced by Dewey: the first one was false individualism, which was in fact egoism; the second one was true individualism, which was constituted by independent thinking and making the individual fully responsible for his/her ideas and faiths, fearing no authority or repression in the pursuit of truth. Hu called this "a sound conception of individualism" (ibid., pp. 244–245). So, a free agent capable of making his/her own reflective deliberation on what to do and how to go about it, who is supposed to be personally responsible for the consequences of his/her self-disclosing and self-enacting actions appeared to have been emerged in Chinese liberalism under Hu's "sound individualism."

In summarizing his own thinking on individual freedom, Hu says, "At present, some people tell you to 'sacrifice your individual freedom in order to seek freedom of the state.' But I will tell you this: 'fight for your own freedom; in doing so, you fight for the freedom of the state. Fight for your own character; in doing so, you fight for the state's character. A bunch of slaves will not be able to establish a state with freedom and equality" (quote from Liu 1999, p. 196). This assertion of Hu is in marked contrast to Liang's collectivist statement on new citizenship mentioned earlier, though the tone of the politics of the felt need is still there. Hu's emphasis of "sound individualism" nevertheless marked the Chinese liberals' first major effort in putting the individual at the center stage of their liberal thought.

If learning the political values, practices, and vocabularies of a foreign culture is like learning a second or third language (what Oakeshott calls the vernacular languages of law and morality), the Chinese liberals since Hu have perhaps started to speak with a relatively clearer tone and focus of the voice of a free agent by releasing the individual from the onerous chains of national salvation and collective priorities, though much still need to be developed in this conception of the individual if one wants to better understand its theoretical and practical implications.

Treating Man as Man and Free Agency

Perhaps Luo Longji, who studied politics in the 1920s at Columbia University and the London School of Economics, was the first in China who managed to put forward a comparatively more developed theory of individualism in Chinese liberalism. His conception of individualism is premised on the respect of personal dignity by treating man as man with constitutional protection of human rights (Luo 2022, 4 Volumes; Cheung 04.12.2022).

Luo asserts that human rights are those necessary conditions that allow man to live as man, and there are three dimensions in this regard: the first dimension relates to conditions that allow the individual to survive and maintain life; the second dimension is for the protection of personal security and safety; and, more importantly, the third dimension is about those conditions that help to constitute man to be human. To Luo, every individual has his/her unique character and personality. If there is no room or opportunity to nurture and develop one's character and personality, one is not living as a human being. In this regard, to take man seriously is to regard each one of them as an end, not as a means. The most fundamental principle in Luo's idea of individualism is to ensure that the individual can develop his/her unique character to his/her best, without which one cannot develop one's personality, which is the sum of the individual's wisdom, thought, language, behavior and so on. A self is really a self only if his/her character and personality are protected and nurtured. This applies to every individual and the acknowledgment and protection of which is the basis of Luo's idea of human rights (Luo 2022, Volume 2, p. 180). Luo therefore argues that in the pursuit of individual character and personality for all citizens, the individual has the obligation to help to create the conditions for all to have equal opportunity to pursue their respective characters and personalities, without subjecting anyone as a means but to regard all individuals as ends (ibid., p. 179).

Under this conception of individualism, Luo believes that human dignity and human rights are not derived from the state or the laws. Instead, the latter are there for the protection of human rights. If one wants to judge how good a state, a legal system, or a society is, the criterion should be found in how well-protected human rights are in that state, legal system, or society (ibid., p.7). Luo further contends that as such, the state must belong to all citizens, with its laws enacted to protect human rights and to restrain governmental powers from abuses. Sovereignty is with the people, and government is by consent, and the laws are there to reflect the public will of the citizens, failing which the citizens do not have the political obligation to obey the laws or the government. No one or organization is above the laws, and all are equal before the laws. To this end, judicial independence and citizens' democratic rights and freedoms must be guaranteed by the constitution.

This treating man as man approach of individualism has since become quite a central thesis in Chinese liberalism. While Luo was perhaps the first Chinese liberal to elaborate on this since the late 1920s (ibid., pp. 2–19), the same thesis was followed up in the post-1949 era by some leading liberal thinkers who fled with the defeated Nationalist government to Taiwan. This theme again has been picked up among mainland Chinese liberals after Mao's Great Proletariat Cultural Revolution. For example, a leading mainland liberal Liu Junning (1999, pp. 183–211) argues that every time when there has been a "discovery of man" found in the development of a civilization, it signifies the blossoming of that civilization; and in the 5,000 years of history of the Chinese civilization, there have only been two eras where we can find the "discovery of man" achieved. The first one was over 2,000 years ago in the ancient periods of Spring and Autumn and Warring States when most classical Chinese thoughts were flourished and developed; and the second was the May Fourth Movement of the twentieth century where the concept of the individual was first clearly emerged (Liu 1999, p.183).

Xiong Zijian, in what is probably the first article-length Chinese study of Hayek's thought and its relations to post-war Chinese liberalism in Taiwan (Xiong 1992), points out that, in the 1950s–1960s in Taiwan, through a study of Hayek's thesis of true and false individualisms and the moral basis of liberalism ([1948] 1980, pp. 1–32), post-war Taiwanese liberals like David Chow, Yin Hai-kuang, and Xia Daoping started to develop a conception of individualism that echoes what Hayek said in *The Road to Serfdom* ([1944] 2007) of respecting the individual man *qua* man, a conception which is not premised on an appeal to the primacy of an abstract individual or on a wholesale rejection of the traditional Chinese culture. I have elsewhere written on how Hayek's social philosophy and critique of totalitarian rule have inspired these post-war liberals in Taiwan to develop their liberalism in the Chinese context (Cheung 2014c, 2017b, and earlier chapters of this book), space here does not allow me to discuss this important topic. I can only point out in this paper that in the preface to *Hayek and His Thought* (Yin et al. ed. 1968), a book edited by Yin Hai-kuang to welcome the visit of Hayek to Taiwan in 1965, Yin referred to Hayek's talk in the National Taiwan University on October 8, 1965, in which Hayek cited Oakeshott's idea of nomocratic society as best to illustrate the political relationship of a free people consistent with his idea of true individualism. What I can manage to do here is to briefly discuss the contributions made to the thesis of treating man as man by another leading liberal Chang Fo-chuan ([1993] 2005), who worked closely with Chow, Yin, and Xia in the 1950s to continue the dialogue of Chinese liberalism in Taiwan when such a dialogue was impossible to take place in the then communist China.

In Chapter 5 of Chang's *Freedom and Human Rights*, he argues that there is a need in modern time to employ our own language to re-articulate a philosophy of man as understood by liberalism (ibid., p. 127). His main contention is that the source of human rights is human's rationality and the individual's self-consciousness, and once one is conscious of his/her own freedom in his/her self-reflective thinking, such an awareness becomes inherent in one's subjectivity, which makes one's own freedom inalienable. Denying this is in denial of the autonomous individual; while violations of an individual's freedom are possible, they are affronts to human dignity (ibid., pp. 127–129).

To Chang, human rationality and self-consciousness are historical achievements. Though it is unclear what they were like in respect of human rationality and self-consciousness before the dawn of civilizations, Chang believes that they are more than just nature-endowed gifts. The more we exercise them to better understand the world around us and ourselves, the more developed they are. When self-consciousness has been developed to such an extent that the self manages to recognize its own subjectivity and its autonomy, one's rationality will bring one to realize that the same subjectivity and autonomy are also inherent in other individuals, and this brings a mutual recognition of each and every individual's subjectivity and autonomy, and calls for the respect of the individual, and hence the idea of treating man as man by respecting the individual's moral subjectivity, the result of which is that the demand for the protection of their right to autonomy is emerged. As such, this right to autonomy is inalienable, because this is what constitutes free agency with moral autonomy.

Like Luo, Chang argues that since the recognition of the individual's inalienable human rights is derived from human rationality and self-consciousness, the state or other collectives cannot be the source of our rights and freedoms. Instead, a state should be the result of a political contract entered into by like-minded free agents with the view to protecting their inalienable human rights through a bill of rights and a constitution. Such protection should be carried out by clearly and properly enacted laws in the state. The state therefore should be an association mainly constituted by laws, and Chang calls it a "legal association" (ibid., p. 214), and the state and the laws must be limited in scope since law can only regulate the individual's external behavior.

To Chang, the inner side of individual behavior, such as his/her moral character, intention, and all that, cannot be regulated by law. This is the case not only because it is difficult for others to know for certain about the inner side of an individual's moral considerations and choices, but it is also difficult to delimit the boundaries of the laws regulating these inner side behaviors. As a result, implementation in this area is always problematic, and abuses are difficult if not impossible to avoid, threatening the protection of human rights as such. Chang therefore argues that the laws in such a liberal state should be formal (not substantive) and prohibitive in nature, they are there to restrict the government, organizations, and other individuals against interfering with citizens' human rights, leaving the individuals to explore their respective moral personalities and individual choices in transactional and practical interactions as freely as possible (ibid., pp. 189–195). Political obligations in such a state are justified only if the laws are all there for the protection of the rights enlisted in the bill of rights in accordance with the political contract formed in the beginning, and these obligations are limited because the laws are both formal and negative, and the individuals are free to engage in their own substantive actions in moral and social affairs so long as they do not infringe against other individuals' legal rights (ibid., pp. 248–249).

From Hu's efforts to release the individual from the chains of collectivist priorities, Luo's emphasis on treating the individual as an end, not as a means, whose unique character and personality constitute the individual's humanity, to Chang's mutual recognition of the free agent's moral subjectivity and inalienable human rights for individual liberty, we can perhaps detect a gradual, continuous enrichment of the theoretical understanding of Chinese liberalism since the May Fourth Movement up to the present time, and these liberals call their thesis "treating man as man." Although there is no evidence to show that any of the above-mentioned leading Chinese liberals has been directly influenced by Oakeshott, I think one can see many parallels (problems too, which will be discussed later) in this treating man as man thesis and Oakeshott's morality of individuality.

To Hu, what constitutes sound individualism are independent thinking and taking full personal responsibility for one's pursuit of one's idea, faith, and action. This individualism puts the individual as the starting point and at the center of its deliberation. I think it is reasonable to say that this is quite consistent with Oakeshott's more philosophically sophisticated formulation of the postulate of a free agent in human conduct where "the starting-place of doing is a state of reflective consciousness, namely, the agent's own understanding of the situation, what it means to him" ([1975] 1991, p. 37). And the agent "is able to imagine [the situation] different from what it is and can recognize it to be alterable by some action or utterance of his own; and when alternatives present themselves to his imagination, he must be able to choose between them and decide upon a performance" (ibid., p. 36).

To Luo, the crucial consideration in his treating man as man approach of individualism is to nurture the development of the free agent's unique character and personality, without which one cannot live like a human being. This again echoes what Oakeshott talks about the free agent's self-enacted development: "as a reflective consciousness, [the agent's] situation is necessarily his own. He is 'free' not because his situation is alterable by an act of unconstrained 'will' but because it is an understood situation and because doing is an intelligent engagement…and it cannot have been imposed upon him by an external agency. He can have come by it only by learning, he acquires only what he accepts and makes his own in an understanding" (ibid., p. 37). In this regard, the independence and uniqueness of the free agent is unreservedly put forward by Oakeshott as follows:

> The 'freedom' intrinsic to agency is…the independence enjoyed by the agent in respect of being a reflective consciousness composed of acquired feelings, emotions, sentiments, affections, understandings, beliefs, convictions, aspirations, ambitions, etc., recognitions of himself and of the world of *pragmata* he inhabits, which he has turned into wishes, and

wishes he has specified in choices of actions and utterances. (ibid., p. 40, emphasis in the original)

The free agent's reflective deliberation is therefore a learning experience, and reflective consciousness of a free agent is, as a result, a historical achievement, something that Chang will heartily accept in his philosophy of man. "In short, the starting-place of doing is the agent himself as a 'historic' self-enacted reflective consciousness" (ibid., p. 37), which is necessarily intrinsic to the free agent with his/her self-understood situation alterable only by his/her further reflective consciousness and engagement in intelligent self-enacted or self-disclosed conduct. As a historical achievement, the strengths of an agent's self-disclosed and self-enacted conduct may have different degrees of substantive "self-directedness." If a high degree of which is enjoyed or practiced, Oakeshott believes that it is then "properly called 'self-determination' or 'autonomy'." (ibid.) In this connection. Chang's thesis of mutual recognition of the subjectivity and autonomy of the individuals in his philosophy of man must assume a high degree of free agency being enjoyed and practiced, and he further argues that once such a high degree of consciousness and mutual recognition is achieved, the idea of inalienable human rights is also established, not because these rights have been all around since the beginning of time, but because such a degree of reflective consciousness cannot be aliened from the free agents concerned (Chang [1993] 2005, pp. 128–129).

The Predicament of Chinese Liberalism

While the extent of the affinity between the Chinese liberals' philosophy of man and Oakeshott's philosophical reflection on the morality of individuality may be contested, I think it is fair to say that although they are trying to learn to speak a foreign language of individualism, these leading Chinese liberals have managed to speak it with quite a high degree of accuracy and eloquence in respect of the nature of free agency. In this regard, I think one may be critical of their originality, yet one will be too harsh to say that the liberalism of these Chinese liberals is "simplistic."

Oakeshott, in my view, is more skeptical than Chinese liberals like Chang, that is why he puts less emphasis on rationality and believes that understanding and misunderstanding are both common in the free agent's reflective consciousness, the exercise of which is more like deliberation and persuasion than rational demonstration.

Oakeshott certainly agrees that freedom is intrinsic to agency, and the agent's reflective consciousness in deliberating and deciding on what imaged and wished-for results to be preferred and to be pursued in his/her self-disclosing and self-enacted conduct is both a learning experience, a historical achievement, as well as a development that discloses the character and individuality of the agent concerned. But whether this intrinsic freedom and unique character of the agent will bring about Chang's claim of mutual recognition of the inalienable human rights of the individual in a moral association is perhaps very much contextual, for "rights" and "duties" of a moral practice are, as Oakeshott says, "Its abstract nouns, when they appear, are faded metaphors, and it is only the uneducated who insist that each must have a single unequivocal meaning indifferent to context" (ibid., p. 63).

As said in the Introduction of this paper, the politics of the felt need has dominated the history of modern China since the late Qing Dynasty, that is why even those who introduced liberalism to China (like Yan Fu) put more emphasis on national salvation and liberation than individual liberty. The hierarchical and collectivist-oriented traditional culture of China is also not a favorable context for individualism. At the time of a crisis, for example on the eve of Japan's invasion of China in the 1930s, a lot of Chinese liberals even went all the way to openly support the dictatorship of the then Nationalist party-state in order to clamor for centralization of power to resist against the Japanese under the overriding purpose of national survival (Zhi ed. 2010).

Oakeshott of course always reminds us that "belligerence is alien to civil association" ([1975] 1991, p. 273). He has given examples to demonstrate this both in *On Human Conduct* (ibid.) and *Lectures in the History of Political Thought* (2006). While Chinese liberalism has been developed in the context of wars, national salvation, revolutions, party-state dictatorships, totalitarian rule, and so on, Oakeshott's philosophical reflection on the different nature of enterprise association and civil association can help us to better understand why such a context has made the introduction of the liberal way of governing to China difficult.

While the integrity of a free agent is compromised if the link between individual beliefs and social and political interaction is severed, the freedom intrinsic to agency cannot be denied so long as reflective consciousness is with the human individual. In exercising this inherent freedom in the individual when deliberating and pursuing his/her imaged and wished-for outcome in a social context, the agent is also related to other agents in certain relationships. That is, they are related either with some common purposes, or with some common rules and practices. If the acting agents agree to pursue an imaged and wished-for common goal and to the strategy to achieve that, they are related to each other in terms of a common purpose; and if there are rules to govern this common endeavor, the utility of those rules is to be decided by the extent to which they are instrumental to the realization of the common purpose. If the common purpose pursued is contingent and transitional, the relationship among the agents in this endeavor will lapse once the purpose is achieved. But if the common purpose and the strategy to achieve it require more durable and sustainable efforts from the agents concerned, then a long-standing enterprise association may be constituted for the pursuit of such an undertaking, in which organizational arrangements may be established for the efficient and effective pursuit of the purpose, with membership, offices, rules, regulations, and so on to be determined or assigned according to their respective perceived utility to the achievement of that chosen common outcome. The integrity of the agent is respected if members are allowed to leave the association once they no longer believe in or share the common purpose; otherwise, free agency is undermined.

If the acting agents in an association are each in pursuit of his/her respective imaged and wished-for outcome; or their common purpose, if any, is arrived at voluntarily by participating agents who can always leave the common undertaking once they cannot share the common purpose or the strategy to achieve it any longer, and there does not exist another overarching, common and substantive purpose for all governing the whole association, then, these agents are related in terms of a set of common rules and practices which constitute the association, but these rules and practices are only procedural considerations qualifying each of the agents' respective actions, without determining any of their respective substantive performances. These common rules and practices can be customary, conventional, transactional, moral, or legal. These rules or practices are not instrumental to the achievement of any of the agents' respective imaged and wish-for outcomes. Instead, they are procedural considerations that may disclose or enact the respective individualities of the agents and the qualities of the agents' chosen substantive performances. These rules or practices also allow the agents to identify themselves as doers and members in the same association, with related rules, procedures, and offices in the association determining the meaning of the rules concerned, revising them, and enacting new ones if and when necessary, through the relevant acknowledged authorities, and settling possible conflicts of interpretation, if any, among members of the association. In other words, this kind of association in theory is constituted wholly by a system of rules, subscription to which will only qualify, not determine, the substantive actions chosen by individual members of the association. The integrity of free agency is not compromised even if the rules are obligatory to all, since the link between individual belief and social interaction is not severed as the rules will only affect the way, not the substance, of how the chosen action of the agent is to be performed. Just like the laws on the highways do not prohibit citizens to choose their preferred destinations, but only qualify them on how to reach their respective destinations without threatening the safety of other road users and so on.

The paradox of the Chinese liberals' pursuit of governing in China in accordance with civil rules and practices is that given the politics of the felt need in modern China, and given the predominantly collectivist ethos embedded in the traditional practices of the Chinese culture, the Chinese liberals have either to undertake their civil project by means of an enterprise association approach, which, if made obligatory in order to be effective, is by nature incompatible with the nature of the civil approach; otherwise, they risk their voices not being heard since they are regarded as quite irrelevant to the urgent issues of national salvation facing the nation. When Sun Yat-sen, the founding father of the

Republic of China, met the father of Chinese liberalism Yan Fu in England in 1905 before the collapse of the Qing Dynasty, the latter advised the former to concentrate on initiating their countrymen to Western liberal values by education when modernizing China. Yet Sun's alleged reply "How long can a man wait for the river to clear?" graphically symbolized the ethos of the politics of the felt need as he was determined to seek a short cut by advocating violent revolutions to help to introduce republicanism to China (Schwartz 1964, pp. 146–147). Sun later became the first revolutionary leader who opted for the Leninist party-state approach and cooperated with the Chinese Communist Party to fight against the warlords who dominated China in the 1920s, hoping that in doing so, his Chinese Nationalist Party could unify China, after which his ideals of citizens' rights and constitutionalism might eventually be realized in the motherland. Unfortunately, this turns out not to be the case, and radical revolutionism and party-state dictatorships, not liberalism, have become the dominant trends in modern Chinese politics since then.

Furthermore, this predicament of the Chinese liberals is not helped by the theoretical difficulty of understanding the nature of civil association, how such an association is constituted solely by the recognition of rules as rules (Oakeshott [1975] 1991, p. 148), with the set of rules in the association to form a system of rules (the rule of laws), which constitutes a practice of being "just" to each other in the interaction among the associates. In such an association, the most articulated and obligatory rules are called laws (ibid., pp. 128–129), the authority of which is derived from the procedural rules themselves, not from the approval or disapproval of the members' concerned, even though whether these laws are desirable or not can be deliberated upon, and changes to the laws can be made, but only if they are carried out in accordance with the authoritative framework constituting the association (ibid., pp. 149–177).

As Oakeshott says, "The most difficult feature of the civil condition to identify and get into place has been law" (ibid., p. 181). Like a common tongue and a moral practice, the rule of law in civil association is a "language of intercourse" (ibid., p. 182). As a language of intercourse, the system of civil rules cannot be abstractly pre-designed from scratch. It certainly is a human artifact, acquired through learning from the native language context, enriched and improved through continuous use of this language on every occasion by the associates in all civil intercourses. Individual associate in civil association is solely related to each other in terms of these civil rules, since they are not related by a common, substantive purpose or on any other terms. They may speak the language well and ill. When they speak, they must speak something. That "something" is their substantive performances or chosen actions for the pursuit of their respective imagined, wished-for outcomes. How they speak it, whether dutifully, eloquently, callously, absent-mindedly, rightfully, wrong-headedly, and so on, depends on how they use the language as general considerations relating to their own, self-understood, contingent situations. Adequate subscription to the civil rules is important, since these rules are the only terms that constitute the associates' civil relationships. Suspension of or inadequate subscription to these rules may mean the lapse of civil relationships among the associates, which, in effect, can lead to dissolution of the association. The viability and continuity of civil association, therefore, depend on the continuous, adequate subscription of the associates to the civil rules, and there are offices, rules, and procedures to determine the rules' authority, jurisdiction, as well as authoritative resolution of differences in case there are conflicting interpretations of the rules in dispute. The authority of the rules and the obligation to follow the rules by the associates are, therefore, not dependent on the approval or disapproval of the rules by the associates concerned, but on the authoritative procedures as ascertained by the rule-governed relevant authorities that constituting the terms of association in civil intercourse. The desirability of specific civil rules can be deliberated, and changes can be made if necessary; but this is to be done in accordance with the prescribed, authoritative procedures provided for in the association. Otherwise, disapproval at the most fundamental level can risk dissolution of civil association. Subscription to the civil rules does not sever the link between individual beliefs and social and political interaction, since the rules concerned are non-instrumental to any of the imagined and wished-for outcomes in the substantive performances of the associates, even though they qualify how the associates go about their civil business.

The Prospects of Speaking a Civil Tongue in the Chinese Context

In some respects, Chang Fo-chuan's liberal philosophy of man is perhaps the closest to Oakeshott's philosophical understanding of civil association when compared with other leading Chinese liberals. For example, when characterizing the nature of a modern liberal state, Chang calls it a "legal association" ([1993] 2005, p. 214). To Chang, a liberal state is there to enact and to implement laws for the protection of human rights and for restraining governmental powers from abuses. Citizens are obliged to obey these laws not because they are legitimated by the state or government, but because they have given their consent to the laws since they are there to protect the rights of the citizens. These laws are therefore formal, negative, and prohibitive in nature. And the laws only govern the external behavior of the citizens concerned, leaving the inner side of their behavior free to express their respective self-enacting characters and individualities in the pursuit of their imagined and wished-for outcomes in society.

While Chang's understanding of a liberal state as a legal association in which the laws are mainly formal, negative, and prohibitive in nature appears to be quite compatible with Oakeshott's understanding of civil association as constituted solely by a system of non-instrumental, civil rules which qualify but do not determine the substantive performances chosen by individual associates, what is more problematic is Chang's characterization of the laws as instruments for the protection of human rights, with the obligation to obey these laws subject to the approval and consent of the people under a political contract agreed in their efforts in establishing the state.

As a language of civil discourse of civil discourse, the rule of law in a liberal state is more than its general principles, though general principles such as right and wrong, propriety and impropriety, duty and obligation, fairness and justice, and so on can be abstracted from the practice of such a discourse. But the specific meanings of these principles are very much dependent upon their context, from which they are abstracted. In other words, if these abstract principles are to be concretely meaningful, they will have to reflect the prevailing winds of the moral and political sentiments found in the context from which they come. Relying mainly on "abstract nouns" (Oakeshott [1975] 1991, p. 63) and general principles to conduct civil discourse is a poor way to enrich the civil language, since the more profound meanings of these nouns and principles have yet to be ascertained.

To be fair to the Chinese liberals, their insistence on the importance of the protection of human rights in China is a response to the authoritarian and totalitarian rule of the party-states, firstly under the Chinese Nationalist Party since 1928, and, secondly, under the Chinese Communist Party since 1949. Chang in his *Freedom and Human Rights* persuasively argues that only the individuals should be rights-bearers, not collectives like the state or other organizations ([1993] 2005, pp. 146–150). Given the widespread sufferings borne by the Chinese people under authoritarian and totalitarian rule in modern China, it is likely the case that one prevailing wind in Chinese politics is to protect the individual from the overwhelming, almost unchecked power wielded by the state. Hence, Chang has come to identify that the laws enacted by the state must be formal, negative, and prohibitive in nature, they are there mainly to restrain government from abusing its powers. But given the context of the politics of the felt need, national salvation, and revival, as well as the collectivist orientation of the political culture of traditional China, it is far from certain that there are no competitive meanings as to what human rights shall mean in China, since the rights to survival, to economic growth, to nation building, and so on are all likely candidates as "prevailing winds" in this regard.

As regards Chang's argument that people are obliged to obey the laws only if they have given their consent or approval to them, this is shared by other Chinese liberals who also adopt the treating man as man thesis. For example, Luo Longi argues that citizens do not have the obligation to obey the laws if they do not reflect the public will of the people (see Cheung 04.12.2022). Liu Junning even goes so far as to say that a liberal state is legitimate only if the individuals have voluntarily given their consent to its political structure and to its way of organizing political life in the state (Liu 1999, p. 202). This is contrary to Oakeshott's procedural approach for civil authority where the validity of the laws is not dependent on the approval or disapproval of the associates, but on the system of laws' self-contained assertion of jurisdictional authority. Oakeshott's argument is that since the associates of civil association are only related to each other in terms of the civil rules of the association, the desirability of specific civil rules can be deliberated and changes to the rules can be made only when the overall authority of the system remains intact; otherwise, it is potentially an act of dissociation. If the authority of the civil rules is denied, there is nothing to relate the associates. The Chinese liberals' approval thesis in this regard is to put political contentions above associational authority, this may well encourage political polarization and secession politics, and political crises such as these are never a friend of civil association.

If the Chinese liberals want to speak the civil tongue more skillfully and more eloquently, then, they should try their best to avoid adopting the enterprise association approach to conduct their civil business as far as possible. Likewise, relying mainly on abstract nouns and principles to engage in a civil dialogue can seldom improve the quality of the conversation, for abstractions can only very superficially reflect the prevailing winds in a civil association, yet these prevailing winds are essential in giving concrete meanings to those nouns and principles. Furthermore, contentious politics can be accommodated if the authority of the civil rules is acknowledged. But if political contentions are to deny the authority of the terms of association of the civil state, then it becomes a matter of dissociation, not the continuation of a civil conversation.

If the above observations are not far off the mark, how useful are they for the future development of Chinese liberalism? I do not think that they are directly useful in helping Chinese liberalism to further develop, but they may help to inform the Chinese liberals how not to conduct civil conversation, and to detect what dangers they should be aware of when using the language of civil intercourse.

The only way to make oneself to be more conversant in using a language is to keep on practicing it, and to learn from good examples and literature, and to engage in dialogue with the native speakers as much as one can. The Chinese liberals are learning to speak a largely foreign language when they are introducing liberal values to the Chinese context.

Speaking a foreign language is already a challenge. Translating it under the urgency of the politics of the felt need to make it sound native is even more difficult. It is therefore not surprising to find that the success of the Chinese liberals is limited. But if they are convinced of the merits of speaking this language, to keep on practicing it may ultimately be the only way forward.

Of late, some leading Chinese liberals are trying to learn from Western as well as Chinese resources to further explore their civil conversation. Mainland legal and political thinker Gao Quanxi has adopted a two-pronged approach in further developing Chinese liberal thought (2016, 2022 2 Volumes). On the one hand, he believes that a more in-depth understanding of the transition from the pre-modern to the modern world in the West may help the Chinese liberals to understand first-hand how emergence of some civil associations in the West were achieved. Gao is particularly interested to learn from England's Glorious Revolution and the United States's federalist enactment of the constitution after the War of Independence. Learning from these cases may shed insights on how transitions from revolutions to civil nation building were made possible. And if Oakeshott is right to say that the civil aspect and the enterprise aspect of a modern state are "sweet enemies," and it is unrealistic to always trump theory against practice in politics, then the lessons learned from these Western political experiences may alert us more about the ways peaceful co-existence were achieved rather than how purity of theory is to be pursued no matter what in the practical political world.

In addition to the above, Gao at the same time believes that since China has tried hard to modernize and to learn from Western liberal experiences since the Sino-British Opium War of 1839–1842, she has over the years already accumulated quite a complex layer of practices in attempting to develop constitutional government in China. For example, the aborted attempts to introduce constitutional monarchy in the late 19th and early twentieth centuries before the collapse of the Qing Dynasty; the attempts to enact a constitution for republican China during the Warlords Era (1912–1928) of the Republic of China; the Nationalist government's ambivalent efforts in practicing guided constitutional government and constitutional government on the mainland (1928–1949) and in Taiwan (1949 to 1996 and beyond, which have eventually helped to provide a governing framework to bring democracy to Taiwan); and, the mainland's limited constitutional reforms since 1982 after Mao's Great Proletariat Cultural Revolution.

While most of these experiences are failed or incomplete attempts to turn China liberal and democratic, there are nevertheless important lessons to be learned that may benefit the future development of liberalism in China. One may also add that the "one country, two systems" practice in Hong Kong, where the rule of law has been prevalent as an important legacy from British rule during the colonial period (1842–1997) may also be a good case to study in order to learn how a predominantly Chinese society can make the common law an entrenched tradition in its governing activity. It must, however, be pointed out that since the governing authorities decided to crush the 2019 somewhat violent massive rallies for democracy and self-determination/independence in Hong Kong, the prospects for a liberal Hong Kong are problematic (Cheung 2022). Nevertheless, I still believe that there are useful lessons to be learned in this case for the development of Chinese liberalism in the Chinese context.

Will the above efforts improve the prospects of speaking a civil tongue in China? I am not sure. Predictions in human affairs are always hazardous. Perhaps only time will tell.

References

Arendt, Hannah. 1973. *The Origins of Totalitarianism*. San Diego: A Harvest/HB Book.

Baron, Marcia W., Philip Pettit, and Michael Slote. 1997. *Three Methods of Ethics*. Oxford: Blackwell Publishers.

Bottelier, Pieter. 2018. *Economic Policy Making in China (1949–2016): The Role of Economists*. Milton: Routledge.

De Bary, Wm. Theodore. 1983. *The Liberal Tradition in China*. Hong Kong: The Chinese University of Hong Kong Press.

Caldwell, Bruce. 2004. *Hayek's Challenge: An Intellectual Biography of F. A. Hayek*. Chicago: The University of Chicago Press.

Chang, Carson (張君勱), et. al. 2008. *Science and Life View* (《科學與人生觀》). Hefei: Huang Shan Bookshop.

Chang, Fo-chuan (張佛泉). [1993] 2005. *Freedom and Human Right* (《自由與人權》), revised ed. Taipei: Commercial Press Tai Wan.

Hao, Chang. 1971. *Liang Chi-chao and Intellectual Transition in China: 1890–1907*. Cambridge, MA and London: Harvard University Press.

Chang, Hao (張灝). 1989. *Dark Consciousness and Democratic Tradition* (《幽暗意識與民主傳統》). Taipei: Linking Publishing.

C. Cheung, *Hayek and Post-War Chinese Liberalism*, Palgrave Studies in Classical Liberalism, https://doi.org/10.1007/978-3-031-64888-5

Chang, Hao. 1990. Some Reflections on the Problems of the Axial-Age Breakthrough in Relation to Classical Confucianism. In *Ideas Across Cultures: Essays on Chinese Thought in Honor of Benjamin I. Schwartz*, ed. Paul A. Cohen and Merle Goldman, 17–31. Cambridge, MA and London: Council on East Asian Studies, Harvard University.

Chen, Alber H. Y. 2022. Constitution and Constitutionalism: China. In *Constitutionalism in Context*, ed. David S. Law. Cambridge: Cambridge University Press. (The copy I refer to here is from the original manuscript written by the author rather than from the book.)

Chen, Guying (陳鼓應), ed. 2020. *Silk Spinning by a Spring Silkworm: The Last Words of Yin Haiguang* (《春蠶吐絲:殷海光最後的話語》). New Taipei City: Commercial Press Tai Wan.

Chen, Xujing (陳序經). 1976. *The Chinese and Western Cultural Perspectives* (《中西文化觀》). Taipei: Cowboy Publishing.

Cheng, Yinghong. 2008. Liberalism in Contemporary China: Ten Years After Its 'Resurface.' *Journal of Contemporary China* 17 (55): 383–400.

Cheung, Chor-yung. 2007. *The Quest for Civil Order: Politics, Rules and Individuality*. Exeter: Imprint Academic.

———. 2011. Beyond Complexity: Can *The Sensory Order* Defend the Liberal Self? In *Hayek in Mind: Hayek's Philosophical Psychology*, ed. Leslie Marsh, 219–239. *Advances in Austrian Economics*, 15.

———. 2014a. Hayek on Nomocracy and Teleocracy: A Critical Assessment. *Cosmos + Taxis* 1 (2): 24–33.

———. 2014b. The Critique of Rationalism and the Defense of Individuality: Oakeshott and Hayek. *Comos + Taxis* 1 (3): 3–9.

Cheung, Chor-yung (張楚勇). 2014c. Hayek and Chinese Liberalism: Problems and Prospects (〈海耶克與中國自由主義:問題與前景〉). In *Proceedings of the Conference on Civic Consciousness and Constitutional Democracy* (《公民意識與憲政民主學術研討會》). Taipei: Academia Sinica.

———. 2017a. Treating Man as Man and the Use of Knowledge in Society: The Liberalism of Xia Daoping (〈把人當人與散在社會的知識之利用〉). *Journal of Hubei University of Economics* 15 (5): 120–128.

Cheung, Chor-yung. 2017b. Oakeshott, Hayek and the Conservative Turn of Chinese Liberalism. In *The Place of Michael Oakeshott in Contemporary Western and Non-Western Thought*, ed. Noel K. O'Sullivan, 160–180. Exeter: Imprint Academic.

——— (張楚勇). 2018. *Friedrich Hayek* (《弗雷德希•海耶克》). Taipei: Linking Publishing.

Cheung, Chor-yung. 2020. "China's Hayek" and the Horrors of Totalitarianism: The Liberal Lessons in Gu Zhun's Thought. In *Reclaiming Liberalism*, ed. David F. Hardwick and Leslie Marsh, 281–311. New York: Palgrave Macmillan.

——— (張楚勇). 2022.12.04. A Treating Man as Man Theory of Human Rights and Constitutionalism: Reading *the Collected Works of Luo Longji* (〈把人當人的人權憲政觀:讀《羅隆基文集》〉). *Ming Pao Daily* (《明報》). Hong Kong.

Cheung, Chor-yung. 2022. Free Speech in the Shadow of a Party-State: Hong Kong and Its Public Service Broadcaster. In *International Comparative Approaches in Free Speech and Open Inquiry*, ed. L.C. Sheahan, 141–167. New York: Palgrave Macmillan.

Ching, Julia. 1997. *Mysticism and Kingship in China: The Heart of Chinese Wisdom*. Cambridge: Cambridge University Press.

Chow, David (周德偉). 1975. *Analyzing the Theory of a Great Thinker of Our Time: F. A. Hayek* (《當代大思想家海耶克學說綜述》). Taipei: Cheng Chung Book Store.

———. 2004. *The Philosophy of Freedom and Chinese Confucian Thought* (《自由哲學與中國聖學》). Beijing: China Social Sciences Press.

———. 2011. *Autobiography* (《落筆驚風雨：我的一生與國黨的點滴》). Taipei: Yuan-Liou Publishing Company.

Chow, David (周德偉) trans. 1973. *The Constitution of Liberty* (《自由的憲章》). Taipei: Economic Office of Bank of Taiwan.

Chow, Tse-tsung. 1960. *The May Fourth Movement: Intellectual Revolution in Modern China*. Cambridge, MA: Harvard University Press.

Chow, William C. L. 1995. The Development of Individualism in Modern China. *Chinese Studies* (《漢學研究》) 13 (2): 77–98.

Coats, Jr., Wendell John and Chor-yung Cheung. 2012. *The Poetic Character of Human Activity: Collected Essays on the Thought of Michael Oakeshott*. Lanham, Boulder, New York, Toronto, Plymouth, UK: Lexington Books.

Cristi, Renato. 1998. *Carl Schmitt and Authoritarian Liberalism*. Cardiff: University of Wales Press.

Deng, Zhenglai (鄧正來). 2004. *Rules, Order, Ignorance: Studies on Hayek's Liberalism* (《規則•秩序•無知:關於哈耶自由主義的研究》). Beijing: Joint Publishing.

The *Economist*. 2023. Xi Jinping's Views of Confucius and Marx, November 4–10, 54–55.

The *Economist*. 2023. China's Party-State Capitalism, December 2–08, 65–66.

Ferguson, Adam. 1995. *An Essay on the History of Civil Society*, ed. Fania Oz-Salzberger. Cambridge: Cambridge University Press.

Fu, Sinian (傅斯年). 1945. Roosevelt and New Liberalism (〈羅斯福與新自由主義〉). In *What Is Liberalism* (《什麼是自由主義》), ed. Zhang Zhongdong (張忠棟) et al., 1999, 105–110. Taipei: Tonsan Bookstore.

Fung, Edmund S.K. 2008/2009. Were Chinese Liberals Liberal? Reflections on the Understanding of Liberalism in Modern China. *Pacific Affairs* 81 (4): 557–576.

———. 2010. *The Intellectual Foundations of Chinese Modernity: Cultural and Political Thought in the Republican Era*. Cambridge: Cambridge University Press.

Gamble, Andrew. 1996. *Hayek: The Iron Cage of Liberty*. Cambridge: Polity Press.

Gao, Quanxi (高全喜). 2003. *Legal Order and Liberal Justice: Hayek's Legal and Constitutional Thought* (《法律秩序與自由正義: 哈耶克的法律與憲政思想》). Beijing: Peking University Press.

———. 2016. *Political Constitution and the Future of the Constitutional System* (《政治憲法與未來憲制》). Hong Kong: City University of Hong Kong Press.

———. 2017. *Liberal Politics and Republican Regime* (《自由政治與共和政體》). Hong Kong: City University of Hong Kong Press.

———. 2022. *The History of Constitutional System in China*. 2 vols. (《中國憲制史》). Hong Kong: City University of Hong Kong Press.

Gaus, Gerald F. 2006. Hayek on the Evolution of Society and Mind. In *The Cambridge Companion of Hayek*, ed. Edward Feser, 232–258. Cambridge: Cambridge University Press.

Gellner, Ernest. 1994. *Conditions of Liberty: Civil Society and Its Rivals*. London: Penguin Books.

Gray, John. 1998. *Hayek on Liberty*, 3rd ed. London and New York: Routledge.

Gu, Zhun (顧準). 1997. *Gu Zhun Diaries* (《顧準日記》). Beijing: Economic Daily Press.

———. 2002a. *Gu Zhun: A Self Report* (《顧準自述》). Beijing: China Youth Publishing House.

———. 2002b. *Gu Zhun's Papers* (《顧準文稿》). Beijing: China Youth Publishing House.

———. 2002c. *Gu Zhun's Reading Notes* (《顧準筆記》. Beijing: China Youth Publishing House.

———. 2002d. *Gu Zhun Diaries* (《顧準日記》. Beijing: China Youth Publishing House.

———. 2013. *From Idealism to Empiricism* (《從理想主義到經濟主義》. Beijing: Guangming Daily Press.
Guo, Ping (郭萍). 2017. *A Pioneer of Liberal Confucianism: A Study of Zhang Junmai's Liberal Idea* (《自由儒學的先聲: 張君勱自由觀研究》). Jinan: Qilu Books.
Han, Shu (韓戍). 2015. *The Biography of Chu Anping* (《儲安平傳》). Hong Kong: Oxford University Press.
Hayek, F.A. [1944] 2007. *The Road to Serfdom: Text and Documents*, ed. Bruce Caldwell. Chicago: The University of Chicago Press.
———. [1948] 1980. *Individualism and Economic Order*. Chicago and London: The University of Chicago Press.
———. [1952] 1976. *The Sensory Order: An Inquiry into the Foundations of Theoretical Psychology*. Chicago: The University of Chicago Press, Midway reprint.
———. [1952] 1979. *The Counter-Revolution of Science: Studies on the Abuse of Reason*. Indianapolis: Liberty Press.
———. 1960. *The Constitution of Liberty*. Chicago: The University of Chicago Press.
———. 1967. *Studies in Philosophy, Politics and Economics*. London: Routledge & Kegan Paul.
———. 1973. *Law, Legislation and Liberty: Volume 1: Rules and Order*. London: Routledge & Kegan.
———. 1976. *Law, Legislation and Liberty: Volume 2: the Mirage of Social Justice*. London & Henley, Routledge & Kegan Paul.
———. [1978] 1990. *New Studies in Philosophy, Politics, Economics and the History of Ideas*. London: Routledge.
———. 1979. *Law, Legislation and Liberty: Volume 3: A New Statement of the Liberal Principles of Justice and Political Economy*. Chicago: The University of Chicago Press.
———. 1988. *The Fatal Conceit: The Errors of Socialism*, ed. W. W. Bartley III. London: Routledge.
———. 1994. *Socialism and War: Essays, Documents, Reviews*, ed. Bruce Caldwell. London: Routledge.
Horwitz, Steven. 2001. From Smith to Menger to Hayek: Liberalism in the Spontaneous-Order Tradition. *The Independent Review* 1: 81–97.
Hu, Shih (胡適).1918. Ibsenism. (〈易卜生主義〉). In *Tolerance and Freedom* (《容忍與自由》), ed. Kwang-Che Pan (潘光哲/ Pan Guangzhe), 2019, 196–221. New Taipei City: Commercial Press Tai Wan.

———. 1926. Our Attitude Towards Modern Western Civilization (〈我們對於西洋近代文明的態度〉). In *Tolerance and Freedom* (《容忍與自由》), ed. Kwang-Che Pan (潘光哲/Pan Guangzhe), 2019, 70–91, New Taipei City: Commercial Press Tai Wan.

Hu, Shih. 1928. The Civilizations of the East and the West. In *Whither Mankind: A Panorama of Modern Civilization*, ed. Charles A. Beard, 25–41. New York, London, Toronto: Longmans, Green and Co.

——— (胡適). 1929. When Can We have the Constitution? (〈我們甚麼時候才可有憲法?〉). In *The Tradition of Peking University and Modern China: Pioneering Voices of Liberalism* (《北大傳統與近代中國:自由主義的先聲》), 1998, ed. Liu Junning (劉軍寧), 176–181. Beijing: China Human Resources Publishing.

———. 1935. Individual Freedom and Social Progress: May Fourth Movement Revisited (〈個人自由與社會進步--再談「五四」運動〉), ed. Pang Kuang-che (潘光哲/Pan Guangzhe), 2019, 240–252. New Taipei City: Commercial Press Tai Wan.

———. 1948. We Must Choose Our Direction (〈我們必須選擇我們的方向〉). In *Tolerance and Freedom* (《容忍與自由》), ed. Pang Kuang-che (潘光哲/Pan Guangzhe), 2019, 164–172. New Taipei City: Commercial Press Tai Wan.

Huang, Max Ko-wu. 2008. *The Meaning of Freedom: Yan Fu and the Origins of Chinese Liberalism*. Hong Kong: Chinese University of Hong Kong Press.

Hutton, Graham. 1961. The Individual and Society. In *Agenda for A Free Society: Essays on Hayek's The Constitution of Liberty*, ed. Arthur Seldon, 17–29. London: Hutchinson.

Jiang, Juntian (蔣勻田). The Road of Anti-serfdom (〈反奴役之路〉). In *Hayek and His Thought* (《海耶克和他的思想》, Yin Hai-kung (殷海光) et al., 1968, 157–170. Hong Kong: Culture Book House.

Kateb, George. 2011. *Human Dignity*. Cambridge, MA and London, UK: The Belknap Press of Harvard University Press.

Legge, James trans. *The Four Books: Confucian Analects, The Great Learning, The Doctrine of the Mean and The Works of Mencius*.

Leighton, Christopher R. 2014. Venture Communist: Gu Zhun in Shanghai, 1949–1952. In *The Capitalist Dilemma in China's Communist Revolution*, ed. Sherman Cochran, 119–147. Ithaca, New York: Cornell East Asia Program.

Li, Weisen, Xingyuan Feng, and Liang Sun. 2017. The Diffusion of F. A. Hayek's Thoughts in Mainland China and Taiwan. In *The Diffusion of Western Economic Ideas in East Asia*, ed. Malcolm Warner, 213–234. London and New York: Routledge.

Li, Xiao-bo (李曉波). 2017. The Evolution and Causes of Xia Daoping's Economic Thought (〈夏道平的經濟思路的演進及其原因〉). *Journal of Hubei University of Economics* (《湖北經濟學院學報》) 15 (15): 108–119.

Li, Zehou (李澤厚). 1987. *On the History of Modern Chinese Thought* (《中國現代思想史論》). Beijing: Dongfan Publishing.

Liang Qichao (梁啓超). 1903. On Public Virtue (〈論公德〉). In *The Tradition of Peking University and Modern China: Pioneering Voices of Liberalism* (《北大傳統與近代中國:自由主義的先聲》), 1998, ed. Liu Junning (劉軍寧), 470–474. Beijing: China Human Resources Publishing.

———. 1904. On Private Virtue (〈論私德〉). In *The Tradition of Peking University and Modern China: Pioneering Voices of Liberalism* (《北大傳統與近代中國:自由主義的先聲》), 1998, ed. Liu Junning (劉軍寧), 475–498. Beijing: China Human Resources Publishing.

———. 1998. The Ability to Organize and the Rule of Law (〈組織能力與法治〉). In *The Tradition of Peking University and Modern China: Pioneering Voices of Liberalism* (《北大傳統與近代中國:自由主義的先聲》), ed. Liu Junning (劉軍寧), 167–168. Beijing: China Human Resources Publishing.

Lin, Jianguang (林建剛). 2013. From Laski to Hayek: Western Scholarship in Hu Shih's Changing Thought (〈從拉斯基到哈耶克〉). *Theoretical Perspective* (《理論視野》) Oct.: 61–63.

Lin, Jianhua (林建華). 2012. *Chinese Liberal Thought in the 1940s* (《1940年代的中國自由主義思潮》). Beijing: China Social Sciences Press.

Lin, Justin Yifu, and Dennis Tao Yang. Food Availability, Entitlements and the Chinese Famine of 1959–1961. *The Economic Journal* 2000, 110 (Jan): 136–158.

Lin Yu-sheng. 1973. Radical Iconoclasm in the May Fourth Period and the Future of Chinese Liberalism. In *Reflections on the May Fourth Movement: A Symposium*, ed. Benjamin Schwartz, 23–58. Cambridge, MA: Harvard University Press.

———.1979. *The Crisis of Chinese Consciousness: Radical Antitraditionalism in the May Fourth Era*. Madison: The University of Wisconsin Press.

——— (林毓生). 1988. *The Creative Transformation of Chinese Tradition* (《中國傳統的創造性轉化》). Hong Kong: Joint Publishing.

———. 1989. *Political Order and Pluralist Society* (《政治秩序與多元社會》). Taipie: Linking Publishing.

———. 2019. *The Origins of China's Trend of Radical Thinking and its Consequences*. (《中國激進思潮的起源與後果》). Taipei: Linking Publishing.

———. 2020. *The Spirit of Modern Intellectual Aristocracy: Selected Recent Works of Lin Yu-sheng* (《現代知識貴族的精神:林毓生思想近作選》, ed.

Josephine Chiu-Duke (丘慧芬). Hong Kong: The Chinese University of Hong Kong Press.

Liu, Guisheng, Lin Qan, and Wang Xianming (劉桂生、林啓彦、王憲明), eds. 1999. *The Thought of Yan Fu Revisited* (嚴復思想新論). Beijing: Tsinghua University Press.

Liu, Junning (劉軍寧). 1996. Back to the Individual: Reiterating Individualism (〈回歸個人:重申個人主義〉). In *The May Fourth Movement Revisited* 《五四新論》, Yu Ying-shih et al. (余英時等著), 183–211. Taipei: Linking Publishing.

———. 1998. *The Republic, Democracy, Constitutionalism: A Study of Liberal Thought* (《共和•民主•憲政—自由主義思想研究》). Shanghai: Joint Publishing Shanghai.

Liu, Juning. 2000. Classical Liberalism Catches on in China. *Journal of Democracy* 11 (3): 48–57.

——— (劉軍寧). 2014. *Conservatism* (《保守主義》), 3rd ed. Beijing: Oriental Publishing.

Liu Zehua (劉澤華). 2006. *On the Idea of the Authority of Kingship* (《王權思想論》). Tianjin: Tianjin People's Publishing.

Lubot, Eugene. 1982. *Liberalism in an Illiberal Age: New Culture Liberals in Republican China, 1919–1937*. Westport, CT: Greenwood Press.

Luo Longji (羅隆基). 1931. What Is the Rule of Law (〈甚麼是法治〉). In *The Tradition of Peking University and Modern China: Pioneering Voices of Liberalism* (《北大傳統與近代中國:自由主義的先聲》), ed. Liu Junning (劉軍寧), 1998, 201–214. Beijing: China Human Resources Publishing.

———. 2022. *The Collected Works of Luo Longji, 4 Volumes* (《羅隆基文集》, 4卷), ed. Lui Zhiqiang (劉志強). Hong Kong: City University of Hong Kong Press.

Luo, Yinsheng, ed. (羅銀勝編). 2017. *Remembering Gu Zhun* (《顧準追思錄》). Beijing: Central Compilation &Translation Press.

Ma, Tao (馬濤). 2010. China's Hayek: Comparing Gu Zhun's Thought on Market Economy (〈中國的哈耶克:顧準的市場經濟思想與比較〉). In *Remembering Gu Zhun* (《顧準追思錄》), ed. Luo Yinsheng (羅銀勝), 2017, 328–348. Beijing: Central Compilation &Translation Press.

Mao, Tse-tung. 1965. *Selected Works of Mao Tse-tung*, vol. II. Peking: Foreign Languages Press.

Mises, Ludwig von. [1949] 1966. *Human Action: A Treatise on Economics*, 3rd rev ed. Chicago: Contemporary Books.

———. 1981. *Socialism: An Economic and Sociological Analysis*. Indianapolis: Liberty Classics.

Murray, Gilbert. 1938. *Liberality and Civilization.* London: George Allen & Unwin.

Nardin, Terry, ed. 2015. *Michael Oakeshott's Cold War Liberalism.* New York: Palgrave Macmillan.

Nie, Xin (聶鑫). 2017. *A Study of Republic of China's Nanking Constitution* (《中華民國南京憲法研究》). Hong Kong: City University of Hong Kong Press.

Oakeshott, Michael. [1975] 1991. *On Human Conduct*. Oxford: Clarendon Press.

———. 1991. *Rationalism in Politics and Other Essays*, new and expanded ed. Indianapolis: Liberty Press.

———. 1996. *The Politics of Faith & the Politics of Scepticism*, ed. Timothy Fuller. New Haven and London: Yale University Press.

———. 2006. *Lectures in the History of Political Thought*, ed. Terry Nardin and Luke O'Sullivan. Exert: Imprint Academic.

Polanyi, Michael. 1962. *Personal Knowledge*. London and Henley: Routledge & Kegan Paul.

Price, Don C. 1990. Constitutional Alternatives and Democracy in Revolution of 1911. In *Ideas Across Cultures: Essays on Chinese Thought in Honor of Benjamin I. Schwartz*, ed. Paul A. Cohen and Merle Goldman, 223–260. Cambridge, MA and London: Council on East Asian Studies, Harvard University.

Pye, Lucian W. 1985. *Asian Power and Politics: The Cultural Dimensions of Authority*. Cambridge, MA and London: The Belknap Press of Harvard University Press.

Qian liqun (錢理群). 2017. *Vicissitudes of Time* (《歲月滄桑》). Hong Kong: City University of Hong Kong Press.

Qiu, Feng (秋風). 2014. *Civilization Embedded: Reflections on Chinese Liberalism* (《嵌入文明:中國自由主義的反思》). Jiangsu: Jiangsu Literary Publishing.

Qiu, Weijun (丘為君). 2019. *Enlightenment, Rationality and Modernity: The Enlightenment Movement of Modern China: 1895–1925* (《啓蒙、理性與現代性:近代中國啓蒙運動:1985-1925》). Taipei: National Taiwan University Press.

Ren, Jiantao (任劍濤). 2004. *Liberalism in the Context of Modern Chinese Thought* (《中國現代思想脈絡中的自由主義》). Beijing: Peking University Press.

Ryle, Gilbert. 1963. *The Concept of Mind*. London, UK: Penguin Books.

Schmitt, Carl. 1996. *The Concept of the Political*, trans. with an intro. by George Schwab. Chicago and London: The University of Chicago Press.

Schwarcz, Vera. 1986. *The Chinese Enlightenment: Intellectuals and the Legacy of the May Fourth Movement of 1919*. Berkeley, Los Angeles, London: University of California Press.

Schwartz, Benjamin. 1964. *In Search of Wealth and Power: Yen Fu and the West*. Cambridge, MA: Harvard University Press.

Scruton, Roger. 2006. Hayek and Conservatism. In *The Cambridge Companion to Hayek*, ed. Edward Feser, 208–231. Cambridge: Cambridge University Press.

Sen, Amartya. 1981. Ingredients of Famine Analysis: Availability and Entitlements. *The Quarterly Journal of Economics* August: 433–464.

———. 1999. *Development as Freedom*. Oxford: Oxford University Press.

Shils, Edward. 1996. Reflections on Civil Society and Civility in the Chinese Intellectual Tradition. In *Confucian Traditions in East Asian Modernity: Moral Education and Economic Culture in Japan and the Four Mini-Dragons*, ed. To Wen-ming, 38–71. Cambridge, MA: Harvard University Press.

———. 1997. *The Virtue of Civility: Selected Essays on Liberalism, Tradition, and Civil Society*, ed. Steven Grosby. Indiana: Liberty Fund.

Stephens, Bret. 2013. Reading Hayek in Beijing. *The Wall Street Journal*, May 24, at http://www.wsj.com/articles/SB10001424127887324659404578501492191072734.

Sun Wen (Sun Yat-sen 孫逸仙). 1985. *The Three People's Principles* (《三民主義》). Tai Pei: A Million Copies of the Three People's Principles Publishing Committee.

Sun Yat-sen (孫逸仙) 1924. The Principle of the Rights of the People (〈民權主義〉). In *Selected Works of Sun Yat-sen, Vol. 2* (《孫中山選集》下册), [1956] 1974, 661–764. Hong Kong: Chung Hwa Publishing (Hong Kong).

Sun, Yefang (孫冶方). 1979. *Some Theoretical Questions on Socialist Economics* (《社會主義經濟的若干理論問題》). Beijing: People's Press.

Teng, Weizao, and Zhu Zongfeng (滕維藻、朱宗風) trans. [1944] 1962. *The Road to Serfdom* (《通向奴役的道路》). Beijing: Commercial Press.

Tsang, Steve, and Olivia Cheung. 2024. *The Political Thought of Xi Jinping*. Oxford: Oxford University Press.

Wang, Yuan-yi (王遠義). 2012. The Debate on "Problems and Isms": A New Interpretation (惑在哪裡---新解胡適與李大釗「問題與主義」的論辯及其歷史意義). *Historical Inquiry* 《臺大歷史學報》9) 50: 155–250.

Watkins, Frederick. 1957. *The Political Tradition of the West: A Study in the Development of Modern Liberalism*. Cambridge, MA: Harvard University Press.

Wu, Hui-Lin (吳惠林). 2015. *Hayek* (《海耶克》). Taipei: Wunan Books.

Wu, Jinglin (吳敬璉). 2005. The Path of Economic Studies Is Far from Smooth (〈經濟學道路不平坦〉). In *Remembering Gu Zhun* (《顧準追思錄》), ed. Luo Yinsheng (羅銀勝), 2017, 183–185. Beijing: Central Compilation &Translation Press.

Xia, Daoping (夏道平). 1989a. *Thoughts on Liberal Economics* (《自由經濟的思路》).Taipei: Yuan-Liou Publishing.

———. 1989b. *Me in* Free China (《我在〈自由中国〉》). Taipei: Yuan-Liou Publishing.

———, trans. 1993. *Individualism and Economic Order* (《個人主義與經濟秩序》). Friedrich A. Hayek, rev. ed. Taipei: Yuan-Liou Publishing.

———. 2013. *Collected Essays of Xia Daoping* (《夏道平文集》), ed. He Zhuoen and Xia Ming (何卓恩、夏明編). Changchun: Changchun Publishing.

Xia, Ming (夏明). 2017. Enduring Great Hardship with Slow Advance in a Pioneer Work: Celebrating the Tenth Anniversary of the Establishment of Hayek Association for Chinese Scholars (〈篳路藍縷 匍匐前行:記華人哈耶克學會成立十週年〉). In *Inheritance and Development of Hayek's Thought* (《海耶克思想的繼承與發展》), 60–76. Tai Chung: Feng Chia University Press.

Xiong, Zijian (熊自健). 1992. Liberals in Post-war Taiwan and Hayek's Thought: The Cases of Yan Hai-kuang, Xia Daoping and David Chow (〈戰後台灣的自由主義者與海耶克思想--以殷海光、夏道平、周德偉為例〉). In *A Critical Study of Contemporary Chinese Thought* (《當代中國思潮述評》), 1–49. Taipei: Wenchin Publishing.

Xu, Foguan (徐復觀). [1988] 2013. *Confucian Political Thought and Democracy, Freedom and Human Rights* (《儒家政治思想與民主自由人權》), ed. Harry Hsin-i Hsiao (蕭欣義). Taipei: Studentbook.

Xu Jilin (許紀霖). 2021. *Conflicts from Left to Right: Chinese Intellectuals in The Rapids of Modern Politics* (《左衝右突: 現代政治激流中的中國知識分子》. Hong Kong: City University of Hong Kong Press.

Xu, Zhangrun (許章潤). 2017. *Reason of State and Good Political Regime* (《國家理性與優良政體》). Hong Kong: City University of Hong Kong Press.

Yadav, Vikash. 2023. *Liberalism's Last Man: Hayek in the Age of Political Capitalism*. Chicago and London: The University of Chicago Press.

Yang, Che-te (楊貞德). 2009. *The Turn to the Self: The Individual in Modern Chinese Political Thought* (《轉向自我:近代中國政治思想上的個人》). Taipei: Institute of Chinese Literature and Philosophy, Academia Sinica.

Yang, Jisheng. 2012. *Tombstone: The Great Chinese Famine 1958–1962*. Trans. Stacy Mosher and Guo Jian, ed. Edward Friedman, Stacy Mosher and Guo Jian. New York: Farrar, Straus and Giroux.

Yao Zhongqiu (姚中秋). 2012. The Question on the Critical Point in Institutional Changes (〈制度變遷的臨界點問題〉). In *The Thought of the Austrian School of Economics and Its Application* (《奧地利經濟學派的思想及其應用》), 11–28. Hong Kong: Ovis Press.

———. 2016. *On Confucian Constitutionalism* (《儒家憲政論》). Hong Kong: City University of Hong Kong Press.

Yeh, Wen-hsin. 2007. *Shanghai Splendor: Economic Sentiments and the Making of Modern China, 1843–1949*. Berkeley: University of California Press.

Yin, Hai-kuang (殷海光) trans. [1944] 2011. *The Road to Serfdom* (《到奴役之路》). Taipei: National Taiwan University Press.

Yin, Hai-kuang (殷海光), et. al. 1968. *Hayek and His Thought* (《海耶克和他的思想》). Hong Kong: Culture Book House.

Yin, Hai-kuang (殷海光). 1982. *Collected Works of Mr. Yin Haiguang, 2 Volumes* (《殷海光先生文集》). Taipei: Laureate Publishing.

———. 2009. *Reappraisal of Cultural Change in Modern China* (《中國文化的展望》). 2 Volumes. Taipei: National Taiwan University Press.

Yin, Hai-kuang, and Lin Yu-sheng (殷海光/林毓生). [1981] 1984. *Letters Between Yin Hai-kuang and Lin Yu-sheng* (《殷海光/林毓生書信錄》). Taipei: Yuan Liou Publishing.

Yu, Ying-shih (余英時). 1999. Neither Renaissance Nor Enlightenment: A Historian's Reflections on the May Fourth Movement" (〈文藝復興乎?啓蒙運動乎?-- 一個史學家對五四運動的反思〉). In *Revisiting the May Fourth Movement* (《五四新論》, 1–31. Taipie: Linking.

Zhang, Jinfu (張勁夫). 1993. A Piece of Important Historical Fact Related to Gu Zhun (〈關於顧準的一件重要史實〉). In *Remembering Gu Zhun* (《顧準追思錄》), ed. Luo Yinsheng (羅銀勝), 2017, 24–25. Beijing: Central Compilation &Translation Press.

Zhang, Qianfan. 2021. The Communist Party Leadership and Rule of Law: A Tale of Two Reforms. *Journal of Contemporary China* 30 (130): 578–595.

Zhang, Rulun (張汝倫). 2003. Oakeshott and Chinese Liberalism (〈歐克肖特和中國自由主義〉). In *Conscience and Theory* (《良知與理論》), 176–189. Nanning: Guangxi Normal University Press.

Zhang, Rulun. 2015. Oakeshott in China. In *Michael Oakeshott's Cold War Liberalism*, ed. Terry Nardin, 137–151. New York: Palgrave Macmillan.

Zhang, Shibao (張世保). 2012. Laski or Hayek (〈 拉斯基 還是 哈耶克〉). In *The Problems of Liberalism* (《自由主義諸問題》), ed. Gao Ruiquan (高瑞泉), 3–33. Shanghai: Shanghai Classics Press.

Zhang, Shuguang (張曙光). 1998. A Thinker's Exploration under Adverse Situation: A Study of Gu Zhun's Thought (〈逆境中探索的思想家—顧準思想研究〉). In *Remembering Gu Zhun* (《顧準追思錄》), ed. Luo Yinsheng (羅銀勝), 2017, 191–212. Beijing: Central Compilation &Translation Press.

Zhi, Xiaomin (智效民), ed. 2010. *Democracy or Dictatorship: A Debate Related to Modernization that Occurred 70 Years Ago* (《民主還是獨裁:70年前一場關於現代化的論爭》). Guangzhou: Guangdong People's Press.

Zhou, Guoping (周國平). 2017. Yan Fu and British Philosophy〈嚴復與英國哲學〉. In *What Do the Chinese Lack? Two Case Studies on the History of Accepting Western Philosophy by the Chinese* (《中國人缺少甚麼:西方哲學接受史上兩個案例之研究》), 12–191. Hong Kong: Hong Kong Open Page Publishing.

Zhu, Xuequin (朱學勤). 1999. *Thinkers Missing in the History of Ideas* (《思想史上的失蹤者》). Guangzhou: Huacheng Publishing House.

Index

C. Cheung, *Hayek and Post-War Chinese Liberalism*, Palgrave Studies in Classical Liberalism, https://doi.org/10.1007/978-3-031-64888-5

The manufacturer's authorised representative in the EU is Springer Nature Customer Service Centre GmbH, Europaplatz 3, 69115 Heidelberg, Germany. If you have any concerns regarding our products, please contact ProductSafety@springernature.com

Printed and bound by CPI Group (UK) Ltd, Croydon, CR0 4YY
30/09/2026
02225583-0005